Arendt's Judgment

Haney Foundation Series

A volume in the Haney Foundation Series, established in 1961 with the generous support of John Louis Haney

Arendt's Judgment

Freedom, Responsibility, Citizenship

Jonathan Peter Schwartz

PENN

University of Pennsylvania Press

Philadelphia

Published by
University of Pennsylvania Press
Philadelphia, Pennsylvania 19104-4112
www.upenn.edu/pennpress

Printed in the United States of America on acid-free paper
10 9 8 7 6 5 4 3 2 1

Library of Congress Cataloging-in-Publication Data
Names: Schwartz, Jonathan Peter, author.
Title: Arendt's judgment : freedom, responsibility, citizenship /
    Jonathan Peter Schwartz.
Other titles: Haney Foundation series.
Description: Philadelphia : University of Pennsylvania Press,
    [2016] | Series: Haney Foundation series | Includes
    bibliographical references and index.
Identifiers: LCCN 2015038852 | ISBN 9780812248142
    (alk. paper)
Subjects: LCSH: Arendt, Hannah, 1906–1975. | Judgment—
    Political aspects. | Political participation. | Political science—
    Philosophy.
Classification: LCC JC251.A74 S398 2016 | DDC
    320.01—dc23
LC record available at http://lccn.loc.gov/2015038852

Contents

Preface

In some ways, this book has been fifteen years in the making. Many of the questions that animate it are questions I was thinking about long before I began researching answers to them. Like many other political observers, the events that dominated the beginning of the last decade altered my political consciousness: the contested 2000 election; the 9/11 attacks; the so-called War on Terror; the buildup to the invasion of Iraq; George W. Bush's reelection. These events raised questions for me that I have searched for answers to ever since. What struck me about that period at the time, and has continued to ever since, was the realization that our world is much less intractable than we often think, that decisions and courses of action of specific individuals can have tremendous consequences. A bad or good judgment can change the world. Frankly, I continue to believe that a series of bad judgments were made during this era. Yet, I was also struck by the immense challenges to good judgment that those faced with the responsibility were confronted with, which left me with a grudging admiration for their willingness to act and judge at all. Rightly or not, a period of existential fear gripped American politics after the 9/11 attacks, and those who made decisions, along with those who supported and opposed them, had to make judgments in a climate of deep anxiety in a modern world characterized by opacity, potency, and immense complexity. But more than anything else, I was struck by the fact that people seemed able to honestly arrive at profoundly different conclusions about the world, even though they were often working from a common set of facts. Why was this possible? What were the human faculties that enabled better or worse judgments? How do we even know, finally, when a good or bad judgment has been made? Moreover, while I recognized this obvious, if obscure, possibility of legitimate differences of opinion, I also became convinced that this was not the only factor in play. There were what seemed to be gaps in the practical reason of many individuals, which they tried to fill with what can only be characterized as an ideology: a peculiar way of judging that reduces the complexity of the world to a simplistic normative-theoretical model, allowing the agent to cognitively exclude any dissonant information. All these questions seemed to lead me, almost inexorably, to look to Hannah Arendt for answers.

Defining good judgment is notoriously difficult: two and half millennia after Aristotle, it remains one of the most elusive yet self-evident human faculties. We commonly recognize it as among the great human goods; though we may initially think to place other goods above it, such as peace, justice, virtue, happiness, or liberty, these can only be realized where good judgment exists. When we elect political leaders, it is good judgment more than anything else we hope they will exercise, for though their ideological position may seem more significant, it will be worthless to us if they lack the judgment to bring that political vision into reality. And given the increasing interconnectedness, complexity, and centralization of modern societies and economies, the ecological challenges of our times, and the massive destructive power in the hands of our regimes, judgment perhaps is more important than ever before. Yet, despite the obvious importance of judgment, it is difficult to understand exactly what it is. We can point to examples of good judgment, such as Lincoln, Mandela, or Martin Luther King, and even more often to instances of bad judgment too innumerable to mention. But it is difficult to put a finger on exactly what made one person effective, while others failed. It is clearly not due to simply having more knowledge, since two people may have similar information about a matter and still arrive at very different judgments. Good judgment instead seems to involve a certain kind of insight into circumstances and an ability to summon up just the right response to that insight: a kind of common sense that, while potentially sharpened by greater knowledge, is still something separate from it.

So how then can we define good judgment? Following Kant, we might define judgment as the ability to subsume particulars under general rules. This is a very abstract account, but it seems to capture some of our basic intuitions. The most obvious case of such judgment in political life is a judge's ruling in court, deciding whether the particular case can be subsumed under some law or precedent. However, in the arena of politics judgment seems to extend further than this. When we talk about the proverbial relationship between theory and practice, we are discussing judgment; but the fundamental question about this relationship has always been what constitutes "theory," what constitutes "practice," and how are they related?[1] At the very least, regardless of how we define them, we seem to have to understand judgment as, in some sense, the establishment of a relationship of our mental activities with our activities in the actual world. But this last characterization still seems too abstract to give us real purchase on our question; an analytic approach can perhaps help us orient ourselves in a general way, but it does not give us much to go on.

These perplexities led me to take another approach, examining the ideas of a thinker who I will argue devoted her life's work to concretely understanding the nature of judgment: Hannah Arendt, whose theory of political judgment I believe to be the most significant consideration of the topic since Aristotle. Arendt believed that understanding the nature of political judgment and the sources of its validity required a dramatic rethinking of what theory and practice are, and how they are related to each other. I believe an examination of her thinking on this question can help us come to terms with the question of judgment and, in the process, give us a deeper view of the importance of judgment for politics in our time. Perhaps it may even help us make better decisions in the future, as we still stand at the outset of a century that arguably poses extraordinary political challenges, not just for America, but for the whole world. This, at least, has been my hope in writing this book.

Introduction

In Pursuit of Authentic Political Philosophy

There exists in our society a widespread fear of judging that has nothing whatever to do with the biblical "Judge not, that ye be not judged." . . . For behind the unwillingness to judge lurks the suspicion that no one is a free agent, and hence the doubt that anyone is responsible or could be expected to answer for what he has done. . . . Hence the huge outcry the moment anyone fixes specific blame on some particular person instead of blaming all deeds or events on historical trends and dialectical movements, in short on some mysterious necessity that works behind the backs of men.

—Hannah Arendt, "Personal Responsibility Under Dictatorship"

Hannah Arendt continues to provoke us. That was her intention. She was not interested in making things easy for her readers. This was not to toy with them: there were urgent purposes behind it. All writers have priorities, and among the highest priorities of modern philosophy and political thought has been to convey clarity of thought and idea. Hannah Arendt had other priorities. She wanted to challenge her readers to look at their past and present world anew, to provoke them not to think *what* she thought, but to think *like* she thought. And to the extent her ultimate goal had not been to win arguments or begin schools of thought, but to, so to speak, awaken her readers from their dogmatic slumbers, she was no doubt successful. Yet, achieving this goal came at a price, and that price meant giving up the assurance that she would pass on a stable set of ideas. Did this mean there was no fundamental core to her thought? Was she merely "moving within the gap between past and future," as she often put it, with no central goals or fundamental purposes directing this movement? It will be my contention here that, though she rarely openly discussed it and arguably never published a direct account of it, there was indeed a fundamental goal orienting her thought, and that goal revolved around the question of how to reestablish the possibility of authentic practical reason and political judgment in the modern world.

Arendt's work—provisional, essayistic, intentionally foreign—presents a formidable challenge to anyone who tries to definitively explain its fundamental purposes and meaning. The problems presented by Arendt's style of thinking and writing are in many ways unique to her. Even in her most coherent projects, such as *On Revolution* or *The Origins of Totalitarianism*, many of the most important arguments and conclusions are buried in a dense, historically detailed narrative. She often refused to write in a clear and straightforward manner, at times even seeming to deliberately hold back the central point of her argument. She almost never writes outside of the essay format, and even her monographs are better described as a series of essays that form something like a conceptual mosaic, rather than a sustained, systematic argument.

Compounding the problem of understanding her is a kind of reflexive skepticism in the academic community instigated by her unusual influence and notoriety. In her day, Arendt was a true public intellectual, on the level of Emerson or Dewey, the sort more often found in Europe but rarely in America. She came to prominence with the publication of her first major work, *The Origins of Totalitarianism*, which was a best seller and launched her into worldwide fame.[1] It was acclaimed by many as a work of genius,[2] and Arendt herself joked that she had become a "cover girl" when her pictures began appearing on magazine covers.[3] Her next book, *The Human Condition*, raised her profile even higher, introducing a nearly unheard of level of erudition and philosophical depth into mainstream literature. Yet despite her undeniable fame, her work, largely thanks to its rather literary nature, has perhaps been less consistently influential than that of other recent figures like Rawls, Strauss, or Habermas. Many have found her work to be more suggestive than definitive, her arguments difficult to follow, and the content of her thought, at times, frustratingly obscure. At a conference on her work in 1972, Christian Bay expressed a frustration no doubt common to her readers, saying, "I read Hannah Arendt with pleasure, but out of aesthetic pleasure. She is a philosopher's philosopher. I think it is beautiful to follow her prose, her sense of unity in history, and to be reminded of the great things the Greeks have said that are still pertinent today. I think, however . . . there is a certain lack of seriousness about modern problems in much of her work."[4]

This assessment has no doubt been encouraged by the fact that during her lifetime she was as influential for her social connections and personal magnetism as for her intellectual contributions. A prominent figure in the interconnected communities of New York literary society and postwar Jewish émigrés, the *New York Review of Books* once called her "the éminence grise of the éminences grises."[5] Irving Howe has noted that her personal charisma made her a significant figure in the intellectual world well before she published anything of true significance.[6] "While far from 'good-looking' in any commonplace way," he tells us, "Hannah Arendt was a remarkably attractive person, with her razored gestures, imperial eye, dangling cigarette. . . . She bristled with intellectual charm, as if to reduce everyone in sight to an alert discipleship. . . . Whatever room she was in Hannah filled through the largeness of her will; indeed, she always seemed larger than her setting." In fact, it is difficult to even draw a clear distinction between her personal and intellectual influence, for many of her ideas had social and political dimensions that transcended intellectual life. She has been claimed by conservatives, progressives, and New Left democrats alike. *Origins* is both a basic text of social science research and a touchstone of Cold War politics; *The Human Condition* and *On Revolution* were virtually required reading in the early days of the New Left.[7] And of course the impact that *Eichmann in Jerusalem* had not merely in its own time but in our continuing confrontation with the question of evil in the modern world cannot be overlooked. It is no surprise that she is among the few twentieth-century intellectual figures who has been the subject of a major motion picture. This celebrity has tended to add to the skepticism with which academia often approaches her, epitomized by Christian Bay. The literary quality of her work at times actually counts against its intellectual seriousness, and she has often been characterized by the social science community, for example, as one of the literati: brilliantly imaginative, but too little concerned with evidence.

Part of the explanation for her often abstruse and uniquely literary style of theory ultimately seems to have had to do with a certain idiosyncrasy of thought, which she appears to have been unable to fully master. Mary McCarthy states that, as far as she knew, all of Arendt's books and articles were edited, often by several collaborators, before reaching print, and often over fundamental elements.[8] Arendt's way of thinking seems to have been more organic than systematic, often requiring the help of others to give it a more coherent form. She herself was open about the tentative and even potentially experimental nature of her thinking[9] and even admitted that she was uncertain of how finally to assess them. At the 1972 conference on her work, she concluded the day's discussions, saying, "I would like to say that everything I did and everything I wrote—all of this is tentative. I think that all thinking, the way that I have indulged in it perhaps a little beyond measure, extravagantly, has the earmark of being tentative."[10] Yet, there also seemed to be a kind of ethos behind her writing. She went on to say that she believed that the nature of intellectual activity did not afford the kind of authority that can go beyond such tentative and experimental forays, and that the true purpose of a political thinker might actually only be to teach others to think politically for themselves. During one of the sharpest exchanges of the conference, Bay criticized Arendt's tentativeness, saying, "I was disturbed when Hannah Arendt said that her desire is never to indoctrinate. I think that *this* is the highest calling of the political theorist: to attempt to indoctrinate, in a pluralist universe, of course. . . . Unless we passionately care for certain opinions, I think we will all be lost." In the ensuing discussion, Arendt said,

> I cannot tell you black on white—and would hate to do it—what the consequences of this kind of thought which I try, not to indoctrinate, but to rouse or to awaken in my students, are, in actual politics. . . . I wouldn't instruct you, and I would think that this would be presumptuous of me. I think that you should be instructed when you sit together with your peers around a table and exchange opinions . . . I think that every other road of the theoretician who tells his students what to think and how to act is . . . my God! These are adults! We are not in the nursery![11]

Arendt seemed to believe that theorists somehow had an obligation to hold something back, to somehow avoid robbing those they teach of their ability to think for themselves. She appeared to understand her purpose in teaching as that of helping others to think for themselves by giving them a place to start. Perhaps in a similar way, she seemed careful to maintain a certain distance and tentativeness in her work.

This language of tentativeness and experimentalism might suggest the lack of seriousness Christian Bay chided her over. Yet, this is hardly believable. Arendt wrote with too much urgency and focused her thought on matters that were of momentous political importance for the twentieth century.

There is no contradiction between the urgency of her subject matter and the experimentalism and tentativeness of her thought, if experimentalism was what these urgent matters required. Arendt believed that we now live in a historically unprecedented situation. While she did her best to characterize this new world, she did not believe that she could do this exhaustively or alone. As we will see, the most basic commitment of her idea of political judgment was that judgment concerns reflection upon a world that separates and relates individuals who have it in common, and, as a result, no one individual can ever hope to fully comprehend it by themselves, and the closest we come is by taking into account the reflections of those who hold it in common with us. Thus, if Arendt did maintain a certain tentativeness in her writing, it no doubt involved a desire to open a conversation about the world we have in common rather than to close it.

But this does not mean that Hannah Arendt did not make substantial progress toward developing a positive theory that could address the problems of the modern world. She herself characterized *The Human Condition* as part of a productive element of her political thought in a letter to Karl Jaspers in 1957. Writing as she was about to publish a collection of "transitional essays," she told Jaspers, "I'm afraid you won't like them because they are entirely negative and destructive, and the positive side is hardly in evidence . . . but I wish you were already familiar with [*The Human Condition*], which you will surely like better."[12] Clearly, Arendt believed Jaspers would have liked *The Human Condition* because in her view, at least, it would carry much more of her positive project. But as we will see, *The Human Condition* was only part of this positive project, a project that in fact predated it and which she was never able to complete. That project revolved around the problem of reestablishing practical reason and political judgment in the modern world, and though it remained unfinished at her death, I will argue here that we can reconstruct it from a disparate set of her published, posthumously published, and unpublished writings. While perhaps it indeed remained provisional and experimental, I believe it was well enough developed to carry the possibility of transforming how we think about many of the most fundamental concepts of political thought, including freedom, justice, sovereignty, citizenship, practical reason, and, indeed, the very nature and meaning of political philosophy itself.

In Pursuit of Authentic Political Philosophy

In another letter to Jaspers in 1956, Arendt said, "I am in the midst of [writing] my *Vita Activa* [the working title of *The Human Condition*], and I've had to put completely out of my mind the relationship between philosophy and politics, which is really of greater interest to me."[13] One of the true surprises of Arendt's thought is that beginning in 1954 she returned to this question of the relation of philosophy and politics over and over, yet never published a direct account of her conclusions about the question. There are at least four different occasions between 1954 and 1969 when Arendt formally wrote about the relationship between philosophy and politics. Each of these is a distinct and original attempt to address this question.

The first occasion was in 1954. That year she wrote a long essay, which she presented as a set of lectures at Notre Dame,[14] entitled "Philosophy and Politics: The Problem of Thought and Action After the French Revolution,"[15] the last portion of which Jerome Kohn edited and published as "Philosophy and Politics" in 1990.[16] It is a highly illuminating manuscript and develops several notions that are only gestured at elsewhere by Arendt. In this essay, she sought to explain how the relationship between philosophy and politics could be authentically grasped only through an understanding of the true nature of thought and action. This manuscript appears to have set the stage for all of her later work, and indeed it could arguably be viewed as a kind of roadmap for understanding her work as a whole. The second occasion was in a manuscript called "Introduction *into* Politics," which was edited and published by Kohn in the volume *The Promise of Politics*.[17] Immediately after finishing *The Human Condition*, Arendt attempted to write a book that developed the broader meaning of her genealogy of the life of action in *The Human Condition*. Kohn notes in his introduction that Arendt eventually intended "Introduction *into* Politics" to be a "large, systematic political work, which as one work exists nowhere in her *oeuvre*."[18] In a letter to the Rockefeller Foundation in early 1960 requesting support for the project, she wrote that the projected book "will continue where [*The Human Condition*] ends" and "will be concerned exclusively with thought and action."[19] Part of this project is what eventually resulted in *On Revolution* after she set this larger project aside to focus on the Eichmann trial and on her examination of the *vita contemplativa* in *The Life of the Mind*. Yet, even as she turned to these other projects, she continued to think and write on the question of philosophy and politics, delivering a 1963 lecture course, also called "Introduction into Politics,"[20] and a 1969 course called "Philosophy and Politics: What Is Political Philosophy?"[21] Arendt, who often used her teaching obligations as opportunities to write initial manuscripts of what later became her essays and books, developed these two lecture courses as distinct and unique treatments of the question of philosophy and politics, clearly intending them to be coherent pieces of writing on the question.

It will be my contention here that, though it seems she never felt ready to publish on the topic, this question of the true relationship between philosophy and politics was the ultimate task of Arendt's work, providing a kind of Rosetta stone for understanding the diverse pursuits and subject matter she wrote and thought about. Of course, it has always been obvious that there was some kind of relationship between Arendt's discussions of the life of action in *The Human Condition* and elsewhere and her reflections on the *vita contemplativa* in her various writings on judgment and in *The Life of the Mind*. The nature of this relationship has been the topic of much commentary and speculation since the two parts of *The Life of the Mind* manuscript were published posthumously.[22] At her death in 1976, Arendt, as is well known, had written most of the two books of *The Life of the Mind*, "Thinking" and "Willing," and had planned a final section on "Judging." This final installment was never written, but it seems unlikely, given Arendt's own comments on the nature of the "Judging" section—not to mention extrapolating from the arguments of the first two volumes—that she would have provided there any such account of the relationship between the two major areas of her thought. At no point in either volume of *The Life of the Mind* does Arendt ever promise any such explanation, and in fact it would have been quite a jolting break in the trajectory of argument as it had developed in the previous two volumes. Several sources attest to the fact that Arendt would have drawn on her lectures on Kant's *Critique of Judgment*, which, while quite political, nevertheless have a similar orientation toward that part of her thought that appears as the *vita contemplativa*.[23] Moreover, her projections of the length of the section, which was not intended to be a full third volume, but more likely some kind of extended concluding section to the "Willing" volume, seemed unlikely to have afforded the necessary space.[24] I will eventually argue that the lectures on Kant's *Critique of Judgment* are indeed crucial to understanding how the two parts of her work are related—indeed, that it provides the final piece to the puzzle. Nevertheless, it is still only a piece of a puzzle that requires much more information than is available, not only in the Kant lectures, but also in *The Human Condition* and *The Life of the Mind*.

That Arendt understood *The Human Condition* and *The Life of the Mind* to be her key works addressing the two fundamental spheres of human experience is beyond question. In *The Human Condition*, Arendt is quite clear that the sphere of experience where thought occurs, what she calls the *vita contemplativa*, is distinct and separate from the sphere of experience of action, which she calls the *vita activa*, and she is careful to stipulate that her concern in *The Human Condition* is almost exclusively with the *vita activa*.[25] Writing of the ancient philosophers' discovery of contemplation, and the tradition and way of life it gave birth to, Arendt writes that the *vita contemplativa* "must lie in an altogether different aspect of the human condition, whose diversity is not exhausted in the various articulations of the *vita activa* and, we may suspect, would not be exhausted even if thought and the movement of reasoning were included in it."[26] Arendt goes on to stipulate that "my use of the term *vita activa* presupposes that the concern underlying all its activities is not the same as and is neither superior nor inferior to the central concern of the *vita contemplativa*," describing this distinction in terms of "the various modes of active engagement in the things of this world, on one side, and pure thought culminating in contemplation, on the other."[27] It is clear, then, that Arendt believed that there is an aspect of the human condition that is separate from that of the *vita activa*, which exists somehow outside "the world" and its "various modes of active engagement," and concerns itself with human faculties such as contemplation and thought.

While the text of *The Human Condition* never suggests that she planned to write a book devoted solely to the *vita contemplativa* and its sphere of experience, there are clear indications that she thought it would eventually be necessary. *The Human Condition* seems to end with the equivalent of a "to be continued." Quite abruptly, in the book's final paragraph, Arendt leaves her discussion of the distinctions in the *vita activa* and turns to the matter of thought. The paragraph clearly has no summary or concluding function—at least, not in relation to the concerns of the *vita activa*—and it is therefore difficult to imagine that she had any other purpose in concluding with this paragraph than to suggest that her discussions of the *vita activa* in the book were not a full account of the human condition, and thus that *The Human Condition* was in a certain sense incomplete. After *The Human Condition*'s publication, Arendt regularly described the project of *The Life of the Mind* as a direct sequel to *The Human Condition*.[28] In a letter to Mary McCarthy in 1968 she said that her "preparations for writing about Thinking-Willing-Judging" are "a kind of part II to the Human Condition [*sic*],"[29] while during the 1972 conference on her work, she said, "I feel that this *Human Condition* needs a second volume and I'm trying to write it."[30] *The Human Condition*, thus, at least by the late sixties, was in fact understood by Arendt to contain two parts, only one of which had been written.

Yet, it appears that Arendt always recognized there was a further step necessary beyond this *vita contemplativa* sequel and that this further step was in fact the most important step of all. The crucial issue that originally prompted her to write *The Human Condition* and *The Life of the Mind* had always been the matter of the *relationship* between thought and action and between the *vita activa* and the *vita contemplativa*. Theoretically speaking, this should not be surprising. *The Human Condition* and *The Life of the Mind* focused almost exclusively on their respective spheres of experience and almost completely ignored the question of their broader relationship to each other. Most of the attempts by scholars to flesh out this relationship for Arendt have typically focused on reconstructing Arendt's theory of political judgment out of a diverse set of published essays such as "Truth and Politics" and "The Crisis in Culture," along with various posthumously published materials such as the Kant lectures, *The Life of the Mind*, and, more recently, "Thinking and Moral Considerations" and "Some Questions of Moral Philosophy."[31] Yet, these attempts have remained for the most part speculative and lacking a clear connection with Arendt's work on action, and so much so that some of her most prominent interpreters have concluded that Arendt's work is somehow fundamentally conflicted.[32] The reason for this perplexity, I believe, is that Arendt's interpreters have been trying to make her theory of judgment do more than it was intended to do. To be sure, they are correct that it does somehow provide a connecting link between the sphere of thought and action. Yet, I believe that the broader relationship between thought and action was never adequately sketched out in the work on judgment. On a theoretical level, it needed something else, something that did not focus exclusively on a particular sphere of experience but instead seeks to come to terms with how these two spheres were related to each other.

Why did Arendt never publish this account the relationship between the *vita activa* and *vita contemplativa*? The obvious conclusion would be that she did not really have an answer. But given her continuing unpublished work on the question of the relation of philosophy and politics, this does not appear to be a plausible conclusion, and in fact these writings suggest she felt she understood the general structure of the relationship quite well. But then the question of why she never published an account of the relationship between the two spheres becomes quite perplexing. Frankly, I am doubtful there is any one decisive reason. As we've seen, Arendt's style of theorizing was quite idiosyncratic, verging on eccentric, and she seemed to gravitate much more to the genealogical process of what she called "pearl diving," of digging deeper and deeper into the origins of our historical world, than to the process of attempting to tie up all the loose ends of her explorations. On the other hand, it may simply have been that she ran out of time, dying before she had even finished *The Life of the Mind*.

But whatever the reason, it will be my contention here that Arendt in essence needed to write a second sequel to *The Human Condition*, or perhaps, instead, a *prequel*, which explained the how the two *vitas* were related to each other. To simplify things in the form of an analogy, I want to argue that this reconstructed theory of judgment that has been developed by many of her interpreters, coupled with her articulations of the *vita activa* and the *vita contemplativa*, are like three large chunks of a picture puzzle; but, unfortunately, they do not form a full picture. We still need more pieces. It will be my task in what follows to attempt to reconstruct, at times through well-informed inference, what this prequel would have argued by showing what the relationship between thought and action truly were for Arendt and how she understood it to be a genuine positive response to the modern predicament. For Arendt, this meant coming to understand the authentic meaning of political philosophy.

Considering Arendt in a Different Light

People have, of course, practiced political philosophy for millennia. Is it really believable that they did not know what they were doing? Does understanding the true nature of political philosophy even matter, so long as it produces useful answers to political problems? As we will see, it does matter quite a bit. For as Arendt will show us, what one understands political philosophy to be can have an enormous impact on the answers it produces. Arendt criticized the tradition of political thought for understanding itself in terms of sovereignty: the idea that politics was concerned with who should rule. She would argue that this notion of sovereignty was ultimately derived from a set of assumptions about what thought and action were, and how they should be related. She argued that, beginning with Plato, political thought had fundamentally grasped itself on the model of *techne*, as the application of rules to improve and legitimize political practice. Sovereign rulership became its model because the assumptions of the technical paradigm ultimately suggest that there can only be one right answer to fundamental political questions. The problem with this is that the sovereignty-based model presumes that politics can be made subordinate to philosophy, so that philosophy can prescribe rules and laws to politics. But what if politics could not so easily be made subordinate? What if the two activities were of such different natures that it was impossible to so simplistically understand their relationship? "If we really believe—and I think we share this belief," Arendt once said, "that plurality rules the earth, then I think one has got to modify this notion of the unity of theory and practice to such an extent that it will be unrecognizable for those who tried their hand at it before. . . . These are two entirely different—if you want to call it—'existential' positions."[33]

In *The Human Condition* and *The Life of the Mind*, Arendt's explorations of action and thought showed each was so much more phenomenally rich than the sovereignty-based conception suggests—that their natures, in fact, were so fundamentally different—it was difficult to imagine how they could *ever* be reconciled.[34] "It lies in the nature of philosophy," she wrote, "to deal with man in the singular, whereas politics could not even be conceived if men did not exist in the plural."[35] Politics, Arendt would go on to argue elsewhere, was essentially "non-sovereign."[36] It was characterized by what the Greeks called *isonomie*, or "no-rule,"[37] a political state of being where "men in their freedom can interact with one another without compulsion, force, and rule over one another, as equals among equals, commanding and obeying one another only in emergencies . . . but otherwise managing all their affairs by speaking with and persuading one another."[38] In the 1969 "Philosophy and Politics" course, she appears to arrive at an aporetic conclusion concerning the question of their relation: "If you ask what is the solution to the riddle, I'd answer: in terms of this course, simply the unity that is man: it is human to act and to want to act; it is human to think and to want to think. . . . It is always life that offers the solutions."[39] But her note that this conclusion was only "in terms of this course" is a crucial qualification. Arendt believed there was faculty that had the capacity to reach across the abyss that separated thought and action: the faculty of judgment. Using a creative appropriation of Kantian aesthetic judgment, she arguably conceived the first truly non-sovereign form of political philosophy: an account of political judgment that was neither arbitrary nor universally determinative in its mode of validity, one that could make room for human plurality. Indeed, this non-sovereign political philosophy was at its best when practiced by a diverse, committed, and politically engaged group of citizens.

This, I believe, represents a new way of understanding Hannah Arendt. The traditional interpretative approach has focused on Arendt's civic republicanism. My approach argues that Arendt's work is best understood if the interpretive focus makes room for another, as it were, center of gravity, one that recognizes that both Arendt's civic republicanism and her search for an authentic political philosophy operate in a kind of "virtuous circle." In other words, I want to argue that Arendt's positive project in response to modernity can only be intelligibly reconstructed if it is recognized that there was a second dimension to her thought beyond her civic republicanism, a dimension that centered on theorizing authentic political philosophy. Pivotal to this will then be to show that her account of judgment was much more central to her work than is commonly recognized. Arendt's theory of judgment has received significant scholarly consideration in the years since her death, and, moreover, her interest in judgment has inspired many scholars to consider the question outside the scope of her work, building on her insight that Kant's "Critique of Aesthetic Judgment" can be applied to practical philosophy in general.[40] Virtually all these engagements with her account of judgment take place in numerous scholarly articles and book chapters, and it is somewhat surprising that only one book has claimed to be devoted to the topic, Max Deutscher's *Judgment After Arendt*, which in fact is only partially concerned with her theory of judgment, in the context of his phenomenological analysis of *The Life of the Mind*.[41] Moreover, Deutscher's book is not really about her theory of *political* judgment, and in fact completely ignores the political elements of her theory. Given the volume of work on Arendt's theory of judgment, it is perhaps surprising that no real consensus has ever emerged about the meaning of her theory. As recently as 2010, after literally dozens of pieces had been written and published on the topic, Bryan Garsten perhaps summarized this literature best when he wrote that "we cannot avoid confronting the fact that while her theory of judgment is suggestive it is also notoriously difficult to understand."[42]

At the same time, her theory of political judgment has most often been treated as a kind of appendix to her thought—an interesting possible direction that she pointed toward but that remained obscure and incomplete at her death. George Kateb spends no time discussing it in his book on Arendt, while Margaret Canovan devotes only four pages to the topic in a section devoted to Arendt's account of "thinking."[43] More recent work done by Dana Villa and Seyla Benhabib give it deeper treatment, but it still remains at best in a supporting role,[44] and, in fact, as recently as 2012, Michael McCarthy claimed in his book that "her account of the intelligible connection between thought and action remains obscure. . . . Although practical wisdom is the supreme political virtue, Arendt is surprisingly silent about it."[45] My claim, in fact, is that virtually all Arendt did was examine the nature of this relationship between thought and action, that Arendt's political thought should be understood as always fundamentally concerned with understanding the true relationship between theory and practice.[46] In other words, I propose to present an interpretation of Arendt that places political judgment at the very center of her thought. I will argue that her advocacy for civic republicanism and idealization of the ancients' noninstrumental political action had behind them the goal of renewing practical reason in a modern era that has profoundly undermined it, for her pursuit of authentic political philosophy could only be fully realized when political judgment is practiced in such a republican context. Placing judgment at the center of her work, in other words, will make it possible for us to understand the systematic thread that runs through her diverse body of work.

However, while this can give us a substantial push in the right direction, it cannot fully resolve all of the difficulties involved in interpreting Arendt. Along with the focus on political judgment, this study draws on a wide range of sources that have been heavily underutilized in the literature on Arendt. Once these sources are taken into account, many of the historical and theoretical gaps that have perplexed her readers and made her theory of political judgment difficult to understand are resolved. The reason for the underuse of these sources is mainly that until recently they were not easily accessible. One of the secondary goals of this study is to provide a roadmap of sorts for engaging with these lesser known sources. The only other book to make serious use of these sources was Margaret Canovan's *Hannah Arendt: A Reinterpretation of Her Political Thought*. While it was a fine interpretation of Arendt, it was plagued by two major difficulties. One is that at the time of its publication in 1992, these underutilized sources could only be accessed through on-site archival research at the Library of Congress, and as a result the usefulness of the book was limited because her readers could not refer to these sources. Now that the Library of Congress holdings are available electronically and various other writings and correspondences have been published posthumously, access to her sources is much easier. The second problem, however, is that although Canovan did pay attention to these materials, she did not recognize the centrality of political judgment that in my view they make explicit, nor that Arendt's overall project concerned discovering the authentic nature of political philosophy, and these are the elements of her work that I believe make her most valuable to us.

Looking Ahead

What has yet to be explained, of course, is how exactly this proposed authentic political philosophy constituted a positive response to the modern situation as Arendt understood it. This question is essentially the subject and theme of this book, and its chapters each seek to flesh out the answer. The climax of the book occurs in Chapter 5. There I defend Arendt's theory of judgment against numerous critiques, explain its theoretical power and novelty as a mode of political philosophy only practicable intersubjectively by engaged and committed citizens, and argue that it represented a "solution" (in Arendt's rather unorthodox sense) to the problem of how to found and maintain a new public realm in a modern world dominated by what she called the social realm. This, however, will require a number of interventions, reinterpretations, and refinements of how Arendt has been understood to this point. The four chapters leading up to Chapter 5 develop a series of concepts and concerns that allow this climax to occur. There is an organic, weblike quality to Arendt's thought, which can make the exploration of specific concepts and areas of her work challenging. The 1950s in particular were an extremely fertile intellectual period of her life, and significant ideas seem to have emerged almost simultaneously. Many ideas that occur in one area of her thinking inform other areas, with the result that an appreciation of the meaning and worth of a certain concept may require understanding theories and concepts developed in distant or seemingly unrelated work. This has been the greatest challenge of this book and no doubt represents a significant limitation: there is no specifically chronological or linear thread that runs from Chapter 1 to Chapter 5. The four chapters leading up to Chapter 5 in many ways illuminate each other along with Chapter 5, so that a full assessment of each may require having read the others.

This is especially the case in Chapter 1, whose full significance will not be appreciated until Arendt's analysis of modernity, its politics, and its modes of political judgment are examined in Chapter 4. Chapter 1 offers a new theoretical treatment of what has been called Arendt's "non-sovereign" conception of political action. Arendt's account of human agency and its realization in political action typically occurs within the context of specific historical instantiations, such as the Greeks, the Romans, and the modern revolutionaries, and, as a result, I will argue that past treatments have often had difficulty distinguishing between general characteristics of Arendtian non-sovereign agency and characteristics unique to each historically specific occurrence. Thus, I will approach the question of Arendtian action in two steps: one that occurs in Chapter 1, outlining what I believe are the general characteristics and concerns of Arendtian non-sovereign agency, while turning in Chapter 2 to an examination of the three specific historical instantiations Arendt examined. In Chapter 1, I use a variety of theoretical and interpretative approaches to reconstruct the meaning and purposes behind Arendt's non-sovereign account of political action, which I believe are in many ways not fully spelled out in canonical texts such as *On Revolution* and *The Human Condition*. I triangulate, so to speak, this theoretical account of non-sovereign agency by consulting canonical texts and numerous unpublished and posthumously published texts against what I will argue was her both implicit and explicit critique of Martin Heidegger.

Heidegger will represent a major figure in my interpretation of Arendt, whose centrality both as a foundational thinker and as a theoretical point of departure was so significant to her thought that he will require a brief yet fairly substantial direct engagement himself. What may at times appear to be an almost relentless attack by Arendt on Heidegger in this book belies the far greater Heideggerian philosophical commitments Arendt maintained throughout her work. Nevertheless, it is these points of departure that define her work. I will argue in Chapter 1 that the central motivation behind the development of Arendt's account of non-sovereign political action was an attempt to challenge modern philosophies of history that robbed human beings of their individuality and political potency, leading ultimately to totalitarian politics. Drawing on Heidegger, Arendt located the origin of history not in historically dialectical forces but in the narrative existence of human beings, and the purpose of her account of action was to theorize a form of historical reflection that placed human action once again at the center of history. In other words, I will argue that Arendt's turn to politics was motivated by essentially historical concerns and that she understood history and politics to be essentially linked. I show that Arendt was motivated by the ancient Greek concept of *athanatizein*, to immortalize, the path to which philosophy and politics had taken fundamentally distinct approaches toward. While philosophy pursued a contemplative path, political *athanatizein* was concerned with historical immortality achieved in the common human world, and it could only be attained by changing that world while at the same time caring for and maintaining it. The resulting conception of human agency, I will argue, is one that is extraordinarily potent and dynamic, whose power and remarkableness human beings have often feared and sought to mitigate, especially in the modern era.

In Chapter 2, I turn to the specific occurrences of political *athanatizein* Arendt explored: the Greeks, the Romans, and the modern revolutionaries. Arendt, I argue, had more in mind in her work on these instances than merely to articulate authentic political action. Each of these instances was uniquely influential in the history Western politics, providing the original political language we continue to use to this day. Each experience offered distinctive insights into the deep problem that haunted Arendt's positive project: the problem of how to refound an authentic public realm, a formal "space of appearances," in a modern world whose basic logic systematically undermined that possibility. The reason she pursued the question of authentic political philosophy, I will argue, was because each of these experiences of founding lacked the capacity for thought that only authentic philosophical experience could provide, and which she believed would be necessary in order to found and maintain a new public realm in the modern era.

Chapter 3 turns to Arendt's exploration of the experience of philosophical *athanatizein* and examines her analysis of the impulses, motivations, and internal logic that led it to give birth to the tradition of political thought. We will see Arendt argue that the authentic experience of philosophy occurred in two human activities taking place in utter withdrawal from the experience of engaged human agency in the world: the thinking activity that exists as a two-in-one dialogue I have with myself and the ultimate philosophical goal of this dialogue, speechless wonder or contemplation. It was this experience of contemplation that provided the legitimacy Plato drew on to establish the tradition of political thought. In doing so, Arendt believed the resulting rather crude conception of political philosophy came to base itself on the production analogy of theory and practice, which ignored the characteristics of this relationship that essentially involved speech. On its basis, Plato would establish the concept of rulership and its resulting politics of sovereignty as a kind of master idea of traditional political theory, an idea that even those members of the tradition that attacked Plato never fully escaped. I will argue that when properly understood, Arendt presents a serious challenge to the tradition of political thought in this analysis.

Chapter 4 explores Arendt's account of the rise of modernity and its odd, near-coincidental political compatibility with the tradition of political thought's sovereignty paradigm of politics, along with her analysis of the modern political pathologies that this connection seemed to facilitate. While her critique of the tradition of political thought has long been recognized as crucial to the development of her political thought, its role in her analysis of the modern situation has generally remained somewhat opaque. Using a much more extended set of sources to supplement the incomplete canonical texts, I seek to provide the clearest and most comprehensive account to date of the role and culpability of the tradition's flawed model of the relation of thought and action in modern political pathologies. Modernity was characterized by world alienation, and this alienation led to a series of revolutionary attempts to refound a new public realm in a common world. What thwarted these attempts was the revolutionaries' inability to escape the categories of the tradition of political thought. In the fluid context of revolutionary politics, a variety of specifically modern patterns of thought would become virulently dangerous after having been given political legitimacy by the traditional understanding of political thought. The venerable tradition of political thought, while not itself culpable for the revolutionary experiences that led to tyranny and totalitarianism, was revealed to be highly vulnerable to abuse at the hands of evil men. If there was to be a successful revolution in the modern world, Arendt believed it would have to appeal to a richer and more authentic form of political thought.

Chapter 5 seeks to reconstruct what Arendt believed this authentic form of political philosophy would have looked like. While it is undeniable that this final piece of the puzzle for Arendt's thinking remained incomplete at her death, I use numerous texts and well-researched inference to reconstruct what I believe was bold new way to practice political philosophy, one that was *essentially* intersubjective. In Chapter 5, I defend Arendt's attempt to apply Kant's "Critique of Aesthetic Judgment" to politics. I outline the problems Arendt detected in earlier accounts of practical reason that led to her turn to the third *Critique*. I argue that in his concept of "enlarged mentality," Kant made an original and profound discovery: that the phenomenon of common sense contains a hidden faculty, which Arendt believed anchored the validity of moral and political judgments. With this advanced concept of political common sense in hand, Arendt was able to argue that the rational validity of political opinion was of a different order than that of cognitive rationality, leading to a notion of political philosophy that did not seek a sovereign perspective in relation to political questions. Political philosophy, in Arendt's mind, should not ask "Who is right?" but instead ask "Who is *more* right?":

who had a deeper and broader insight into the world that citizens share in common with each other? In this theory, I argue that Arendt could claim to have truly fulfilled her goal of returning political philosophy to the citizens, for Arendt understood the structure of Kantian judgment to imply that the more broad and diverse the perspectives offered in the process of deliberation, the better the resulting judgments will be.

In the concluding chapter, I will take stock of Arendt's ideas. First, I offer some concluding critical comments on Arendt, her project, and her ideas. I briefly consider the historical, theoretical, practical, and methodological limitations of what Arendt accomplished, and then seek to begin a discussion of its position in relation to current political thought. After this, in the final portion of the book, I confront the common critique of Arendt that her apparent goals of renewing the political action and judgment of modern citizens are of limited practical value in modern liberal capitalist society. I argue that in the context of modern commercial democratic regimes this critique is largely accurate, given that the clear goal of liberal politics has historically been to remove most of the responsibility for the preservation and realization of political goals from the majority of citizens by politically organizing them through market and institutional mechanisms. However, I then seek to think beyond where Arendt concluded her work by considering how her political ideals relate to an analysis of modern society she perhaps died too soon to appreciate: the likely unsustainability of contemporary liberal political economy in the near future. I argue that in the likely future context where the vast majority of citizens will not be able to expect robust economic advancement and relatively unlimited career choices and prospects, the traditional liberal reliance on markets and institutions will become much less effective, and therefore modern political regimes will need to rely much more on the political judgment and direct political action of their citizens. The sustainable future of civilization, in other words, may very well depend on our ability to realize something like Arendt's non-sovereign ideal of republican political freedom at a federated global level.

1 | Action, Politics, Genealogy

Hannah Arendt's theory of action has both inspired and perplexed her readers. Its revival of the ancient idea of publicly performed freedom reintroduced a lost dimension into political theory, one that insisted that free human action, at its highest level, was more than merely doing as one pleases in private life. Authentic action, according to Arendt, was something visible in the public realm, carrying a genuine potency capable of changing the world. Given its centrality to her thought and its radical character, it has, not surprisingly, been a target of significant critique. In this chapter, I want to attempt to turn aside some of the more serious criticism of Arendt by offering a new interpretation of her theory of action. I believe that a great deal of the criticism of her thought originates in a misunderstanding of the role and meaning of her theory of action, especially her attempt to revive the ancient ideal of noninstrumental political action. Though it may come as a surprise, I believe this criticism is rooted in a failure to understand Arendt's long-standing concern over the problem of history and her unique practice of historiography.

There are at least two misunderstandings of Arendt that I believe the account of Arendtian action offered here can resolve. First, many critics have interpreted Arendt's attempt to revive the noninstrumental ideal of political action as a deliberative, participatory, and performative activity, which situates politics from a kind of quasi-aesthetic perspective. They argue that Arendt—drawing strongly on the logic of Aristotle's assertion that *praxis*, as the highest human activity, cannot have a *telos* beyond itself, but is *a-telos*, an "end in itself"—believed that any instrumental or teleological activity must therefore be kept out of politics. As a result, readers have often understood her as suggesting a dichotomous relationship between political action and instrumental activity, with the implication that social concerns such as poverty or discrimination cannot be a concern of genuine politics. Politics should instead be free to engage in a deliberative and performative disclosive activity of individual identity.[1] Readers have often found the idea that there could ever be such a sharp separation established between social concerns and the political odd and possibly unintelligible. Even Mary McCarthy, her close friend, editor, and literary executor, once told Arendt, "I have always asked myself: 'What is somebody supposed to do on the public stage, in the public space, if he does not concern himself with the social? That is, what's left?'"[2] A second misunderstanding concerns her theory of judgment. Some critics have argued that there is a contradiction in her accounts of judgment, and indeed that this contradiction is so fundamental that the only conclusion one might draw is that she must have had two different theories of judgment.[3] These critics assert that her texts indicate that there was an earlier, more political and practical account of judgment in such places as the *Between Past and Future* essays, and a later much more contemplative and historical account offered in texts such as *The Life of the Mind*.[4]

But suppose Arendt understood politics and history to be much more closely related than these critics think? Might it be possible that Arendt was simply viewing judgment from two different perspectives: one from the side of politics and the *vita activa*, and the other from the side of history and the *vita contemplativa*? I argue here that Arendt's political and historiographic concerns were in fact intimately linked, and it was the recognition of this link that prompted her to develop a unique genealogical approach. There were a set of long-standing modern conflations about the nature of politics and history that Arendt hoped to deconstruct, and her first step in doing this was through reconceiving the very nature of historical reflection. Thus, while it is no doubt true that her work was primarily focused on politics, we will see in this chapter that it was her concerns over history both as a political problem and as a methodological problem that originally prompted that concern with politics. In her work, she would seek to reassert the primary place of human agency in history, and when the implications of this project are adequately appreciated, many misunderstandings of her thought, I believe, are cleared up. On the account I propose, what defined political agency for Arendt had much more to do with the historical significance of a specific deed or event, and little to do with whether instrumental activity was involved in the deed. As for the notion that there is a conflict in Arendt between political judgment and historical reflection, her approach shows that she understood history and politics to be coterminous. Thus, what appears to be a conflict turns out merely to be a shift in perspective.

What results from this assertion of the primordial place of human action in history is an incredibly strong notion of human agency—stronger even than many readers already familiar with her work may realize. The difficulty understanding Arendt's approach presents, however, is that she never explicitly formulated it, and therefore it must be gleaned from a number of disparate texts. As a result, the argument of this chapter must inevitably be somewhat long and dialectical. Pivotal will be understanding the central role her teacher and mentor Martin Heidegger played in the development of her approach, whose ideas she adopted but also heavily revised. It will therefore be necessary to discuss Heidegger's contributions to Arendt's ideas in some depth, before turning to her departures from him and their consequences. First, however, it will be helpful to have a sense of Arendt's basic genealogical approach.

The Problem of Origins

A genealogy is a narrative that seeks to comprehend and explain a historic occurrence or circumstance by uncovering its origins or fundamental causes. This, of course, is an extraordinarily perplexing endeavor. How does one, after all, find these sources? What are the criteria for judging their relevance? On what authority does the genealogist make her claims? Perhaps unsurprisingly then, Arendt is often accused of contradicting herself or engaging in a mode of theorizing that was overly messy. This was to be expected: the chief goal of a genealogist is to pursue what Heidegger called *aletheia*, the fundamental experiences that lay at origins of history. Arendt was much more concerned with capturing those experiences adequately than she was with conceptual and logical consistency, which ultimately is more a consequence of the simplicity of our articulations of concepts than the authenticity of our explorations of lived experience.

The problem of genealogy seems to have been forced on Arendt by her analysis of the modern situation, and specifically what she felt was the complete failure of the tradition of political thought to cope with that situation. The tradition's "moral, legal, theoretical, and practical standards," she claimed, "together with its political institutions and forms of government, broke down spectacularly" in the first part of the twentieth century.[5] As a result, we now lived in an era without a "testament," or tradition, which "selects and names, which hands down and preserves, which indicates where the treasures are and what their worth is."[6] She believed Tocqueville captured the historical moment best when he wrote that "since the past has ceased to throw its light upon the future, the mind of man wanders in obscurity."[7] As a result, we are "confronted anew . . . by the elementary problems of human living-together."[8] The elemental nature of such problems must present unique difficulties for historical reflection. If tradition has failed, there is no authority to appeal to in order to establish the validity of historical claims and the significance of events. As a result, a historian in this era ultimately has nothing to guide her but her own judgment. This, to say the least, is a daunting prospect, and Arendt recognized the almost unavoidable presumptuousness in this era of the kind of historical reflections she pursued. She called this activity "thinking without a banister."[9] It was her way of indicating that the practice of genealogy was the only place genuine historical reflection could begin in our era. The historian must go back to the primordial experiences that preceded the tradition and awaken those experiences in order to make history intelligible again.

One of Arendt's earliest discussions of her approach came in her reply to Eric Voegelin's review of *The Origins of Totalitarianism*.[10] Voegelin criticized her for incorporating value judgments too deeply into her analyses of totalitarianism, arguing that the "morally abhorrent and the emotionally existing will overshadow the essential."[11] Arendt rejected this criticism. She insisted that this qualitative aspect of the analysis formed "an integral part of it. This has nothing to do with sentimentality or moralizing, although, of course, either can become a pitfall for the author. If I moralized or became sentimental, I simply did not do well what I was supposed to do, namely, to describe the totalitarian phenomenon as occurring, not on the moon, but in the midst of human society." She argued that, for instance, her use of "the image of Hell" to describe the Nazi death camps was not meant "allegorically, but literally . . . a description of the camps as Hell on earth is more 'objective,' that is, more adequate to their essence than statements of a purely sociological or psychological nature."[12] For Arendt, in other words, descriptions of historical phenomena cannot be separated from their qualitative context.[13]

She was significantly influenced in this approach by the "critical interpretation of the past" done by Heidegger and her close friend Walter Benjamin.[14] Heidegger and Benjamin showed Arendt a mode of genealogical practice that could bring the original meaning of vital words in our language back to life through thought and imagination. They had argued that words carried behind them authentic experiences that often are lost with passage of time. These experiences could be revived and used to shed light on the past and, consequentially, also on the present world where tradition can no longer illuminate the most important aspects of lives.[15] She called this mode of genealogy "pearl diving":[16]

> [Pearl diving] works with the "thought fragments" it can wrest from the past and gather about itself. Like a pearl diver who descends to the bottom of the sea . . . to pry loose the rich and the strange, the pearls and coral in the depths and to carry them to the surface, this thinking delves into the depths of the past. . . . What guides this thinking is the conviction that although the living is subject to the ruin of time, the process of decay is at the same time a process of crystallization . . . as though they waited only for the pearl diver who one day will come down to them and bring them up into the world of the living.[17]

For Arendt, the break in tradition meant that there was no longer an "Ariadne thread" that connected our political language to our commonsense experiences.[18] Our political words were "empty shells,"[19] which, because they had lost their moorings in authentic experiences, could be redefined at will so long as they served to support some "functionalized" theory.[20] While pearl diving could not "retie the broken thread of tradition," it could perhaps "discover the real origins of traditional concepts in order to distill from them anew their original spirit."[21]

However, what distinguished Arendt was a determination to anchor her genealogical studies in an unprecedented assertion of the role of human agency in history. Arendt first articulated this agency-based approach in *The Human Condition*, arguing that historical "events," which for her always involved the "deeds" of acting human beings, were "*sui generis*"[22] and characterized by "absolute, objective novelty."[23] It is in the nature of events and deeds "to break through the commonly accepted and reach into the extraordinary, where whatever is true in common and everyday life no longer applies because everything that exists is unique and *sui generis*."[24] Arendt believed that the invention of the telescope was one such event. While many of the elements of the modern scientific outlook, such as the development of nominalist ontologies, the idea of an Archimedean thought experiment, and skepticism about the veracity of the senses preceded the telescope's invention, it required an act of pure human natality—the uniquely human capacity to begin something new—to turn these disparate elements into a potent historical "event." In other words, according to Arendt, there *must* be an act of sheer human spontaneous natality at the heart of all historical trends and processes. Such acts must appear from the viewpoint of historical causality as "miraculous."[25]

> Every act, seen from the perspective not of the agent but of the process in whose framework it occurs and whose automatism it interrupts, is a "miracle"—that is, something which could not be expected. . . . History, in contradistinction to nature, is full of events; here the miracle of accident and infinite improbability occurs so frequently that it seems strange to speak of miracles at all. But the reason for this frequency is merely that historical processes are created and constantly interrupted by human initiative, by the *initium* man is insofar as he is a human being.[26]

To assert this strong objectivity on behalf of the deeds and events of historical phenomena—an objectivity anchored in a powerful assertion of spontaneous human agency and initiative—Arendt clearly must have had an alternate conception of the meaning of historiographic "truth." This historiography was drawn from Heidegger's philosophy, but it would involve a series of highly original and imaginative critiques and revisions of that philosophy.

Arendt's Heideggerian Foundation

The relationship of Arendt's thought to Heidegger[27] has been dealt with elsewhere by writers such as Seyla Benhabib, Lewis and Sandra Hinchman, Jacques Taminiaux, and Dana Villa.[28] While I have learned a great deal from this work, in my view none of them sufficiently addresses my specific purpose here. I want to examine how Arendt appropriated and revised Heidegger in order to show that politics and history were intimately connected and that her interest in this connection was grounded in her determination to reassert human agency in history. Heidegger's abiding and formative impact on Arendt is, at this point, one of the most easily established relations of influence between significant intellectual figures available. To see how extensively and avidly Arendt read Heidegger's work, one can consult Bard College's Hannah Arendt Collection, which provides online copies of marginalia from her personal library showing that she took notes in at least twenty-five of Heidegger's works.[29] Consulting her papers at the Library of Congress shows that in the early 1950s Arendt taught courses on Heidegger and was regularly consulted by his translators. Heidegger was arguably the key figure in her philosophical training; she attended some of his most famous and important courses and had an intermittent romantic relationship with him through much of the mid to late 1920s.[30] Indeed, while Karl Jaspers supervised her dissertation, Young-Bruehl notes that "both the way in which Arendt wove Jaspers's orientations though her work and the language in which she expressed her ideas owe a much greater debt to Heidegger."[31] In a letter from the 1950s, which described the project that would become *The Human Condition* and which attests to the crucial impact of Heidegger's classes and philosophical tutelage on her own thought, she told Heidegger that "I would not be able to do this . . . without what I learned from you in my youth."[32] Arendt, moreover, attests to the extraordinarily influential nature of the early Heidegger courses she attended in a celebratory essay for Heidegger's eightieth birthday, noting that "Heidegger's 'fame' predates by about eight years the publication of *Sein und Zeit* . . . indeed it is open to question whether the unusual success of this book . . . would have been possible if it had not been preceded by the teacher's reputation among the students, in whose opinion, at any rate, the book's success merely confirmed what they had known for many years."[33]

Heidegger pioneered an approach to philosophical argumentation that used phenomenological analysis to establish transcendental arguments about the nature of human existence, a mode of phenomenology Arendt directly appropriated in her own approach.[34] In its most basic sense, phenomenology is simply the attempt to describe human experience as authentically as possible. Heidegger's innovation was to link this descriptive procedure to the establishment of competing explanations. Certain phenomena may have popular explanations attached to them. Phenomenology can be used to describe an experience or phenomenon in such a way that the more popular explanation is somehow undermined and an alternative explanation—typically one the phenomenologist is advocating for—is presented in a more convincing light.[35] When Arendt, for instance, asserted that "Hell on earth" is a more objective description of the Nazi death camps than any mode of description based on scientific methodology could provide, she was utilizing just such a phenomenological argument.

Heidegger's use of this phenomenological approach was extremely ambitious in scope. He proposed to "raise anew the question of the meaning of Being,"[36] arguing that this question had been put aside long ago in ancient Greece and given an answer that has remained fundamentally the same throughout the history of Western philosophy.[37] To someone unfamiliar with metaphysical philosophy, this may seem like an outlandishly elementary proposition. Being, after all, seems self-evidently to be whatever there is. On the other hand, to metaphysical philosophers, Heidegger would seem to be making no sense at all, since a variety of different answers to the question of what Being is have been given: for Plato, Being was the eternal forms; for Augustine and Thomas Aquinas, it was God; for Nietzsche, it was the will to power. The problem with this objection, Heidegger argued, is that metaphysics is answering a different question than he is asking about Being. The metaphysicians had answered the question of *what* Being is, while Heidegger proposed to raise anew the question of the *meaning* of Being. The attempt to say *what* Being is treats Being as if it is some sort of entity. But Heidegger points out that Being is no thing, but a quality that all things possess. The problem with attempting, as metaphysics had, to say "what Being is" is that it begs the question. When we attempt to articulate what something means, we attempt to explain it in terms of more simplistic and basic experiences and concepts. But if Being is the most basic quality of all things, if it is already present in everything, then any attempt to explain it cannot appeal to anything more basic. As a result, attempts to answer the question of *what* Being is already presuppose an understanding of Being. Thus, any "theoretical" approach to the question will come up short, because in attempting to conceptualize Being, modern science and metaphysical philosophy are attempting to define Being as a thing, rather than as the most basic quality of things.

In *Being and Time*, Heidegger sought to approach the question of the meaning of Being phenomenologically: because Being is always already presupposed in all human existence, he proposed to examine how it shows itself in human experience. What is significant in this proposition for understanding Arendt's account of politics and history is that Heidegger has rejected as yet another version of metaphysics the idea that the physical universe, its matter and forces, can adequately describe Being. Metaphysics had always defined Being as what persists through all contingent changes, and thus, to the extent modern science defines matter and forces as what is present through all change, modern science has a metaphysical conception of Being. Heidegger argued that before this assertion can be justified, we must examine Being as it appears in human experience, for that is where our understanding of the meaning of Being is drawn from. If, as Heidegger proposed to do, we examine the way Being manifests itself in human experience, he believed the naturalistic metaphysic of modern science will reveal itself to be inadequate. The consequence of this for Arendt is that her grounds for claiming a kind of objectivity for historical phenomena, deeds, and events that falls outside naturalistic ontology are greatly strengthened, because in the context of human experience Being, according Heidegger, encompasses both nature and history as exclusive ontological domains.

In order to show that our understanding of Being can only be grasped through the phenomenological analysis of human experience, Heidegger developed powerful philosophical arguments concerning the nature of human experience and the beings that human beings are. His most significant argument was his observation that human beings are *essentially* contextual.[38] This is a fundamental commitment Arendt adopted from Heidegger, and she provided one of the most concise and penetrating formulations of Heidegger's perspective in the opening chapter of *The Human Condition*. In these opening pages, Arendt appeared to be continuing her exchange with Voegelin. Voegelin had attacked an offhand statement Arendt had made that "human nature as such is at stake" in his review of *Origins*, arguing that this was nonsensical, since human nature could never be changed. In her reply, Arendt challenged the very idea that there existed such a thing as a human nature in Voegelin's Platonic sense.[39] Her reasoning had to do with the nature of the existential threat she believed totalitarianism posed to human beings. If there was such a thing as an unchanging human nature, then the threat of totalitarianism was greatly diminished, since human nature could never fundamentally be altered or diminished. The essential capacities of human beings would only have to wait for a set of historical circumstances that allowed them to express their freedom again. Arendt suggested that we do not know if there is such a thing as human nature, and, furthermore, we have no grounds for believing the essential characteristics of human beings could not be altered in a fundamental way. As she remarked, "Historically we know of man's nature only insofar as it has existence, and no realm of eternal essences will ever console us if man loses his essential capabilities."[40]

Arendt expanded on this argument in the opening moments of *The Human Condition*. "The problem of human nature," she writes, "seems unanswerable in both its individual psychological sense and its general philosophical sense. It is highly unlikely that we, who can know, determine, and define the natural essences of all things surrounding us, which we are not, should ever be able to do the same for ourselves—this would be like jumping over our own shadows."[41] At first blush, this statement of the impossibility of comprehending human nature by drawing an analogy to "shadow jumping" seems like nothing more than a literary flourish. Yet, seen against the background of Arendt's existentialism, it turns out to be a penetrating formulation of Heidegger's thought: "nothing entitles us to assume that man has a nature or essence in the same sense as other things. In other words, if we have a nature or essence, then surely only a god could know and define it, and the first prerequisite would be that he be able to speak about a 'who' as though it were a 'what.' The perplexity is that the modes of human cognition applicable to things with 'natural' qualities . . . fail us when we raise the question: And who are we?"[42] Thus, in Arendt's words, human beings, "no matter what they do, are always conditioned beings,"[43] by which she means that the only certain statement that can be made about human nature is the fact that it always draws on, is dependent upon, and indeed is unintelligible without a context that transcends and gives meaning to it. A rock would always be rock, whether it had a context or not; but if a human being, however, could somehow exist without a context—if perhaps she was born and lived alone, somehow, in the vacuum of deep space—she could never truly be a human being.

Heidegger's most well-known formulation of this idea comes in his characterization of humans as "Being-in-the-world."[44] Humans cannot be the sort of beings they are unless they always already find themselves in a meaningful context. There is virtually no doubt that Arendt drew this concept directly from Heidegger's *Being and Time* when she formulated her own concepts of worldliness and common sense. The Bard College collection shows that Arendt's German copy of *Being and Time* was heavily used.[45] Moreover, in an article critically engaging Heidegger's account of human action written around the time she formulated the ideas that would result in *The Human Condition*—her book dealing most extensively with worldliness— she raises the key critique of the tradition of political thought that is found in *The Human Condition*. The problem with the tradition of political thought, in her view, was that it has always sought to deal with human beings in the singular, while politics is essentially concerned with the condition of human plurality, the fact that "men, not Man, live on the earth."[46] Foreshadowing the central role that worldliness would play in *The Human Condition*, Arendt writes in this article that "it may be—but I shall only hint at this—that

Heidegger's concept of 'world,' which in many respects stands at the center of his philosophy, constitutes a step out of this difficulty."[47]

According to Heidegger, there could be no particular objects, no things at all, unless they were conditioned by a meaningful world that provides a background of intelligibility to them.[48] This worldly background, which we only become aware of indirectly, is not a thing in itself but somehow a condition of things. The idea of "world" seems to be constitutive of many intuitive experiences. When we say things like this or that would mean "the end of the world," typically we don't have in mind the total annihilation of the planet. Often this phrase might be limited to the end of our particular civilization or even our personal lifestyle or long-term goals. The "world" means more to us than objects that surround us: it involves all our human meanings and involvements, things that cannot be reified into objects but somehow seem to be attached to objects from out of our world. Heidegger would occasionally use the German phrase *es weltet* to describe this experience, which literally translates as "it worlds," that is, that the world *worlds at us and around us.*[49]

If this is true, it would then present modern scientific epistemology with serious complications. It implies that there will never be any truly "theoretical" position—no final Archimedean point, in Arendt's words—for no matter what methodological and experimental precautions are adopted, they will always be rooted and have their origin in some kind of human worldly background. Moreover, it would also suggest that the whole framework of "value thinking"—which Arendt and her teachers were so critical of—would become untenable. Since meaning comes out of a world that always conditions our activities and reflections from an ever present background, there is in principle no way to ever give a satisfactory account of any particular "value." Whatever we label a "value," such as justice, beauty, goodness, or greatness, proceeds out of the meaningful background and never fully captures what that background implies. The attempt to objectify a meaning by labeling it a "value" only guarantees that it will lose its power to illuminate why we do and think the things we do in our lives.[50]

Heidegger deals with the framework of being-in-the-world primarily in the first division of *Being and Time*. While there are seemingly endless phenomenological refinements Heidegger carefully adds to the notion of being-in-the-world, for my purposes, I will focus on only two such specifics Heidegger develops, both of which clearly influenced Arendt's thought: what

Heidegger calls our "thrownness," and what he calls "being-in." Thrownness is the "factical" life situation in which human beings find themselves in their unique social, political, historical, and relational circumstances.[51] Heidegger uses the word "factical," as distinct from "factual," in order to emphasize that the concrete facts of our lives are not just objective circumstances that have only a contingent bearing on us; they are, as Arendt emphasizes, conditions of our existence. We are, existentially speaking, *thrown* into the particular world we inhabit, thrown into who we are and what possibilities we have available to us. Arendt adopts this notion in her account of worldliness. A world is not merely a community; it also includes the structures and concrete conditions of our civilization.

Our ability to engage with the worldly situation we are thrown in is what Heidegger calls "being-in."[52] Being-in seems clearly to have been a primary source for Arendt's idea of "common sense," which she refers to as the sixth sense, which fits our five senses into the common world. Since it is clear that Heidegger's concept of being-in-the-world is the source of Arendt's fundamental political category of worldliness, there can be little doubt that "being-in" and "common sense" for all intents and purposes refer to the same basic existential structure, particularly since Heidegger devotes so much of *Being and Time* to "being-in."[53] Heidegger articulates being-in as our ability to be and feel at home in our concrete worldly surroundings. Being-in has the sense of "inhabiting," "residing," "dwelling," "to be accustomed to," and "to be familiar with."[54] As we will see later, Arendt believed that being-in, or common sense, has atrophied in the modern era, and that the modern attempt to replace it with what she called "common sense reasoning," an orientation based on the basic structure of the human mind and body, is what would ultimately lead to a variety of modern political pathologies. In Chapter 5, we will see Arendt attempt in her theory of judgment to theorize the possibility of reestablishing some form of common sense.

While the first division of *Being and Time* was thus clearly of great importance to Arendt, the second division is arguably even more so. As we will see, it is from the second division that Arendt makes her most distinctive departures from Heidegger. *Being and Time* was famously intended by Heidegger to have four more divisions. Heidegger eventually abandoned the project's more ambitious objective, which would have required the final four divisions. This ultimate objective had been to work out the meaning of Being by appealing to the experience of Time.[55] Heidegger had proposed to do this by examining first the being that already has an understanding of

Being—however vague that understanding may be—what Heidegger calls *Dasein*, his word for human beings.[56] In *Being and Time*, Heidegger approached human beings and their experience of Being in two steps: in the first division he looks at the basic existential structures of human experience, while in the second division he articulates the new qualities these structures take on when they are reinterpreted from the perspective of what he called "ecstatic temporality," his term for how time manifests itself in human experience.[57] While the existential structures of our being-in-the-world provide the background conditions that allow us to start to bring the meaning of Being into focus, Heidegger believed that it is only after we reinterpret these background conditions from our primordial experience of time as "temporality" that we finally come into genuine contact with Being. He argued that the common way of thinking about time as a linear progression or sequence of events actually drew on a primordial experience of time that we always already have before developing this more theoretical notion of time. This temporality is "ecstatic" because in each element of this experience of time (past, present, or future) we "stand out" from our worldliness and "into the truth of Being,"[58] that is, we somehow exist in an existential position that is removed from our worldliness, because it brings into focus the limits or "horizons" of that worldliness.[59] Heidegger believed that when we can confront our primordial temporality, it will allow us to experience Being in its authentic meaning. This confrontation with Being will give insight, depth, and authenticity to our worldly involvements.

According to Heidegger, the past, as an aspect of temporality, is rooted in our existence as essentially historical beings, what he calls our "historicity."[60] By saying we are "historical," Heidegger is not simply asserting that there were a sequence of well-known events that our civilization's historians have documented and placed in bound narratives. He means that our lives are always grasped as narratives that stretch out from birth to death.[61] It is these unique stories that allow us to have an identity—to become a "who" rather than a "what."[62] The history books written by historians are only possible because we first and foremost originally experience our own individual lives as narratives.[63] However, the ability to grasp ourselves as a "who" with a unique life story requires a direct confrontation with our ecstatic temporality.[64] This is crucial for understanding Arendt's account of historical methodology: there is an essential link between our existence as narratively structured agents and the histories we produce. Our histories are narrative because we ourselves are narratives.

But while our past plays an important role in providing a traditional and cultural background or "heritage,"[65] it is only by confronting our future that we truly experience Being in its immediacy, in such a way that our story becomes truly our own unique story. This primordial future is not our goals and plans in life. We only confront Being when we confront the absolute limit of our own being-in-the-world: death. Recall that Heidegger had argued that Being is not a thing but the most basic and fundamental quality of all things. Being is therefore literally nothing: "no-thing."[66] In other words, Being is that mysterious aspect of all things that is both its ground—the source from which it all came—but also completely opaque and mysterious, beyond human comprehension because it is the fundamental condition of all such comprehension. As a result, it cannot be thought, but only left in question, as the mysterious groundless ground, the nothing, of all things. This nothingness underlying all things can only be confronted when we confront our absolute mortality, the fundamental nothingness that awaits all of us in death.[67] When we do this, we receive a "moment of vision"[68] that allows us to fully live in our present by resolutely choosing the life we were originally thoughtlessly channeled into by the patterns of our worldly possibilities.[69] This ability to choose what we have already been, in terms of both our own lives and our civilization's heritage occurs in the mode of what Heidegger calls "resoluteness."[70] Resoluteness allows the moment of vision to take some kind of articulate form in what Heidegger had called "discourse," the linguistic and communicative element of our being-in. After we have faced up to our death and placed this moment of vision in some kind of articulate and expressive form or "discourse," we come to have what he calls "primordial truth" or "disclosedness," and later, after *Being and Time*, *aletheia*, the word for truth he borrows from the Greeks, which meant truth as "uncoveredness" or "unconcealment."[71]

For Heidegger, since all truth is conditioned by an existential point of view, all truth always reveals only certain facets of Being.[72] One might take for example an artwork such as Edvard Munch's *The Scream*. From a scientific point of view, it would be a "correct" statement about the being of *The Scream* to define it as canvas with dried paint on it. In that sense, science has indeed "revealed" something about the painting. Yet, at the same time, it has concealed something about the painting; indeed, it might be argued that it has concealed much more than it has revealed. Consider the way the world is revealed or disclosed in *The Scream*. Munch captures in its bizarre surreality and strangeness the way the world "worlds" when we experience moments of horror. In these unforgettable moments, the "worlding" of the world seems to slow down to a crawl in an odd slow-motion effect, making people around us become shadowy figures, little more than part of the landscape, doing utterly meaningless things. Thus, it may indeed be scientifically "correct" that *The Scream* is only a canvas with dried paint on it, but its *aletheia*, what it reveals or opens up—its essential truth about its being—is also much more than that.

But while art may provide an exemplary instance of Heideggerian *aletheia*, Heidegger believed *aletheia* went far beyond art, leading ultimately to a confrontation with the meaning of Being itself, which he believed was the source of human freedom and could only be approached through what he called "thinking." It is a well-established fact of twentieth-century philosophical history that both Heidegger's and Arendt's projects were inspired by and responding to Aristotle's practical philosophy, especially as it was articulated in the *Nicomachean Ethics* in Heidegger's case, while it appears Arendt drew broadly on the *Ethics*, the *Politics*, the *Rhetoric*, and the *Poetics*.[73] It is by now clear that *Being and Time* should be interpreted as an attempt to establish the priority of Aristotle's account of action, or *praxis*, as the fundament of human existence.[74] The first division of *Being and Time* seems clearly intended to establish this assertion. Yet, free human action is never achieved in the first division. The closest we come to action is in the context of technical activities, Aristotle's *poiesis*, what Arendt would eventually call "work." All human activity in the first division, while certainly inescapable and fundamental, is still essentially thoughtless and inauthentic, at best employing theoretical or technical means/ends thinking, because it does not reflect on the essentially mysterious grounds of our being-in-the-world.[75] It is only in the second division, after *phronēsis*, or what Heidegger would later come to call authentic "thinking," has been faced up to through a confrontation with mortality that our practical activity takes on the quality of action, or *praxis*.

A crucial upshot of this—one that Arendt will relentlessly attack—is that Heidegger believes that free human action has less to do with the specific choices, activities, or concrete courses of action we choose to take, and more to do with how our everyday activities, which are thoughtless and conformist in nature, can be transfigured and take on a deep and profound quality—a quality that makes it truly free action—only when we reflect on and confront the meaning of Being. Michael Allen Gillespie argues: "In this respect, this phronetic moment of vision looks more like a conversion experience than a deliberative judgment. Heidegger reads Aristotle more through

Paul, Augustine, Eckhart, and Luther than through the Aristotelian ethical tradition. . . . This phronetic moment of vision brings about not merely a transformation of the world but first and foremost a transformation or conversion of *Dasein* itself."[76] As we will see, this conception of human freedom as an essentially reflective or contemplative endeavor is what ties Heidegger most closely to the philosophical tradition and is the fundamental point of departure for Arendt. Of course, from Heidegger's perspective this is still ultimately a practical philosophy—indeed, all philosophy is ultimately practical, in Heidegger's very broad, existentialist sense. But Arendt, for her part, rejects this claim: she will go on to argue that contemplation and action are two very different activities, and their relationship—if indeed there is one at all—is extremely obscure. In her critique of Heidegger in the "Willing" volume of *The Life of the Mind*, she characterizes Heidegger's notion of action as "a kind of 'acting' (*handeln*) which is polemically understood as the opposite of the 'loud' and visible actions of public life. . . . This acting is silent, a 'letting one's own self act in its indebtedness,' and this entirely inner 'action' in which man opens himself to the authentic actuality of being thrown, can exist only in the activity of thinking."[77]

It is true that Heidegger's work in the 1930s seems to suggest a more activist and political stance, but there is no evidence that work from this period had any direct philosophical influence on Arendt, and Heidegger himself soon seemed to move on from it. By the end of the 1930s, Heidegger's conception of *praxis* and *phronēsis* would, more than ever before, become increasingly more contemplative and quasi-religious. Heidegger would continue to articulate human freedom as having less to do with concrete acting in the world, and more to do with how we can establish an authentic relationship to Being through what he called "thinking." Thus, in the "Letter on Humanism," Heidegger continues to argue that true action only occurs in the authentic thinking of Being, saying that such thinking is a mode of action that is "the simplest and at the same time the highest, because it concerns the relation of Being to man."[78]

A Political Critique of Heidegger

Arendt's approach would be based on a number of politically inspired appropriations and revisions of Heidegger, one that I will argue has far-reaching consequences for how we think about history, politics, and human agency in general. For Heidegger, the public structures of our existence—our world, history, civilization, public realm—represent sources of conformity and inauthenticity. These are the things we have in common with others, and we therefore naturally become inauthentic when we thoughtlessly take over these conditions. We get lost in "what one does." To the extent we become differentiated from our existential history by establishing our unique identity in a confrontation with mortality, action is therefore only realized in contemplation. In this contemplative conception of agency, Heidegger has thus essentially collapsed the distinction between thought and action: action is ultimately only our ability to think Being. The resulting theory of history this conception of historicity leads to is one that gives little potency and significance to concrete human deeds, emphasizing instead general trends or "sendings from Being," as Heidegger called them, which in many ways determine and give meaning to the specific acts of human beings.

Arendt, by turns, would seek to challenge each of these propositions. In her critique of Heidegger, she sought to reintroduce human agency, and in turn politics, back into historical reflection, articulating an account of history and politics that would return genuine potency and meaning to the concrete deeds of human agents. In her view, Heidegger's existentialism had failed in its attempt to escape metaphysics, for even though it left many of the fundamental metaphysical categories behind, it nevertheless remained bound in a more primordial way by the philosophical tradition's prejudices denigrating human action. This point has relevance to one of the key interpretative questions Arendt scholars have confronted: explaining the relationship between *The Origins of Totalitarianism* and *The Human Condition*. Seyla Benhabib, Margaret Canovan, Michael H. McCarthy, Hanna Fenichel Pitkin, and Dana Villa have all dealt with this question at length.[79] These two books seem in many ways to be related to each other in only the broadest thematic ways. What led Arendt to write a book so different in so many ways from the earlier book? I will argue in the following that, while there is no doubt that politics was the fundamental concern of Arendt's work by the time of *The Human Condition*, it was originally her concern over the political and methodological problems of history raised by her work in *Origins* that instigated her turn to politics. Arendt's political thought, in other words, was her to solution to what she believed was a problematic tendency of modern history to denigrate and largely ignore human agency.

As we will see in Chapter 4, a nexus of political and historiographic problems confronted Arendt after *Origins*, involving the relationship between totalitarianism, revolutionary politics, and modern conceptions of the philosophy of history. Arendt had recognized that totalitarian political movements invariably arose with revolutionary aspirations and were typically animated by what she called an "ideology," by which she meant a conception of historical necessity or law.[80] Much of her critique of modernity involved deconstructing the notion of ideology as a politics of historical movement: she would insist that history was located not in dialectical trends but in concrete human deeds. But this critique of modern historical thinking carried historiographic implications: any historiography she employed would have to reflect this emphasis on human agency and to eschew historical explanations originating from grand historical trends. As we will see, she was able to achieve this through her critique of Heidegger.

Arendt departed from Heidegger on two fundamental points. First, adopting Heidegger's concept of worldliness, she wrote, as I noted earlier, that "the problem that has plagued political philosophy almost throughout its history . . . [was that philosophy has always dealt] with man in the singular, whereas politics could not even be conceived of if man did not exist in the plural. . . . It may be—but I shall only hint at this—that Heidegger's concept of 'world' . . . constitutes a step out of this difficulty."[81] But Arendt was unhappy with the significance Heidegger gave the world, arguing that, contra Heidegger, worldliness was not a source of inauthenticity and conformity, but instead a realm where human beings can truly realize their identity in free human action.[82] "Thus we find the old hostility of the philosopher toward the *polis* in Heidegger's analyses of average everyday life . . . in which the public realm has the function of hiding reality."[83] Second, she argued that, while Heidegger's concept of historicity—the narrative agency of human beings—was true, his conception of action as an essentially contemplative activity was profoundly flawed. She writes that Heidegger's conception of historicity "shares with the older concept of history the fact that . . . it never reaches but always misses the center of politics—man as an acting being."[84]

Arendt and Heidegger have, in essence, diametrically opposed accounts of how human beings become "whos"—how they come to have unique life stories. For Heidegger, human beings only come to have authentic life stories when they resolutely confront their ultimate groundlessness in death. Historicity, in other words, is for him rooted in the condition of mortality.[85] Though certainly unimaginable without a recognition of the condition of mortality, Arendt nevertheless finds historicity to be rooted in a condition that is diametrically opposed to Heidegger's account: in birth, or what Arendt calls the condition of natality.[86] Arendt equates human natality, the ability to be born, with the human capacity for action, which she defines as the ability to begin something new:[87] "With the creation of man, the principle of beginning came into the world. . . . The fact that man is capable of action means that the unexpected can be expected from him, that he is able to perform what is infinitely improbable. And this again is possible only because each man is unique, so that with each birth something uniquely new comes into the world."[88] In other words, it is this capacity to act and to begin that Arendt believes forms the content of our life stories. Our lives are made up of a series of unique happenings—events and deeds that constitute our "whoness." While, like Heidegger, this relationship between action and historicity becomes the condition of history for Arendt, it affords a very different sensibility than Heidegger gave it. In Arendt's words: "But the reason why each human life tells its story and why history ultimately becomes the storybook of mankind . . . is that both are the outcome of action."[89] And as a result, because Heidegger's conception of history deals not merely at a psychological but instead at an ontological level, Arendt's account of action carries extraordinary potency, in a way Heidegger's contemplative notion of action probably never could, offering unique potential to radically alter our existing circumstances every time we perform an act.[90]

Arendt believed that part of the reason Heidegger arrived at these conclusions was that, especially in *Being and Time*, Heidegger drew his phenomenological conclusions from modern society and politics, a context that in her view greatly resisted potent human agency. In *The Human Condition*, Arendt set out to use Heidegger's "pearl diving" approach against him, attempting to unearth authentic experiences of historically potent human political agency that had been lost in the past. What she discovered was that Heidegger's view of the public realm and common world remained deeply bound to the philosophical tradition's historical prejudices against it. This refusal to leave those prejudices behind meant that while his existentialism may have successfully escaped the metaphysics of presence, his philosophy could not truly achieve an understanding of authentic human agency and, as a result, could never truly ground historical reflection.

Arendt's only significant published discussion of her theory of history comes in her essay "The Concept of History." While the essay contains a clear indication that politics was essentially related to history, Arendt makes much more explicit statements about the relationship in her 1969 lecture course "Philosophy and Politics: What Is Political Philosophy?"; in what follows, I want to use the 1969 course to supplement "The Concept of History" in order to better understand how she related politics and history. In the 1969 course, Arendt suggested that a fundamental tension exists in each human being between the faculty for thought and the faculty for action. It is, of course, relatively common in the modern era to understand there to be a gap of sorts between theory and practice, which must be bridged or reconciled. The idea that there is an *essential* tension between them is much more perplexing. However, Arendt argued this was not a flaw in humanity; in her view, it made human beings intensely interesting creatures, capable of combining faculties and engaging in activities that, from a phenomenological perspective, appear to have almost nothing in common.

This tension between thought and action arises out of their respective predominance in two fundamentally distinct and mutually exclusive spheres of experience. While action's sphere of experience was our engaged activity in the world, thought's sphere of experience took place in a mysterious gap in time between past and future that was utterly and existentially withdrawn from the common world. These spheres of experience gave rise to two authentic ways of life, each directed toward the realization of either thought or action. The *vita activa* sought to actualize action, and the activity it developed to do this was politics. The *vita contemplativa* sought to actualize thought, and the activity it developed was philosophy. These pursuits were anchored in competing conceptions of the Greeks' highest aspiration, captured in the mysterious Greek word *athanatizein*. In the 1969 course, Arendt notes that *athanatizein* was virtually impossible to adequately translate, as it was open to multivocal interpretations and took in a variety of disparate practices, but settles for rendering it as "to immortalize."[91] "The common root of politics and philosophy is immortality . . . not in the sense that the philosophers finally defined it, but only in the sense that both endeavors spring from the same desire of mortals to become or, since that is impossible, to partake in immortality, to get their share of it."[92]

Arendt asserts that a kind of competition developed among the Greeks over the best path to *athanatizein*.[93] For the philosophers, *athanatizein* meant contemplation, "to dwell in the neighborhood of those things which are forever."[94] Philosophy was oriented by the condition of mortality, since it pursued the things that exist beyond human life and its world, "the things which are eternal."[95] This philosophical orientation, she claimed, begins as far back as Plato's argument in the *Phaedo* for the immortality of the soul. Since death was the separation of the soul and body, and the philosophers pursued the eternal, the philosophers were therefore in love with death: "the philosopher qua philosopher will wish to die . . . those who hold fast to philosophy will pursue only dying and having died."[96] According to Arendt, the philosophers sought to live their lives in this gap between past and future and to realize the activities of the gap without reference to human affairs. And from out of this pursuit of immortality, the philosophers found a kind freedom all their own, a "philosophical freedom,"[97] which was elevated far beyond the activities of the world of acting women and men. Thus, in this respect Heidegger's contemplative account of human action and identity, far from distancing him from the philosophical tradition, was what bound him most closely to it.[98]

In competition with the philosophers, the Greek political actors pursued a very different kind of *athanatizein*. The tradition of political thought was formulated and structured by the philosophers, and Arendt therefore believed that their contemplative approach to immortalizing had in one way or another framed Western political theories. The problem with this, she argued, was that politics had its own unique and foundational practice of *athanatizein*, which had nothing to do with contemplation, but instead had to do with action, with free activity in the concrete circumstances of the human world.[99] Political actors did not strive to immortalize themselves through contemplation but instead through the performance of great deeds in a public realm where their peers could judge the acts, deciding whether those deeds deserved to become the content of history.[100] Thus, the essential characteristic of political action was its concern with the specific kind of immortality that comes from historical greatness in the human world.

However, the historical problem with this uniquely political form of *athanatizein* was that those who actually lived and took part in this activity— the "men of action," as she called them—rarely took the time to theorize about it. As a result, most of Western political thought was done by philosophers who disdained the political form of immortalizing and the activities of the men of action.[101] Philosophers could not grasp the actors' obsession with fame and power, since in their view it was "absurd" to think that humans could ever live up to what was highest in the cosmos,[102] and came to view political theory, in the words of Pascal, as like "laying down rules for a lunatic asylum."[103] "Hence," she writes, "the old paradox was resolved by the philosophers by denying to man not the capacity to 'immortalize,' but the capacity of measuring himself and his own deeds against the everlasting greatness of the cosmos."[104] Arendt's political writings were an attempt to provide the fullest articulation yet given of what the Western men of action had actually been doing in their pursuit of immortality.[105] To do this, she focused on what she believed were the three originary attempts to achieve political *athanati-zein* in Western politics: the Greeks, the Romans, and the modern revolutionaries.[106] Each instance displayed a unique version of political action, contributing formative elements and ideals to Western politics and culture that continue on in our political language.[107] Chapter 2 will examine these three different instances of political action. Presently, however, I want to provide a general account of what Arendt understood this political version of *athanatizein* to involve.

Politics and the Human Condition

What does it mean to *be* a narrative—*to live a life as a story*? If humans are "whos" and not "whats," they can therefore never be given labels, never meaningfully be placed in conceptual boxes. They are too interesting, too dynamic. Unlike the animals, who remain members of species that revolve eternally in the cycle of the cosmos, humans are "'the mortals,'" according to Arendt, "the only mortal things there are . . . individual life, a *bios* with a recognizable life-story from birth to death, rises out of biological life . . . [and] is distinguished from other things by the rectilinear course of its movement, which, so to speak, cuts through the circular movements of biological life."[108] The only way of coming to terms with the "whoness" of a human being is by learning their story, which always transcends any definition that we use to try to capture them with.

Any narrative must have a setting. When we read a novel, we take the setting as simply given: the setting is the condition of the novel. Human life is narrative because it enters a setting that is simply given: just like the stories we tell that derive from it, human experience can describe the setting—the human condition—but it cannot ever get beyond that condition, for we are not gods who live eternally but beings whose existence unfolds in time as a story. As we have seen, Arendt's claim about the narrative character of human existence grows out of her understanding of the conditioned nature of human beings. To say that humans are essentially conditioned beings means that they are creatures who have limits, and that these limits are *essential* to what and who they are. Humans can never get beyond them, just like they cannot jump over their own shadows. What we can do is articulate those limits, try to take their measure, and attempt to understand how they structure and condition our experience. Human life is conditioned by such existential structures as temporality, mortality, embodiment, scarcity, language, natality, plurality, earth-boundedness, historicality, and even its own technology.[109] These are not objective facts, in the conventional sense. They are conditions of our consciousness, and we can only understand them by understanding how they structure our consciousness. There is, so to speak, no transcendental subject of knowledge. Even when Arendt moves farthest away from the human condition in her account of the thinking activity, this activity is still "conditioned," in this case by what Heidegger had called "temporality," and what Arendt calls the "gap between past and future."

In *The Human Condition*, Arendt proposed to pursue these questions by first making a number of distinctions between the various types of activities humans perform in their worldly conditions. It will be necessary to bracket for the moment the question of the *vita contemplativa*, where many other activities are performed outside our worldly conditions. In Chapter 3, when we turn to examine the philosophical way of life, thinking and contemplating will be of primary importance, but even in the context of worldliness it is not really possible to escape the relevance of the activities of the mind. For Arendt insists that the life stories humans construct out of the events of their lives would be impossible without the ability to reflect about the meaning of those events with the activity of thought, thus recognizing that Heidegger was at least half right: humans are both mortal *and* natal, both acting *and* thinking beings.

Arendt begins her discussion of the worldly activities in the prologue to *The Human Condition* with the at first blush strange proposal: "What I propose . . . is very simple: to think what we are doing."[110] This, of course, implies a rather odd proposition: that we somehow do not *know* what we are doing. Arendt immediately begins making a series distinctions between various human activities. She argues that there are three fundamental conditions to which human beings, as conditioned beings, are subject: the natural necessity of the life process, the worldly human artifice, and the condition of plurality. Corresponding to each of these conditions are, respectively, the three essential human activities: labor, work, and action.[111]

Labor is the activity humans perform in order to survive the driving necessity of natural metabolism. "[Labor] corresponds to the biological process of the human body, whose spontaneous growth, metabolism, and eventual decay are bound to the vital necessities produced and fed into the life process. . . . The human condition of labor is life itself."[112] Unlike the other activities, labor is cyclical and endless, like nature itself, making it the activity we share with animals, and thus when humans exist as laboring beings she calls them *animal laborans*.[113] "Of all human activities," she writes, "only labor . . . is unending, progressing automatically in accordance with life itself and outside the range of willful decisions or humanly meaningful purposes."[114]

Work, on the other hand, establishes a "bulwark" against natural necessity. It creates a space for humans to escape labor by providing "an 'artificial' world of things, distinctly different from all natural surroundings. Within its borders each individual life is housed, while this world itself is meant to outlast and transcend them all. The human condition of work is worldliness."[115] At the most abstract level, Arendt distinguishes work by the fact that it has a definite beginning and ending, and this ending is always characterized by a finished product. As the only human activity that employs the teleological means/end category, it thus involves a form of specialized knowledge that can be taught and reproduced.[116] As an "artificial" teleological activity, its process always involves doing violence to what is naturally given in order to bring about a worldly space to block out natural necessity.

Finally, action "corresponds to the human condition of plurality, to the fact that men, not Man, live on the earth and inhabit the world. While all aspects of the human condition are somehow related to politics, this plurality is specifically the condition—not only the *conditio sine qua non*, but the *conditio per quam*—of all political life."[117] Labor and work find their significance and meaning in the activity of action, which redeems these activities from futility by producing stories that give them meaning.[118] Action is able to accomplish this as a result of several unique qualities it possesses. In its purest sense, action is the human capacity to begin a new process or chain of events within the human world.[119] It is by far the rarest of the human activities—vanishingly rare, in fact. In contrast to work, action is ateleological, an activity that is not done in order to produce something beyond it, but is instead an end in itself.[120] Each action is *sui generis*: it always has a meaning that is completely distinct from any act that has come before it.[121] Each action discloses the "who" rather than the "what" of the actor.[122] This is because each human being is unique and unlike any other that has come before. The stories created by the deeds of actors disclose this unique "whoness." By its nature, action produces and establishes relationships among humans, and this results in a "web of human relations."[123] As a result of these qualities, action inevitably is boundless and unpredictable: each course of action undertaken will impact the other individuals in the web of relationships, eventually coming to have a meaning far exceeding anything the actor could have imagined or foreseen.[124] Arendt therefore argues that action has a process character: while we are bound to the natural world through labor by the processes of natural necessity, through action we begin new processes in the web of human relations.[125] Arendt asserts that the "web of human relations" established by action exists as a kind of overgrowth on the worldly human artifice: together the two constitute what she calls the "common world." Arendt claims that the objective world produced by work gives stability to the web of human relations—which by nature is ephemeral and unstable—and allows the deeds done by actors to have lasting significance and, potentially, immortality.[126]

Arendt argues that action is essentially conditioned by speech, claiming that without speech action would be meaningless. They are like two sides of a coin: action creates new realities, and speech discloses those new realities.[127] She writes that action "is humanly disclosed by the word, and though his deed can be perceived in its brute physical appearance without verbal accompaniment, it becomes relevant only through the spoken word."[128] Readers often find this fundamental association of speech and action odd, since clearly labor and work can involve the use of speech. What Arendt appears to mean by this is that action is the activity humans possess to create stories, and thus meaning. Storytelling would be inconceivable without speech, while the products of work and the abundance of labor seem not necessarily so.[129] Arendt refers to them as *essentially* speechless because, in her view, while work and labor may use speech in contingent circumstances, each could be performed without speech and would still maintain its same essential character.[130] These distinctions should not be interpreted too literally, however, as if there is necessarily a strict dichotomy between instances of work and action: there is no reason the same act may not be *both* a moment of work and a moment of action. The distinction between the two activities does not occur at a logical level, but instead at an essential and ontological level. To take a relatively recent example, the invention the personal computer, for instance, demonstrates characteristics of both work and action.

The only other activity that Arendt believes is essentially conditioned by speech is thought, which she argues takes place in the "two-in-one" dialogue of the thinking ego, and which we use to frame and make sense of the events of our life stories.[131] Arendt recognized this essential relation of thought and action to speech as far back as her first manuscript in 1954, which confronted the question of the relation of thought and action, saying that to partake in thought and action "meant to be aware of being human in an articulate, specific sense. Action without speech was violence; since it could not disclose its meaning in words, it remained senseless and meaningless. Thought, on the other hand, [could be so little conceived as proceeding without] speech that one single word, *logos*, was used for both 'word' and 'thought or argument.'"[132] Arendt, in other words, came to believe that human freedom and the capacity for speech—whether expressed in the context of the philosophical freedom of thought or in the performance of great actions in the human world—were so essentially related that it was literally impossible to comprehend one without the other.

Excursus: The Concept of Non-Sovereign Agency

This essential relationship between human agency and speech led Arendt to attack one of the central pillars of traditional political thought: the concept of sovereignty. The notion of non-sovereign freedom takes its bearings from Arendt's insight that political action is misconceived when it is articulated in terms of the sovereign engagement of a unified and unconditioned will.[133] She insisted that this understanding of political action inevitably leads to the identification of political action with violence, since, in her view, only violence could unilaterally enact the intentions of a unified will.[134] It was this sovereign understanding of action that led to the tradition of political thought's fabricative model of political judgment, which imagines the relationship between thought and action to involve the execution by those who are ruled of a preconceived idea produced by a ruler. Arendt believed that the moment action is conceived in unilateral terms of willful execution, it has lost contact with the phenomenal evidence associated with action, which always involves the creation of new realities and moves within a human web of relationships that responds to and creates a new, unintended set of circumstances other than what the actor intended. Arendt's insights into the non-sovereign conditions of human agency have inspired recent scholarship by Joan Cocks, Sharon Krause, Patchen Markell, Dana Villa, and Linda Zerilli.[135] These scholars have sought to explore how agency must be reconceived when such conditions as its essential relation to speech, plurality, worldliness, relational relativity, and unpredictability are taken into account. I want now to pause and explore this notion of non-sovereign agency, paying special attention to the unique insights I believe Arendt can offer it.

It is vitally important to understand that—based as it is on Heidegger's fundamental ontology—Arendtian action is not merely epiphenomenal. Each act of human agency carries tremendous potency. Arendtian agency asserts that action is not retroactively achieved through contemplative reflection or located outside phenomenal reality in a noumenal realm, but instead has the potential to monumentally impact the concrete human world. As such, action is incredibly rare, happening at best only a few times in any given human life. As the subject matter of the narrative of a human life, action forms the content—the acts, deeds, events—their stories recount. It is the specific, concrete, and *sui generis* actions an actor undertakes that reveals the "whoness" of the actor, their unique identity. Only that actor and that actor alone would have summoned up that unique, particular response to the circumstances that were presented to them in the world. The action is something completely original to the actor, something that could never have been predicted on the basis of antecedent causes. Arendt argues that action is exclusively characterized by its extraordinariness, and thus human historical reality is the story of *events* enacted by human agents.[136]

Arendt's notion of action has both inspired and perplexed her readers. Many struggle with how her account of human agency can be intelligible once our ability to predict the outcome of our acts becomes so ambiguous. If we have no control over the outcome of our actions, does this not render our agency moot? I want to argue here that this is not necessarily so. Instead, it only significantly attenuates and complicates it, that the actor's agency involves trying to, in Arendt's words, "force things into a certain direction."[137] Because action is something that is *essentially* intersubjective, it appears as if any description of the causality of action could never be characterized in terms of a simplistic cause/effect logic.[138] Thus, the first presumption that has to be abandoned is any easy understanding of the causality occurring in human agency in terms of fabrication—of an effect achieved by our acts that is the result of an antecedent mechanical or efficient cause.

If human ontology truly is at its basis a narrative or story that conditions our epistemological and historical frameworks in the way Heidegger suggests, then the sense of causality associated with it has to be reconceived in a much more sophisticated manner. Contemporary philosophers such as Charles Taylor, for instance, have noted the likely impossibility of ever performing a complete reduction of historical phenomena to physical mechanism.[139] But even beyond the metaphysically contested nature of causality, our phenomenal conception of causality has always been marked by much more sophistication than the mechanistic conception of cause and effect. Aristotle, for instance, famously theorized a fourfold phenomenology of causality, none of which—not even *causa efficiens*—coheres exactly with the modern mechanistic conception of causality. In his essay "The Question Concerning Technology," Heidegger embraced this conception of causality, arguing that authentic human causality is never sovereign causality: it recognizes that human action never truly enacts its will, but instead has the sense of cultivating and abetting that which proceeds out of *physis* or Being, for example, in parenting, advising, or farming.[140] Arendt, however, developed a more dynamic notion of the causality of human agency. Unlike Heidegger and Aristotle, Arendtian action does not just abet what is already proceeding out of Being; it is itself natal. It is the beginning of something new.

In order to conceptualize this dynamic conception of causality, we might preliminarily refer to Kant's discussions of causality in the *Critique of Pure Reason*. Kant understood mechanism (cause and effect) to be only one category of a threefold categorical account that included both "*substantia et accidens*" and what he calls "community" or "interaction."[141] This last category of interaction is much closer to the kind of causality Arendt understands human action to have, although her version is much more dynamic and potent. Kant refers to it as the notion of "a dynamic community," that is, the fact that within a given community of phenomena they all are reciprocally interacting and determining each other and this interaction has to be understood dynamically and not successively.[142] Kant illustrates the idea by pointing to gravitation, the fact that it makes no sense to understand the relation between the earth and the moon solely in terms of the earth exerting a force on the moon or vice versa; rather, they interact by exerting a common force on each other. In other words, the notion of causality involved here is, as Kant says, "not successive but instantaneous."[143] The notion of causality that I believe Arendt had in mind in her notion of non-sovereign action should be understood much more in terms of this sort of dynamic interaction than in the fabricative (i.e., sovereign) conception of cause and effect that arises out of causality's mechanistic aspect.

It is easy to find examples of dynamic causality in human life. Team sports are an obvious case of dynamic causality. A good quarterback or point guard can never sovereignly and unilaterally enact his will. Rather, his leadership and decision-making abilities in fluid situations enable the team to execute together. There is an interaction and dynamism among the players that seems impossible to reduce to cause and effect. Another example is found in the art of persuasion. People in sales often point out that skilled salespeople know when to stop selling their customers; they have to find the right moment to let customers choose for themselves to buy the product. These are, of course, necessarily simplistic examples geared toward illustration, but the basic idea is easily applied to our relationships in general. The point is that relationships are dynamic: any action requires a very subtle comprehension of the state of affairs the act will bring about *between* individuals affected by the action. When I relate to another person through action, I do not enact my will on them. Arendt insists throughout her work that the only effect action has is to establish relationships;[144] in other words, the moment I act in relation to another person, that person *simultaneously reacts* to me. What results is not an effect, but a new dynamic state of affairs. Something arises between us, a relationship, that is fundamentally dynamic—what Arendt calls "a space of appearance" that separates and relates us—whose ultimate meaning I could never have exactly predicted and whose outcome I can never be certain of. And that ultimate meaning can only be revealed by the story of the relationship. This is why, as we will see later, Arendt's conception of practical reason in analogy to artistic judgment is so apposite. In a similar way to great art, the actor can never be completely certain of what their actions will ultimately mean. Yet, it is indicative of a skillful actor—an actor with what Machiavelli called *virtù*—to be capable of deliberating on a course of action that will end in a meaningful story, a story that reveals the actor's "whoness," just as skillful artists will almost always find their work meaning something other than they intended at the beginning.

In truth, Arendt's articulations of human agency are much closer to phenomenal reality than anything produced in traditional accounts. An action can be the most exhilarating experience of one's life. For younger people, first dates can be exhilarating and nerve-racking because each one possesses a clear potential for action: the events of the night may set off a life-defining chain of events. Action, in fact, constitutes those rare moments in life—weddings, births, career choices, interventions, conversion experiences—where we know we are "laying it all on the line," so to speak, risking our life as we currently know it in order to initiate a course of action that expresses our "whoness," our unique identity, in a richer and deeper way than how our lives existed before. Action is certainly not equivalent to our capacity for free choice:[145] whether or not I choose to spend my Sunday morning working out, sleeping in, or going to church is far from an instance of action. Indeed, it is not even clear if there *is* an unambiguous moment of choice involved in a particular action. Arendt notes that, while action clearly involves some kind of initiation on the part of the actor, it also has to be "carried through," and this carrying through is just as much a part of the act or event.[146] When a recent college graduate acts in undertaking to go to graduate school or decides to start his own business, it is not clear that there was ever one specific moment of choice or initiation; rather, there might be a series of progressive choices and courses of action undertaken that when taken together amount to an action. What matters is not the specific instances, but rather whether there is a self-defining act that the actor can recount in the story of his or her life.

Moreover, while this "carrying through" of the action can be performed by the actor to a certain extent, it can probably never be done completely alone: other actors must also help see the action through with that actor. Since action always occurs in what Arendt calls the "web of human relationships," the meaning and thus the final outcome of the act is never up to the actor alone—who can at best force events in a particular direction—but probably even more so to other actors with whom he or she interacts.[147] Consider the recovery movement. Very often, the fact that addicts or trauma victims were able to transcend their history and begin establishing a meaningful life for themselves and their family could never have been predicted on the basis of existing antecedent causes. In fact, very often those who know them best have long since given up hope that they will ever change. The recovery movement illustrates the profoundly intersubjective nature of action that Arendt continually points to: Addicts are the initiators of the act, they take the first step; but in many ways it is the support—the "carrying through," as it were—that they receive from their peers in the movement that allows them to, if not overcome completely, at least gain some kind of power over their addictions or traumas.[148]

But all this does not mean that Arendt understood action to be an unadulterated good—far from it, in fact. Arendt was quite aware that action has dark and dangerous elements: suicide or abandonment, after all, are certainly moments of action.[149] Action is often the source of the greatest tragedies of our lives, moments where something precious is lost or destroyed. Indeed, in a variety of places, including *The Human Condition*, Arendt also points to the burdensome character of action.[150] Her polemically laudatory comments in *The Human Condition* and elsewhere at times obscure the fact that action undertaken in the wrong spirit can be a profoundly dark activity, whose results may be both dangerous and immoral (Hitler's "final solution," after all, was no doubt an action).[151] Arendt believed humans were generally ambivalent about their freedom, often experiencing it as heartbreaking and overwhelming,[152] and in modernity this has led to a "flight into impotency, a desperate desire to be relieved entirely of the ability to act."[153]

There in fact seems to be an essential element of the tragic in Arendt's conception of human agency. The victories achieved in our life stories only have meaning against the experience of failure; moments of joy have a bittersweet depth drawn from the knowledge of griefs that preceded them and that inevitably await us. The heroism and elitism that Arendtian action is often simplistically interpreted with are, in fact, leavened by a recognition of the persistence of sorrow and defeat in a world of profoundly flawed and mortal human beings. It seems that what animated Arendt's reflections on the limits of the human condition was a desire to give the full scope of human agency its due, to reckon with the fact that it is our sadness and disappointments as much as our accomplishments and moments of joy that make us fully human and thus capable of appreciating others with the courage to act.

This essentially tragic element of human action was the basis for Arendt's challenge to the modern understanding of politics as sovereignty and its fundamental objective: success. Arendt believed there was something inhuman in the modern obsession with the idea that success defined the fundamental criteria of action. Because of its essential conditioning by speech, the defining characteristic of action can never be the sovereignty of success, but instead non-sovereign political categories such as historical greatness and commitment to the preservation of the common world. This, of course, does not mean that success is not a factor in actors' deliberations concerning courses of action. But it does imply that success cannot be the fundamental criterion of political judgment, for success can never redeem action. A successful course of action—genocide, for instance—may successfully achieve the short-term intentions of the actors, but it will never be redeemable in speech. The judgment of (authentic) history will inevitably come to view it as despicable. To illustrate this, Arendt often quoted a favorite line from Cato: "The victorious cause pleased the gods, but the defeated cause pleased Cato."[154] What she means by this is that, in the course of history, tragedy and defeat may be as world disclosing and world preserving as any victory. "Man," she writes,

> cannot defend himself against the blows of fate, against the chicanery of the gods, but he can resist them in speech and respond to them, and though the response changes nothing . . . such words belong to the event as such. If words are of equal rank with the event, if, as is said at the end of *Antigone*, "great words" answer and requite "great blows struck from

on high," then what happens is itself something great and worthy of remembrance and fame . . . our downfall can become a deed if we hurl
words against it even as we perish.[155]

If we consider defining political moments of recent memory, it is indeed
evident that success or failure is not what defines the significance and meaning of the event itself and its consequences for our world. The election of
Barack Obama may have been a moment of success in American race relations, but it was not merely the success of the endeavor that bore its meaning: it was what the event disclosed to and about American politics at that
moment. Yet historically, certain moments of defeat in American race relations were at least as world defining: the violence done to the peaceful pro-
testers of the civil rights movement or the assassination of Martin Luther
King probably did more to force American politics to consistently recognize
the question of race than anything Barack Obama will ever do. This, of
course, does not mean that success is not often a necessity; it does, however,
mean that success could never be the essential criterion of human agency.

Political *Athanatizein*

I turn now to how Arendt reintroduced human agency back into historical reflection, a project that centered on reviving political *athanatizein*. Benjamin Constant famously drew the distinction between the liberty of the
moderns and the liberty of the ancients. The liberty of the moderns, perhaps
best exemplified by Rawls currently, is a private liberty that politics protects
through the guarantee of certain basic rights and liberties and, increasingly,
on certain baseline conditions of social equality. Arendt remains the most
prominent modern proponent of the liberty of the ancients, which located
the arena of free human action not in a private sphere made secure by politics
but in the arena of politics itself. According to Arendt, political action had
once afforded a much more profound, meaningful, and consequential realm
of human freedom than modern private liberty, which, having located freedom in private life, in her view rendered freedom impotent and insignificant
and therefore unremarkable.

Many readings of Arendt's political thought focus on what she calls the
"condition of plurality": her current Wikipedia page (ca. 2015), for instance,
characterizes her political thought by pointing to her statement of the "*conditio per quam* . . . of all political life": the fact that "men, not Man, live on the

earth and inhabit the world."[156] Though broadly accurate, I argue here that focusing on plurality does not capture the full meaning of what Arendt had in mind by the notion of the political, that the political for her was better described as an articulation of the conditions of political *athanatizein*. The condition of plurality is based on the fact of the narrative agency of human beings and expresses the fact that the world is filled with a plurality of unique life stories. As we've seen, like Heidegger, Arendt believed this narrative ontology of human beings was the primordial source of history: "That every individual life between birth and death can eventually be told as a story with a beginning and end is the prepolitical and prehistorical condition of history, the great story without beginning and end."[157] The deep question this condition poses is how these stories, which in her view are so distinctive that they are literally *sui generis*,[158] can escape the isolation and solipsism this absolute individualism implies and be related to each other in a way that could afford the possibility of historical immortality. She sought to do this by articulating the activity, action, that humans perform to provide the content of these stories and by defending the ability of a common world and public realm to provide an intersubjective space of reality where actors can enact their life stories before their peers. I argue in the following that only action performed in a public realm, political action, is capable of achieving historical greatness, that is, political *athanatizein*.

The interpretation of Arendtian political action offered here implicitly takes a position on a point that has been somewhat ambiguous in the literature on Arendt: to wit, whether there could be any kind of action performed in the private realm, that is, nonpolitical action. I believe the notion that Arendt thought action could only take place in the political arena is largely based on a lack of precision in her writing in *The Human Condition*, imprecisions she clarifies elsewhere. In *The Human Condition*, Arendt draws a sharp distinction between the public and the private realm. Because of her interest in reasserting the significance of the public realm, she is often thought to have taken a dim view of the private realm. This notion is reinforced by the fact that when she initially discusses the public realm in *The Human Condition* she seems to identify it with the idea of the "common world." [159] The "common world" is the general concept Arendt develops to explain how the absolute plurality of individual "whos" can be related to each other. The common world, in Arendt's words, has the power "to gather them together, to relate and to separate them."[160] Thus, if the common world is indeed identical to the public realm, then it seems true that there could be no action in the private sphere. However, there is good reason to believe that this section of the book was either not fully thought through or simply badly written.

To begin with, Arendt is not nearly as contemptuous of the private realm in *The Human Condition* as is often thought. Her concern, rather, was that the distinction between the public and private realms had become muddled in the modern era, and it was this "social realm" to which she directed her contempt. She believed, in fact, that the private realm was a sacred space withdrawn from the world that humans needed desperately, a realm that sheltered them from the cold light of the public realm, and indeed it was the role of politics to protect this realm as much as it was to protect the public realm.[161] She believed one of the tragedies of modern capitalism was the re-defining of private property away from the idea of a "privately held place *within the world*" and toward the idea of capital accumulation.[162] Moreover, in later writings she clearly distinguishes between "the [common] world *and its public space*,"[163] and repeatedly indicates the existence of action in the private realm. In her lecture course, "Some Questions Concerning Moral Philosophy," written a few years after *The Human Condition*, she explicitly indicates the existence of "nonpolitical action, which does not take place in public."[164] And even in *The Human Condition* there are indications suggesting the existence of this kind of action in privately situated settings, such as when she states of "action and speech" that the modern era has "banished these into the sphere of the intimate and the private."[165] Thus, the common world is better understood as including *both* our public and private relationships. While it is probably the case that *truly* private action is impossible—since action necessarily must be performed with and before others—it is likely that most action is of a kind of quasi-public nature. Most of our relationships probably involve some kind of informal public realm or space of appearance.[166] In "Introduction *into* Politics," Arendt states that "wherever human beings come together—be it in private or social, be it in public or politically—a space is generated that simultaneously gathers them into it and separates them from one another. . . . Wherever people come together, the world thrusts itself between them, and it is in this in-between space that all human affairs are conducted."[167]

This is most clearly evident in how Arendt describes the idea of a "space of appearance." Arendt identifies a space of appearance with reality as such: a space between the actors where phenomena can intersubjectively appear to them.[168] This space of appearance is a broad phenomenon and can appear wherever people act and speak together: "The space of appearance comes into being wherever men are together in the manner of speech and action, and therefore predates and precedes all formal constitution of the public realm and the various forms of government, that is, the various forms in which the public realm can be organized. . . . Wherever people gather together, it is potentially there, but only potentially, not necessarily and not forever."[169] The space of appearance is therefore not necessarily a formal phenomenon, but instead "its true space lies between people living together for this purpose [of acting and speaking together], no matter where they happen to be. . . . Action and speech create a space between the participants which can find its proper location almost anytime and anywhere."[170] Thus, any formally instituted public realm is based on a more original, primordial, and informal public realm that precedes it and enables its continuation in the world. In other words, while action in the public arena is the raison d'être of politics, other less elevated and significant forms of action can occur in private relationships characterized by more informal spaces of appearance.

The language Arendt uses can often be overly mysterious, but the idea of a space of appearance simply seems to be her way of capturing the nature of relationships. The notion of a space of appearance indicates that relationships can exist among an indeterminate number of individuals: it can arise between two friends, in a family, a group (churches, companies, political movements), or even a nation. Something arises between the individuals involved in any kind of relationship, something they never fully control, that separates and relates them to each other. A space of appearance is incredibly significant to human beings because action can only appear, and therefore exist, within it. The significant events of our lives only have meaning if there are other people who occupy a common space of appearance with us, who have a relationship to us, who can see and appreciate those events. Action needs a space of appearance to illuminate it; it provides a kind of intersubjectively constituted spotlight for our actions.[171] At the same time, Arendt also argues that only action can bring a space of appearance into being: "Action, moreover, no matter what its specific content, always establishes relationships."[172] Thus, relationships are somehow the result of action, but also the only place where action can occur.[173] There seems therefore to be a kind of reciprocal and dynamic causality to the relationship between action and the space of appearance, where each brings the other into being.

There are therefore a number of essential distinctions that need to be recognized when coming to terms with what Arendt means by the common world. The common world as a whole is an amalgam of two human conditions. The first is the web of human relationships that is almost infinite in its relativity and instability and is constituted by an almost endless variety of shifting and multidimensional relationships or "spaces of appearance." The second is the human artifice: our laws, institutions, technology, scientific and historical documentation and literature, and works of art that provide a civilizing bulwark against natural necessity and without which human life descends into savagery.[174] Contra the simplistic view sometimes attributed to her, work for Arendt entails much more meaningful endeavors than is typically implied by the mundane idea of a "production process." It is difficult to overstate the value Arendt attributes to these products of work: these "islands of stability" are literally the primordial wellspring of human civilization. Action, though guided by goals and intentions, could never properly be thought predictable, and even when careful plans are worked out they quickly become irrelevant, since action never produces a finished product but rather sets off a chain of events in the web of human relationships. One might think of the endless shifting alliances in the television show *Survivor* as an example of what would become of our culture without the human artifice: human culture with no products of work to stabilize it quickly degrades into tribalism and endless infighting.

Arendt's "Common World"

	Web of Human Relationships	*Human Artifice*
Private Realm	Family, friends, etc.	Homes, possessions, etc.
Public Realm	Political actors and citizens	Laws and institutions, historical documentation, public infrastructure

Arendt's sharp distinction between the public and the private has been attacked from the standpoint of social justice in variety of ways; in particular, feminist critics point out that the assertion of a private sphere has been used as a cloak for various kinds of barbaric practices and domestic abuse.[175] Essential as the public realm is to the political activities of judging and acting, Arendt also recognized the political relevance of the private realm. This political relevance comes from another faculty involved in historical reflection: the faculty of thought, which, as we will see later, Arendt insists can only be performed in private, in withdrawal from our worldly entanglements. This emphasis on freedom of thought partly explains her determination to maintain the distinction between the two realms. While it is arguably true that Arendt did not take these objections seriously enough, one doubts she would have altered her view significantly. She believed that how and where various communities draw the distinction between the public and private is a matter those communities' own citizens should judge over.[176] But perhaps even more significant, one thing her research on totalitarianism appeared to have taught her was that this distinction *must* be drawn: while feminist critics in particular level a powerful critique, one must wonder if the idea that "the personal is political" is a dangerously slippery slope.

There is no doubt, however, that Arendt saw the revival of an authentic public realm to be the most urgent purpose of her work. While the private realm seems to be constituted by a wide variety of different informal relationships or spaces of appearance, the public realm is a formally articulated and institutionalized space of appearance, giving unusual stability and endurance to that space.[177] While *The Human Condition* generally focused on the Greeks' experience of their public realm, how the public realm is organized and articulated often differs from society to society. In "Introduction *into* Politics," the book she attempted to write in 1958–1959 about the broad relationship between thought and action, Arendt outlined a number of forms the public realm can take. Her ideal is what she calls a "political public realm."[178] As Chapter 2 will discuss in more depth, Arendt believed there were three original instances of political public realms: the ancient Greeks, the republican Romans, and (for brief periods) modern revolutionary actors. These public realms were "political" because their citizens were primordially involved in the maintenance of their public realms. Historically, however, most public realms have been nonpolitical public realms. The church in the Christian era afforded a kind of public realm, though because of Christian theology it was a much less authentically *political* space.[179] The same was true for the early modern era of emerging capitalist expansion, which found its own public realm in the exchange market.[180] As we will see later, the public realm of the modern world is generally what Arendt calls the social realm. The social realm is a form of public realm where the distinction between the public and the private has lost its meaning, and, as a result, many of the activities that historically were thought to belong in the private realm have

been allowed into the public realm.[181] The social realm is a space of appearance, no doubt, but one that has lost the original political capacity to memo-
rialize and disclose the "who" of the actors and instead has become a place of
conformity, hypocrisy, and corruption.[182]

While clearly most action thus probably occurs in private life, Arendt
understood political action to be the highest kind of action. The most direct
and unequivocal definition of political action she ever gave came at the conclusion of her 1963 lecture course "Introduction into Politics," where she
stated simply that "action [is] political if performed in the public realm."[183]
What is so special about performing action in the public realm? In "What Is
Freedom?" she tells us: "[The public realm] is the realm where freedom is a
worldly reality, tangible in words which can be heard, in deeds which can be
seen, and in events which are talked about and remembered, and turned into
stories before they are finally incorporated into the great storybook of human
history."[184] In other words, what makes the public realm special is that only
by acting within it is it possible to achieve the kind of *athanatizein* specific to
politics: the immortalization of history.

However, it seems clear that this was only a partial definition. Merely to
act on the public stage is not enough to achieve historical greatness: it also
matters what one achieves and why. Understanding how and why this is can
clarify the problem with more aesthetic interpretations of Arendtian political
action discussed at the beginning of this chapter. The problem that seems to
infect these interpretations is that they seem determined to assume a strict
dichotomy between activities that are telos and *a-telos*, between an activity
performed for some higher goal or purpose and an activity that was an end in
itself. Of course, this is to some extent understandable: Arendt, after all, had
clearly distinguished between work, which operates under conditions of
means and ends, and action, which has no finished product, but is an end in
itself. Thus, the logic runs that any instrumental or teleological activity occurring in politics must, according to Arendt, have an activity outside it that
"redeems" it, and this redeeming activity is what true political action must
therefore be. All elements of instrumentality should thus be kept out of political activity. The implication seems to be that most of what we consider to
be the concrete concerns of politics, such as public policy or social justice,
must be relegated merely to administration, so that politics can be free to
engage in a deliberative and performative-disclosive activity of individual
identity. This dichotomous understanding of the relationship between action
and instrumentality is based on the fundamental assumption that there are

only two, mutually exclusive ways of conceiving of activities, that is, they are either telos or *a-telos*.

However, it is possible there is a third option, an option suggested by none other than Plato himself. At the beginning of book 2 of the *Republic*, Plato proposes a sophisticated, threefold division of human goods.[185] He has Glaucon suggest that there are things that are good for their own sake, such as joy; things that are only good for their consequences, such as physical training; and things that are *both* good for their consequences and good for their own sake, one of which, Glaucon suspects, might be justice. This third option, in other words, was an activity that was *both* telos and *a-telos*. In essence, I suggest that this distinction between action and work should be understood not on a logical level but instead at an *ontological* level. Mirroring their dynamic versus instrumental modes of causality, action and work should not necessarily be seen as mutually exclusive activities, but instead could potentially be the very same activity grasped at two distinct ontological levels. Does Arendt ever provide examples of political actions that are ontologically both telos and *a-telos*? There are in fact a number of such examples, but the clearest might be her acknowledgment, as Patchen Markell has argued elsewhere,[186] that instances of work, which are teleologically governed by means/ends logic and always involving doing violence to something given, can also at the same time be instances of action. In "The Concept of History," she points out that "insofar as the end product of fabrication is incorporated into the human world . . . its use and eventual 'history' can never be predicted. . . . This means only that man is never exclusively *homo faber*, that even the fabricator remains at the same time an acting being."[187] The most well-known instance of this is given in *The Human Condition*, when she pointed to the invention of the telescope, clearly an instance of the activity of work, as an exemplary "event": an action whose unforeseeable consequences established a new state of affairs in the world, altering the Western world irrevocably and ushering in modernity through its initiation of modern science.[188] In other words, I would argue that what Arendtian political action might involve in concrete terms is much broader than has often been assumed. Since fabrication is her fundamental category for dealing with the question of violence, it is then evident that she did not reject all instances of violence as possible instances of political action. After all, she repeatedly points to the French Resistance as an exemplary political action, which obviously involved quite a lot of violent activities,[189] not to mention, as we will see in Chapter 2, the empire-building activities of Romans.

When we understand the special sense in which Arendtian political action is ateleological, the occasional accusation that it is aestheticized or narcissistic evaporates. Arendt continually noted that political action is *essentially* always concerned with maintaining and preserving the world.[190] In the 1963 "Introduction into Politics" course, she refers to political action as having *amor mundi*, and writes, "What do I mean by 'politically minded'? . . . Very generally, I mean by it to care more for the world, which was before we appeared and which will be after we disappear, than for ourselves, for our immediate interests and for our life."[191] Only political action is capable of changing the world, and it therefore is the only kind of action that is capable of preserving and maintaining the world when necessary.[192] She writes that "the world . . . is irrevocably delivered up to the ruin of time unless human beings are determined to intervene, to alter, to create what is new. . . . Because the world is made by mortals, it wears out, and because it continuously changes its inhabitants it runs the risk of becoming as mortal as they. To preserve the world . . . it must be constantly set right anew."[193] Political action, in other words, has to somehow change the world by beginning new initiatives, and yet it also must affirm and maintain that same world. This is why Arendt argues that politics is never concerned with our individual interests: to act politically is always to act for the sake of a common world that separates and relates the individual actors within it, always with the goal of preserving and affirming that world while also changing it in the hope that our action will leave behind a mark of some kind in that world.

True political actors, then are always acting *both* for the opportunity to achieve immortality *and* to maintain and preserve the common world.[194] In Arendt's view, only action geared toward caring for the world was action worthy of political *athanatizein*. Some of Arendt's most articulate discussions of this dual-natured sense of the ateleology of political action come in a 1955 set of lectures on Machiavelli. Given that these lectures occur during the same time she was researching *The Human Condition* and anticipate many themes discussed in later essays such as "What Is Freedom?" we can be sure that the ideas in the Machiavelli lectures were foundational for her more apparently "aesthetic" account of political action in *The Human Condition*. Consider this passage:

> [The] greatness of this world is constituted through *virtù* and *fortuna*. *Fortuna* is a constellation in the world which is visible only for *virtù*; *fortuna* is the appearing of the world, the shining up of the world, the

smiling of the world. It invites man to show his excellence. . . . World and man are bound together like man and wife: action fits man into the world like eyes fit us to see the sun. . . . Action shows the world's *fortuna* and man's *virtù* at one and the same time.[195]

This passage is certainly a highly aestheticized moment in Arendt's account of Machiavellian political action. She writes that Machiavelli "never asks: What is politics good for? Nobody [else in the tradition] leaves out this question altogether. [For Machiavelli,] politics has no higher aim beyond itself."[196] Yet, she also goes on to point to the dual nature of ateleological political action. Gesturing toward its concern with preserving and affirming the world, she writes: "Machiavelli says success is the end of all action, 'from which there is no appeal.' . . . But success has [to be] for the sake of . . . Italy or the state or the realm of the secular or the world. The meaning comes from the same world in which politics is being conducted. . . . Without Italy, your victory has no meaning."[197] At the same time, she continues to insist that politics remains centrally concerned with the greatness of the actor: "The chief concept of political action . . . is glory, glory for a people or a prince or for whoever in involved in the business of the world. Glory shines . . . [it] does great enterprises all for eternal fame and present glory."[198] Somehow, the two elements—the teleological concern for preserving the world and ateleological concern with the immortality of the deeds done in the name of preserving it—are so deeply intertwined they are impossible to separate from each other. In "What Is Freedom?"—an essay that drew directly from the Machiavelli lectures—Arendt formulates the point succinctly, saying that the "end or *raison d'être* [of the political] would be to establish and keep in existence a space where freedom as virtuosity can appear . . . in events which are talked about, remembered, and turned into stories, before they are finally incorporated into the great storybook of human history."[199] Thus, while the idea of an "aestheticization of politics" draws on a certain aspect of Arendtian political action, ultimately it fails to capture what she truly had in mind. Political action is *a-telos* not because it is narcissistic, but because it has no higher goal or purpose beyond itself: it affirms the world in order to immortalize itself, and it immortalizes itself in order to affirm the world.

Concretely speaking, this conception of political action aligns with many intuitions we have about political greatness. If we consider, for instance, the rankings of U.S. presidents by historians, Abraham Lincoln and Franklin Roosevelt tend to top the list. The criteria for these evaluations are remarkably similar to what Arendt proposes: great presidents were presented with major threats to our common world and were able to measure up to those moments. Presidents who receive middling rankings tend to effective leaders who, had they been presented with similar circumstances, might have done just as well. It is possible they are not considered truly great presidents simply because there was no challenge—no *fortuna*—for them to measure their political *virtù* with. On the other hand, poor presidents seem to be those who failed to measure up to the moment, such as Herbert Hoover's mishandling of the Great Depression or James Buchanan's ineptitude during the pre–Civil War period.

Presidents are, of course, uniquely positioned to be able to perform political action and achieve political *athanatizein*, but political action is not limited to the activities of elites. Whistleblowers such as Edward Snowden or Daniel Ellsberg are likely cases of political action in Arendt's sense. Consider the case of Ellsberg's release of the Pentagon Papers, which Arendt herself discussed in "Lying and Politics." All the criteria of political *athanatizein* are present in his case. Ellsberg initiated his action by himself, challenging a vast power structure that in his view was damaging the American common world by systematically misleading the public and undermining its constitutional principles. The act bears all the hallmarks of action: Ellsberg acted into a situation whose outcome he could not possibly have foreseen. His act, though initiated by himself, could not have been carried through if other actors were not willing to join him, such as the media outlets who choose to report on and publish the papers in spite of intimidation from the White House. Finally, the consequences of the act were so far-reaching that we arguably may still be experiencing them. The Watergate scandal was in many ways a direct response to Ellsberg's act, and the consequences of that scandal for our contemporary political culture are still felt in countless ways. Moreover, because Ellsberg was in a far less powerful position than a president, one has to consider the greatness of the deed to be all the more remarkable. These are of course highly individualistic instances of political action, but political action in groups can be even more potent. Arendt often pointed to the French Resistance during the Second World War, but one might also think of how we remember the "greatest generation" of World War II, the civil rights movement, or the Polish Solidarity movement, all of which involved numerous nameless individuals whose actions were worthy of political *athanatizein*.

History, Politics, and Human Agency

To return to the questions that prompted this discussion of Arendt's political and historical thought: What has it taught us about her approach? First, it has taught us that the origins and meaning of history are not in world historical processes but in a dynamic conception of human agency. The world we inhabit was made by the actions of human beings, actions whose ultimate consequences they almost never imagined would have occurred. But in order to affect the world in this dramatic way, this action must be political, that is, it must somehow have gained access to a public realm. Only action in the public realm has the necessary potency to alter the world enough to become the content of history. Second, it should be noted that there is a distinction in Arendt's articulation of political action that she probably should have made more explicit. This is between the basic phenomena of political action and the criteria of historical judgment used to evaluate it. Of course, action is done all the time in the public realm, but that certainly does not guarantee its political *athanatizein*. Arendt's description of political action as "care of the world" bears little resemblance to the tyranny and corruption often witnessed on the public stage. These acts of tyranny surely are political actions, in the sense that they are acts done in the public realm, but they do not achieve political *athanatizein*—they cannot gain historical greatness—because they fail to achieve the criteria of historical judgment: they did not care for and preserve our common world.

Thus, for Arendt, human agency must be taken very seriously by historical narratives. Truly authentic history *must* be recounted and traced back to events grounded in genuine acts of human spontaneity, and the criteria that judge the significance of those events have to do with whether those acts contributed to the preservation of our common world. This is why Arendt always seeks to ground her historical narratives in concrete events and deeds, such as her insistence that modernity began with the invention of the telescope. Critics often find this idea an oversimplification, and in many ways it is: the modern world was a result of a wide variety of social, intellectual, political, technological, and economic factors. Yet, whether Arendt is right about the telescope or not, her critics have to a certain extent missed the broader lesson she wanted to teach. Her intention had not been to claim that no other elements were at the roots of the modern era, but instead had been to give human agency it due in history, to show that historical trends and processes, real as they may be, always have an origin in the actions of human beings and not solely in gigantic historical processes.

It should be clear by now that the fundamental motivation behind her thought was a relentless protest against modern ideologies and paradigms of thought that see human beings as little more than the products of complex social and historical determinants over which they have little control. While there are no doubt many such forces at work in history, from Arendt's perspective their relationship to our world must always be traced back to an act of sheer human natality. In the end, this may present a standard that is either unreasonably high or impractical; but as corrective to a variety of general trends in modern thought and contemporary political and historical reflection, its importance seems obvious. And, moreover, it represents a potentially valuable corrective to the approaches of a discipline like political science, whose methods arguably often seem to operate at a significant distance from genuine human agency.

Though I have attempted to provide numerous illustrations for the ideas in this chapter, as a kind of preliminary conceptual framework it has unavoidably been necessary to operate at a fairly high level of abstraction. Arendt, however, had a wealth of examples of her own. She spent a great deal of time carefully examining at least three distinct examples of her ideal of political action in the history of Western civilization: the ancient Greeks, the republican Romans, and the modern revolutionaries. In Chapter 2, we will consider the unique role each played in her understanding of the history of Western politics, along with what each taught her about the possibilities for politics in our own era.

2 Arendt's Politics of Founding

It is no coincidence that the word "citizen" was treated as a sacred appellation by the "men of action" Hannah Arendt studied. In the preface to *Between Past and Future*, Arendt discussed the idea of freedom that animated the word "citizen" by pointing to the experiences of René Char, who joined the French Resistance after the fall of France in World War II and was unexpectedly thrown into public affairs. For Char and his comrades, that time during the Resistance was the most important period of their lives. After the war, when politics returned to the stale old struggle of competing ideologies, there was a vague sense among the former comrades-in-arms that "they had lost their treasure."[1] "What was this treasure?" Arendt asked. What made that time so precious for the members of the French Resistance, and why could they never again, according to Char, quite clearly locate it in public or private life? The mysteriousness of the power that period held for the actors in the Resistance, she argued, lay in the absence of what she called a "testament" that named the treasure, a "tradition . . . which selects and preserves, which indicates where the treasures are and what their worth is." In her political thought, Arendt set out to name this treasure. She believed it had been the same experience as that of the other Western men of action, who pursued political *athanatizein*, arguing that because they were actors and not thinkers the men of action rarely took the time to theorize the nature of their pursuit.[2] Political thought therefore fell to the philosophers, who (with a few tepid exceptions) detested politics and denigrated its form of *athanatizein*. Arendt claimed that our civilization's political language—words such as "freedom," "equality," "citizenship," *res publica*, and "politics" itself—came from these original political experiences of the men of action. But as the memory of those experiences faded, new meanings, often derived from the tradition of political thought, were given to those words. Arendt proposed to use her genealogical approach to go in search of the primordial experiences of political action that lay behind our political language, discovering in the process a very different experience of political freedom than that which these words have accrued over time.

In her 1969 course "Philosophy and Politics: What Is Political Philosophy?" she explained what she had been in search of in her political studies. "The past and its relevance," she writes, "are by no means identical with the tradition and its sacredness. The past is present first of all in the language we speak. All of our terminology in these matters, especially in political matters, is first Greek, second Roman, and third belongs to the revolutionaries of the Modern Age."[3] Arendt is here summarizing much of her work on politics during the previous two decades. Each of these three original political experiences gave Arendt essential insights into the nature and possibilities of authentic politics. These were primordial experiences of what she variously called political action, public happiness, public freedom, or simply citizenship.[4] The modern revolutionaries, as Arendt argues most comprehensively in *On Revolution*, showed why it has been so difficult to perform authentic political action and to realize the political experience of true citizenship in the modern era. In *The Human Condition*, Arendt showed that the Greeks, as the originators of the political experience of citizenship, offered a kind of purity in that experience that has never existed since. Finally, in "Introduction *into* Politics" and "What Is Authority," Arendt indicated how the Romans demonstrated that the political experience of citizenship could become a source of stability and enduring freedom in the world, and, as a result, she appeared to view them as a kind of historical ideal of political action and citizenship. These three original instances of Western politics are among the few examples of what Arendt called a "political public realm," a public realm based on the active participation of its citizens (see Chapter 1). This was not accidental: I will argue here that Arendt believed that her positive project could only begin in such a political public realm.

We will see two themes throughout this chapter's discussion of the authentic Western experiences of politics that help us understand what Arendt was attempting to do in her work. On the one hand, the question of founding—of how to found a new public realm—was clearly the master idea of her political writings. The modern revolutionaries were confronted with it and largely failed to accomplish it, due to the characteristic thought patterns of modernity. The Romans deified the act of founding, but this fact made them a poor example of founding since for them the act of founding existed in the primordial past. Thus, it was to the Greeks Arendt turned to understand how to refound a public realm. On the other hand, the question of how such a public realm could be maintained in a modern world whose politics are so subversive to its existence meant that the mere act of founding was not enough, and this, I will argue, was what ultimately lay behind Arendt's concern with understanding the authentic nature of political philosophy. Only understanding the true nature of political judgment, as the authentic relationship between thought and action, could keep a new public realm—a new space for "public freedom"—in existence. As we will see, this was where Arendt believed the Greeks failed: while their politics had a space for the faculty of judgment, Arendt believed that their judgment lacked the depth afforded by the faculty of thought, and this was the reason for the unstable nature of their politics. The modern revolutionaries' fatal error was also related to a flawed relationship of thought and action: in this case, the modern conception of that relationship drawn from the tradition of political thought's productive paradigm of political judgment, which in turn led them to interpret the politics of founding in terms of sovereign political violence. Only the Romans demonstrated an enduring politics that entailed a fully realized experience of political judgment. Unfortunately, the Romans' experience of the relationship of thought and action was mediated through their unique experience of tradition, which made thought much more politically accessible to them than it seems to be for moderns; and moreover, like all other historical occurrences, the Romans' politics were unique and unrepeatable. Thus, while her genealogies of the politics of founding could be instructive, her project would eventually have to imagine an unprecedented possibility: to realize, perhaps for the first time, a political public realm that consciously practiced political philosophy. In other words, her pursuit of the true nature of political philosophy was essentially related to a desire to understand the human faculties necessary to found and maintain a new public realm in the modern world. As this book's ensuing pages will show, the act of founding and preserving a space for public freedom and the question of authentic political philosophy presuppose each other: neither can exist for long without the other. Whether or not this was a virtuous or a vicious circle remains unclear: it appears Arendt never fully solved this problem in her work.

Greek *Isonomie*

Bound up with the problem of founding is a theoretical insight that Arendt was arguably the first to formulate: the idea that politics was essentially non-sovereign. Later, we will examine what led Arendt to challenge the idea that politics (as the phenomenon concerned with the exercise of power) was a matter of sovereignty, or, in Aristotle's formulation, a matter of "ruling and being ruled." We will see that Arendt's long-standing concerns over the nature and failures of revolutionary politics—both in totalitarian regimes and beyond them—led her to reject the idea that politics was a matter of sovereign rule. She would argue that it had been the conceptual frameworks underlying the legitimacy of sovereign politics that had led to the most disastrous revolutionary activities. What lay behind these failures, she argued, had been a model of politics, drawn from the tradition of political thought, which grasped political action on the model of the productive paradigm, and imagined that the founding of political regimes and public realms was a matter of work and artifice. What she discovered in the Greeks was arguably the first and only political society that understood the non-sovereign politics of founding.

The activity of founding lay at the very center of the Greeks' politics, existing, according to Arendt, as "an almost commonplace experience."[5] This constant activity of founding public realms was based on her recognition of their very different conception of power, a kind of power that was based on action and its dynamic capacity to establish relationships, and not (or at least, not essentially) on the instrumental cause/effect framework of work. Power is "what keeps the public realm, the potential space of appearance between acting and speaking men, in existence" and is generated by the "gathering together" and "acting together" of human beings. It is "actualized only where word and deed have not parted company, where words are not empty and deeds not brutal, where words are not used to veil intentions but to disclose realities, and deeds are not used to violate and destroy but to establish relations and create new realities."[6] If action is the origin of power, then the legitimacy of the sovereign conception of politics—drawing as it does on the framework of the activity of work—is undermined, and what is indicated is then a very different account of the nature of political power, a non-sovereign conception of politics as "no-rule." The Greeks, according to Arendt, exemplified this politics of no-rule.

Arendt's story of the origins of Greek politics predates the polis, beginning with the Homeric poets and the ancient historians. Arendt presents the ancient poets and historians, prior to the emergence of philosophy and politics, as the first practitioners of *athanatizein*.[7] The ancient historians represent a primordial ideal for Arendt in that, unlike either of the later forms of *athanatizein*, they appeared to draw on action, thought, and judgment in full measure. In ancient Greece, philosophy and politics in various ways ignored certain of these faculties while giving priority to others. Philosophy pursued thought and contemplation, "to dwell in the neighborhood of those things which are forever," and this concern with the eternal led the philosophers to reject the notion of immortality offered by the historians and poets for what they perceived as their impure concern with ephemeral human affairs. Politics, on the other hand, sought through the establishment of the polis to actualize action and achieve immortality without the help of the *vita contemplativa* represented by the person of the poet or historian.[8] Relying heavily on the comments of Pericles about the nature and meaning of the polis, Arendt argued that the citizens in the Greek polis were convinced that its organization meant they no longer needed the poets to immortalize them. They believed that through the "incessant" political talking that occurred in the agora, the greatness they could achieve would be all the greater since they alone were the ones doing the immortalizing.[9]

According to Arendt, the Greeks understood their political activities in the polis in fiercely agonistic terms, as the primary space of self-disclosure, a place where their individual excellence could be judged by and measured against their peers in a kind of "organized remembrance."[10] Demonstrating their excellence or "virtuosity" through political action was seen as the primary means to achieving political *athanatizein*.[11] Because of this, the Greeks understood politics as fundamentally an activity where everyone had an equal right to show their excellence, and where no one could assert rulership over anyone else—a space where actors could move freely among their peers. The original political experience of the polis found its expression in the Greek word for political equality, *isonomie*, which literally means "no-rule."[12] When citizens entered the public realm, they left behind the distinctions and inequality that characterize the private realm and established conditions of equality through the institutions of the public realm.[13]

The Greeks' political experience recognized the natural inequality of the individual citizens, a recognition that Arendt believed was based on their intuitive sense of the fundamental political condition of plurality.[14] Because of the condition of plurality, the Greeks recognized that (Aristotle's claims

notwithstanding) there was nothing fundamentally political about human beings as individuals. The fact that they are so radically plural means that these
unequal actors must somehow be "equalized,"[15] that they stand in need of
being "relativized" by a public realm that can separate and relate them to each
other.[16] All of this was the basis for the sharp distinction they drew between
the public and private realms, which corresponds to the distinction Arendt
drew between liberation and freedom.[17] The private realm represented the
sphere of the household where we must gain liberation from—and thus gain
sovereignty over—natural necessity, and therefore whatever equality we have
there is derived from our basic natural needs as animals. The Greeks believed
they had the opportunity for true freedom when they entered the public
realm, which they experienced as a kind of "second life."[18] This second life
was believed to be free from coercion. Arendt writes that the Greeks believed
that politics "begins where the realm of material necessity and physical brute
force ends."[19] In this situation of "no-rule," the original meaning of politics
was "that men in their freedom can interact with one another without compulsion, force, and rule over one another, as equals among equals, commanding and obeying one another only in emergencies . . . but otherwise managing
all their affairs by speaking with and persuading one another."[20] It is this high
premium placed on persuasion over coercion in their political life that defined the Greeks' political experience.

The Greeks were uncompromisingly strict in separating the private realm
where household maintenance of life occurred from the public realm where
citizens went to act and move among their peers. Coercion and rulership
belonged to the private household and almost never in the public realm, because activities that involved coercion, such as labor or any form of work's
instrumental means/ends logic, were not appropriate to the political sphere
since they could never be matters of persuasion. This, however, did not mean
that matters involving material necessity or warfare and violence could not be
discussed insofar as they pertained to public affairs, though, as we have seen,
many critics have read Arendt as suggesting otherwise.[21] Rather, to be political, she argued, concerned not the *content* of public affairs but the *manner* in
which they were conducted. What mattered politically was not *what* was
done, but *how* it was done. In "Introduction *into* Politics," the manuscript
written immediately after *The Human Condition* and before *On Revolution*,
Arendt acknowledges this, stating that "in the *polis*, providing for life's necessities and defending itself were not at the center of political life but were political only . . . to the extent that decisions concerning them were not decreed

from on high but decided by people talking with and persuading one another."[22] Indeed, Pericles, whom Arendt regularly lionized as an exemplar of Greek political action, helped enact an entitlement system that was intended to encourage greater participation in the agora among poorer citizens of Athens. In the 1972 conference on her work, she acknowledged that there are no specific delimitations on what can be politically deliberated over: "at all times people living together will have affairs that belong in the public realm . . . what these matters are at any historical moment is probably utterly different."[23] She then freely admitted that social questions could therefore be a target of political action; her stipulation, however, was that the social issue at stake had to be relevant toward liberating citizens for participating in political action.[24]

Arendt points out that the Greeks were well aware that other forms of organization, such as responsible tyranny, were more efficient and were willing to avail themselves of these modes when absolutely necessary.[25] They purposely held to the messier, more imprecise "political" way of life, however, because only such a way of life allowed for their conception of freedom as "no-rule." And while it may have been true that Greek political organization was less efficient, it nevertheless allowed for a kind of political judgment that was inherently superior to that of any possible tyrant. No single individual, no tyrant, could provide the insight into their common world that their "incessant talk" could give. Arendt believed that in the context of the endless deliberations of the agora the Greeks discovered political judgment. She argued that this political judgment took advantage of the fact that each actor is located at a different point in the common world. Through experience in polis life, the Greeks developed what she calls "impartiality," the ability to gain an enlarged mentality, which, as we will see in Chapter 5, is another word for having the common sense essential for political judgment.[26]

But by allowing each citizen to offer their *doxa*, or opinion, the Greeks came to believe that they did not need the help of the *vita contemplativa*'s defining faculty of thought, which the historians had always employed along with judgment.[27] This intensely political version of judgment, which sought to ignore thought and reflection in deliberating on courses of action, seemed to be effective in achieving the glory that the citizens of the polis sought, but it also appeared to be rather reckless and unstable. Arendt's assessment of the Greek polis experience, in fact, was decidedly less sanguine than is commonly believed, her lionizing comments in *The Human Condition* notwithstanding. One aspect that clearly troubled her was the growing alienation of politics from philosophy in the Greek polis, which suggested that political action within it would become superficial, short-sighted, and reckless.[28] This problem played itself out in another aspect of Greek politics that troubled her: the Greeks' agonistic and highly individualistic form of political action. Noting that the citizens of the Greek polis seemed too individualistic, competitive, and obsessed with heroic traditions and aspirations, she wrote that this agonistic spirit "eventually was to bring the Greek city-states to ruin because it made alliances between them well-nigh impossible and poisoned the domestic life of the citizens with envy and mutual hatred (envy was the national vice of ancient Greece)."[29] This agonism came to dominate their politics, so that in Athens (as articulated through the speeches of Pericles) the major foreign policy objective seemed to be concerned with gaining glory at the expense of their rivals and at any cost.[30] She quotes Pericles saying that "even if we should be defeated, the memory will be left intact that we ruled over more Hellenes than any other polis, that we sustained the greatest wars against them, united or separated, and that we once inhabited the greatest and the richest polis." Still, Arendt believed that, while there was a recklessness and hubris to the Greek polis, there was still a kind undeniable greatness to their activities. She goes on to assert that "Pericles was seized (and Athens with him) of the hubris of power. No one has trusted power so much as Pericles, never was it as overestimated in its possibilities. Or was it? Don't we still remember this short, ridiculously short period of Athenian history through the centuries? Despite all her follies?"[31] Assessing their enduring legacy, Arendt writes that "it is the greatness and also the tragedy of Athens and of Pericles . . . that they thought of politics, or rather that activity that corresponds to the polis, as something which could attain immortality directly without the intervention of the poets and historians."[32]

With this history in view, the "attitude of the philosophers toward the polis," and indeed toward realm of human affairs in general, comes to seem in many ways justified. Politics was characterized by "temporality, instability, and relativity," while philosophy concerned itself with the "stability, permanence, and finality" of the eternal things of the cosmos.[33] Human action, particularly in the Periclean era of visceral hubris from which the ancient political philosophers emerged, may have achieved greatness on its own terms, but at what a cost, and especially when the philosophers had for some time embraced the contemplative experience of *thaumazein* (wonder) as the highest path to *athanatizein*. Arendt illustrates this by setting up an opposition between Pericles and Solon, who, in the 1969 lecture course, exemplifies, along with Socrates, the political relevance of the thinking faculty and the *vita contemplativa* in general—a kind of political path not taken by Athenian politics. Solon, like the ancient political philosophers after him, placed heavy emphasis on moderation, or "putting within limits," while Pericles represented the ideal of "striving for excellence at any price."[34] Arendt believed that, like Solon, Socrates' ultimate goal had been to reunite philosophy and politics, "to bring philosophy down from the sky to the earth."[35] It was the increasing loss of faith in the worth of thought that had led to rancor both among the various cities and between the citizens. "What Socrates [tried] to introduce into polis life is thinking itself, not a special philosophical doctrine, but the principle that everything should be examined in thought."[36] Thought, Arendt argued, was for Socrates a dialogue I have with myself—a two-in-one within my thinking ego. Without this dialogue, she was convinced that politics inevitably becomes superficial.[37] Socrates wanted to teach his fellow citizens that "living together with others begins with living together with oneself . . . only he who knows how to live with himself is fit to live with others."[38]

Socrates' death, of course, demonstrated that he had failed in this goal, and, by the time of Plato and Aristotle, philosophy and politics had little common.[39] They sought forms of realization that had no relation to each other: politics sought realization solely in the world of human affairs through action, while philosophy sought realization in the gap between past and future, an existential position utterly removed from that world, in the activity of thought leading to contemplation, or *thaumazein*. After it became evident that the political world could not be ignored, explicitly demonstrated by the death of Socrates, Plato sought to subordinate politics to philosophy, and this, according to Arendt, was the origin of all traditional political philosophy.[40] Politics had been *a-telos*, just as philosophy was: it provided a public realm where acting men and women could perform great deeds. Plato sought to give political action a telos, an end beyond itself, which was to support and protect the contemplative way of life of the philosophers. According to Arendt, "this consideration of action under the category of end and means brings action into a dangerously close relationship with fabrication."[41] The introduction of a telos into political action was the origin of the ideal of the politics of sovereign rulership that has dominated the tradition of political thought ever since.

In Chapter 3, we will see that Arendt's critique of the tradition of political thought revolved around Plato's introduction—and Aristotle's acceptance—of the ideal of rulership as the correct model for understanding the relationship of thought and action and, by extension, of philosophy and politics. The analogies Plato drew on in formulating this political ideal were all drawn from nonpolitical elements of Greek life. The idea that rulership reflected the appropriate model of political relationships was a radical argument on Plato's part and would have been perceived as bizarre by his fellow Athenians, who only understood sovereign rule to be appropriate in the context of the private household. Moreover, in formulating the explicit relationship of thought to action that is entailed in this relationship of ruling, Plato appealed to the ideal of the craftsman who conceives a model and then may carry it out himself or allow associates to do it for him.[42] In either case, thought and action have "parted company," as Arendt puts it, because it is not necessary that the one who thinks be the one who acts. We will see in the coming pages that authentic political judgment *essentially* means that the one who acts must also be the one who judges and thinks. All this, of course, relates to the Chapter 1's claims that Arendt's political thought was ultimately concerned with the question of history: that her discussions of action were at their core concerned with the relationship of human agency to historical judgment. We now see how philosophy and politics parted ways in the polis. When she said she was searching for their relationship, what she meant was a return to the original practice of history done by the ancient poets and historians, which predated that parting. The political judgment of authentic political philosophy, in other words, is ultimately a judgment about the historical greatness of an act or deed.

Still, it stands to reason that if the Greeks, in their political thoughtlessness, had not been so cavalier and profligate in their political activities, Arendt may never have been able to discover the phenomenon of founding. In the Romans, she would find a people who exemplified the thoughtfulness and gravity that the act of founding required in order to endure.

The Legacy of Rome

Arendt's account of Roman politics is an underresearched aspect of her thought. To date, only Dean Hammer has published an article-length treatment of the topic.[43] Hammer's work is illuminating, but it understandably lacks the full contextual engagement with Arendt's broader set of ideas I am attempting here. Though Arendt occasionally referred to the Greeks and Romans as the "twin peoples of antiquity,"[44] her published writings would lead one to think that Roman politics represented a relatively minor area of her thought. The only significant treatment the Romans received in work she published during her lifetime occurs in her essay "What Is Authority?" But in fact Roman politics were very important to Arendt. Previously, I pointed out that Arendt had intended to write a larger, more systematic treatment of her political thought after she published *The Human Condition* and had worked on this larger project throughout the period from 1954 to 1969. While a part of that eventual work became *On Revolution* and various of her later essays, the broader project was never completed. What we now know of that broader project indicates that Rome would have played a pivotal role in it. The recently published "Introduction *into* Politics," written when she was still working on the more systematic work in 1958–1959, spends roughly equal amounts of time dealing with the Greeks and Romans. The Romans seemed to be a bridge of sorts for Arendt between the examples of political action found in *The Human Condition* (1958) and *On Revolution* (1962); indeed, there are convincing reasons to conclude that Rome represented a kind of political ideal for her.

To begin with, Arendt's political involvement in postwar Europe suggests this. Arendt had argued in *Origins* that the only right all humans possess is "the right to have rights," the right to be a citizen in a concrete political community that articulates specific, concrete political rights. This argument would initially indicate a certain skepticism toward cosmopolitanism, and, indeed, she was quick to point out that any world government could be very dangerous.[45] Yet, Arendt spoke positively of the idea of "world citizenship" as late as her essay on Jaspers and in the 1970 lectures on Kant's political philosophy. Moreover, she was highly active in the European integration movement in the fifties.[46] Indeed, it appears that much of the impulse to develop the language of "non-sovereignty" was related to her desire to theorize notions of political organization that did not strictly adhere to the idea of national sovereignty. She appears to have viewed Rome as an example of how these apparently conflicting ideas of world government and non-sovereignty were once reconciled. "Introduction *into* Politics," in fact, suggests Arendt believed that some kind of non-sovereign association of republican states could perform the same function as republican Rome.[47]

Arendt's formulation of the modern predicament and her hopes for escaping it are also suggestive of a Roman ideal. One of her most explicit statements of this came in a colloquium she chaired for *Christianity and Crisis* in 1966, entitled "Remarks on 'The Crisis Character of Modern Society.'"[48]

Quoting Tocqueville's statement that "the past ceases to throw light upon the future, and the mind of man wanders in obscurity," Arendt claimed that the series of crises that the members of the colloquium had witnessed to that point in the twentieth century were symptomatic of a general crisis of the modern world. The realities of our world are now "enormously changed and daily changing," regularly giving birth to "unprecedented developments." "If," she remarked, "the series of crises in which we have lived since the beginning of the century can teach us anything at all, it is, I think, the simple fact that there are no general standards to determine our judgments unfailingly, no general rules under which to subsume the particular cases with any degree of certainty." We must, she believed, find a way to deal with these crises and unprecedented developments without "trusting the validity of the so-called lessons of history." Doing so "is difficult and uncomfortable, but it also contains great challenges and perhaps even promises." Her hope was that from "out of this turmoil of being confronted with reality without the help of precedent, that is, of tradition and authority, there will finally arise some new code of conduct." This notion of a "new code of conduct" is highly suggestive of Roman politics' unique ability to wed political freedom with authority and tradition. Its ability to do this was based on a distinction Arendt drew between sovereignty and authority. This may appear a rather counterintuitive idea, since Western political thought has traditionally identified sovereignty with authority. But Arendt argued that these ideas were distinct. Authority came from Roman political experience and indicated an obedience that was freely given. Sovereignty was an invention of the tradition of political thought. It indicated a politics of rulership and coercion, regardless of whether that coercion came from the force of reason or of violence. Arendt argues that Greek political philosophy would in all likelihood have remained utopian in character if the Romans had not decided to embrace and integrate it into their politics.[49] The tradition of political thought played very little role at all in establishing Western civilization, according to Arendt. In fact, the tradition merely mischaracterized what was achieved through Roman political action, but because the Romans adopted Greek political philosophy as their highest authorities in matters of theory, the conceptual framework of the tradition spread to wherever the Roman Empire spread. As the centuries passed, sovereignty became increasingly confused with authority.

Roman political action had several distinctive characteristics from the Greeks that allowed it to establish the Western world. Greek political action possessed a kind of purity and simplicity that Arendt used for polemical purposes in *The Human Condition*. This purity resulted in a foreignness to modern ways of thinking about politics that was highly productive for highlighting political phenomena that modern individuals might not otherwise take seriously. But Arendt, as we have seen, had no delusions about the political instability and conflict in Greek political life. Roman politics, on the other hand, was much more stable and less individualistic. It seemed to embody in its very nature the civic friendship that Socrates, Plato, and Aristotle had believed could have saved the Greek polis.[50] In "Ruling and Being Ruled," Arendt writes that "[against the Greek experience] stands the spirit of polity which flourished in Rome rather than Athens. The Roman spirit embodies and exults—to a degree it is difficult for us to recapture—the great overflowing joy of companionship among one's equals."[51] While all forms of political action have certain essential features in common, Roman political action was uniquely authoritarian and conservative. It is a testament to Arendt's ability to transcend standard political categories that this recognition in no sense implied that Roman political action was any less free or authentic than other forms of political action, including that of the Greeks. The common world was the most sacred thing imaginable to the Romans. While the Greeks tended to emphasize the virtuosity of political action in an agonistic public realm—a place to demonstrate one's *areté*, or excellence—Roman political action gave priority to the care and preservation of the common world. While the Greeks sought immortality in performing great deeds that would be memorialized by the polis, the Romans sought immortality by taking part in and carrying forward the original act of founding the Roman world. Arendt writes that "the foundation of a new body politic—to the Greeks an almost commonplace experience—became to the Romans the central, decisive, unrepeatable beginning of their whole history, a unique event." Thus, "at the heart of Roman politics," she writes, "from the beginning of the republic until virtually the end of the imperial era, stands the conviction of the sacredness of foundation, in the sense that once something has been founded it remains binding for all future generations. To be engaged in politics meant first and foremost to preserve the founding of the city of Rome." This veneration for an authoritative founding origin was alien to the Greeks, who treated even Homer, "the educator of all Hellas," with a glibness that would have shocked the Romans.[52]

Roman political action was performed under the auspices of institutions that constantly tied it back to the foundation of Rome. Arendt describes these institutions as "the Roman trinity of religion, authority, and tradition."[53] Religion was central to the Romans' politics. Indeed, religion and politics were considered nearly identical in Rome, because "the binding power of the foundation" was rooted in the fact that "the city . . . offered the gods of the people a permanent home."[54] Tradition preserved the authoritative beginning through a body of myths, legends, and authoritative examples and precedents—"the testimony of the ancestors." Authority represented the political force of religion and tradition. Authority was located in the Senate, an institution that was understood to possess no actual political power, but was instead conceived as "a council of elders" representing the *maiores*, the greater ones and ancestors, and was endowed with the right of "augmentation and confirmation" of the proposed undertakings of political actors. Arendt writes that "the strength of this trinity lay in the binding force of an authoritative beginning to which 'religious bonds' tied men back through tradition" and that "to act without authority and tradition, without accepted, time-honored standards and models, without the help of the wisdom of the founding fathers was inconceivable." Political judgment was thus oriented through a tradition that connected the Romans closely to their common world. All political action had to find an authoritative precedent or example, and to act without such authority was considered impious and dangerous.[55] This did not mean that political action lost its *sui generis* character: authorities "'augment' and confirm human actions but do not guide them," and any political action itself offered the possibility of becoming an example and precedent in its own right. Precedents and examples, rather, lent political action "gravitas," the ability to bear the weight of Rome's sacred foundation. Getting a share of immortality, then—the purpose of all politics—was not, as with the Greeks, a function of leaving memorials behind that would be remembered by future generations. It instead involved leaving behind examples for the Roman traditions that allowed one to "[grow] closer to the ancestors and the past," and thus to the sacred foundation of Rome, and, as a result, old age rather than mere adulthood was considered "the very climax of human life."[56]

These unique characteristics gave Rome an expansiveness that would have been impossible in many other political contexts. To appreciate this, one need only recall Arendt's thoroughgoing political opposition to all forms of modern imperialism in *The Origins of Totalitarianism* and her various attacks on the Vietnam War. Modern imperialism, according to Arendt, was driven by economic necessities rather than political conditions, and as a result came to see politics in terms of "expansion for expansion's sake."[57] From the viewpoint of authentic politics this was "megalomania," "insanity," and a "contradiction to the human condition," since, in her view, politics fundamentally involves limitations.[58] Her apparent admiration for Roman imperialism would thus seem like a flagrant contradiction, but the truth is that Rome seems to have developed a form of politics that could be highly expansive without overstepping the inherent limits of political life. Arendt argues that because Roman political action always revolved around the preservation and carrying forward of the original foundation of the city, the idea of beginning a completely new body politic—in the manner that the Greek city-states seemed to on a regular basis—was nearly inconceivable. Roman historical consciousness was rooted and found its intelligibility in this "unique" and "unrepeatable" event, an event involving action taken on the part of the gods and superhuman "effort and toil" on the part of those who founded it. And unlike the Greek gods whose permanent home was on Mount Olympus, the permanent home of the Roman gods was in the city of Rome itself. Thus, the only way Rome could have understood expansion was in terms of "adding to the original foundation" until "the whole of the Western world [was] united and administered by Rome, as though [it] were nothing more than a Roman hinterland."[59]

This would likely have kept any other body politic from significantly expanding; however, two aspects of its politics seem to have made Rome an exceptional case. One was the political stability provided by the Roman trinity. The second had to do with the way the foundational myths and legends of Rome gave it a self-consciousness that was unusually politically inclusive in antiquity. Reflecting on the role of legends in human history in *The Origins of Totalitarianism*, Arendt writes:

> Legends have always played a powerful role in the making of history. . . .
> Legends were the spiritual foundations of every ancient city, empire,
> people, promising safe guidance through the limitless spaces of the future. Without ever relating facts reliably, yet always expressing their true
> significance, they offered a truth beyond realities, a remembrance beyond
> memories. . . . In this sense, legends are not only among the first memories of mankind, but actually the true beginning of human history.[60]

If she is correct, there are few instances in which legends have had a more far-reaching impact on human history than in the case of the Romans. Drawing on Theodor Mommsen's enormous, Nobel Prize–winning work on Rome, Arendt argues that the Romans' literature shows that they located the

city's foundation not in the violent actions of Romulus, but more primordially in the stories surrounding the Trojan War, particularly as it was emblem-
atically embellished by Virgil in the *Aeneid*.[61] When the Trojans, under the
command of Aeneas, came to the Italian peninsula after the destruction of
Troy, they were confronted by the native Latins, led by Turnus, who claimed
to be another Achilles. In this case, however, the Trojans won the war, and
Turnus was defeated by Aeneas; but instead of ending in the total annihilation of one or the other of the two combatants, the *Aeneid* ends with an alliance and a treaty between the warring parties.[62] The Roman foundation myth
ends in reconciliation because the Trojans themselves had once been decisively defeated and were thus able to take the standpoint of those they
defeated.

Arendt argues that this foundation myth structured the basic self-
interpretation of Roman politics. The foundation myth expressed itself most
explicitly in the distinctively political way the Romans understood legislation
and foreign policy. For the Greeks, both of these activities were pre- or ex-
trapolitical. The Greeks understood political action to take place within
strictly circumscribed boundaries that excluded any form of violence or coercion. As result, the sphere of the household, as the realm driven by biological
necessity requiring a kind of benign despotic rule by the household head, had
to be strictly excluded from the political realm. The household head was only
free when he left the realm of coercion and moved freely among his peers in
the political realm. Just as in the realm of domestic policy, foreign policy,
because it was also perceived fundamentally to be a realm of coercion, violence, and necessity, required strict exclusion from the political realm. Thus,
for the Greeks, the word for law, *nómos*, had the sense of being like the walls
of the city, which circumscribed the area in which citizens could be free.[63]
Outside those boundaries, violence and coercion were simply the principle on
which any course of action was based. Thus, on Arendt's interpretation, the
Melian Dialogue simply expressed the common Greek understanding of
where foreign policy is located in relation to politics: outside it.[64] The Romans, by contrast, had a dramatically different understanding of the relationship between politics, law, and foreign policy. Unlike the Greeks, for whom
politics was conceived as a kind of "island" in a sea of necessity and coercion,
the Roman *lex* meant "lasting ties" and "contract." Arendt writes that for the
Romans "a law is something that links human beings together, and it comes
into being not by *diktat* or by an act of force but rather through mutual
agreements. Formulation of law, of this lasting tie that follows the violence of

war, is itself tied to proposals and counterproposals, that is, to speech, which in the view of both the Greeks and Romans was central to all politics." Thus, legislation and the laws themselves were understood by the Romans to be political by nature, in stark distinction to the Greeks, who understood legislation to be "so radically disconnected from truly political activities" that the lawgiver did not even have to be a citizen, but could be contracted from the outside to supply the city's needs like an architect or sculptor.[65] Thus, we see once again that it was perfectly acceptable in Arendt's view for instrumental activities to be instances of political action, and that what counted as political action was not constant but instead depended on the interpretations of the specific body politic where it was performed.

From out of this capacity to politicize law and foreign policy, Arendt argued that the Romans established Western civilization as what came to be a massive "common world," the scale of which had never been seen before in human history. "There is no doubt," she writes, that "the idea of a political order beyond the borders of one's own nation or city, is solely of Roman origin. The Roman politicization of the space between peoples marks the beginning of the Western world—indeed, it first created the Western world as *world*. There had been many civilizations before Rome, some of them extraordinarily rich and great, but what lay between them was not a world but only a desert."[66] These experiences gave birth to a strikingly cosmopolitan ideal for such a conservative body politic: the *societas Romana*, "an infinitely expandable system of alliances initiated by Rome, in which peoples and lands were not only bound to Rome by temporary and renewable treaties, but also became Rome's eternal allies."[67] From out of this *societas Romana* sprang the ideal that to this day still encompasses the Western ideal of political judgment: *humanitas*, or humanism.[68]

In her essay "On Humanity in Dark Times," Arendt explains the politics of the Roman ideal of *humanitas* as "the political fact that in Rome people of widely different ethnic origins and descent could acquire Roman citizenship and thus enter into the discourse among cultivated Romans, could discuss the world and life with them." The crucial point here, Arendt is quick to note, is that *humanitas* was not simply a matter of individual cultivation, as the modern notion of "humanism" is often understood to be. It was a matter of political activity, a crucial element of the cultivation of the political judgment exercised by Roman citizens.[69] For Arendt, the essential characteristic of judgment is what she calls "impartiality," a standard of judgment distinct from the epistemological ideal of "objectivity."[70] Impartiality does not seek to escape the perspectivalism of living in a common world, but instead seeks to take into consideration as many of those perspectives as possible. According to Arendt, different historical bodies politic have utilized various strategies in the cultivation of impartiality. For the Greeks, impartiality was achieved within the boundaries of the agora: "Since for the Greeks the public political space is common to all (*koinon*), the space where the citizens assemble, it is the realm in which all things can first be recognized in their many-sidedness. This ability to see the same thing first from two opposing sides and then from all sides [is] an ability ultimately based in Homeric impartiality."[71] Roman impartiality, however, while it encompassed the Greeks' impartiality, went beyond it. While the Roman cosmopolitan ideal of *humanitas* obviously involved deliberation among an extraordinarily diverse set of citizens as participants in the deliberations of the public realm, the ideal itself grew out of a sense of impartiality that was rooted in the traditions, values, and religious practices that informed Rome's historical consciousness and political judgment. As a result, the common sense connection of the Romans to their common world was extraordinarily deep and intuitive. According to Arendt the Romans had incorporated the Socratic recognition of the need for thoughtfulness in political judgment by carrying forward the traditions and narratives of their ancestors. Because their traditions informed their activities in such an effective and natural way, their political judgment required very little genuine thought and reflection, but instead simply the analogizing of "examples" to courses of action through the practice of seeking authoritative gravitas. Arendt argued that in the Roman era tradition bridged the gap between past and future where thought occurs, offering the connection to the past that thought provides, and, as a result, made thinking largely unnecessary.[72]

If politics is always essentially concerned with the preservation of a public realm and common world, the effectiveness of Roman political judgment is nearly incontrovertible. Throughout her work, we see Arendt insist that political judgment can never be effectively evaluated in terms of the criteria of success or failure. Yet, even by this measure the effectiveness of Roman political judgment is difficult to deny, since it established the most expansive, stable, and enduring political regime in human history. But even taking into account the broader historical criteria to which Arendt is referring in her political thought, to an extraordinary degree the Romans seem to have achieved their true *political* goals of preserving and adding to the sacred foundation of the republic, and thus to have gained a large share of immortality.

But eventually, like all human things, Arendt admits that Roman political judgment eroded, and the Romans' political effectiveness declined. The Roman trinity could not stabilize the Roman *lex* indefinitely, which in its drive to establish ties and alliances would have gone on growing forever.[73] Rome eventually collapsed through overreach, but its heritage passed to a successor, Christianity.[74]

The Rise of Revolutionary Politics

Arendt continues the story through the post-Roman era, arguing that the concept of authority soon became much more ambiguous in the Christian era. While the Roman trinity provided the foundations for Western civilization, the meaning of the trinity was mistaken for the theoretical heritage of the Greek political philosophies, and this had far-reaching consequences. Arendt suggests that the passing of the Roman principle of authority to the Christian church is a historical event that approaches the miraculous, given the "anti-political and anti-institutional tendencies" of the original content of the Christian faith. Christianity, as a religion whose initial impulses were in rebellion against the public realm and political life in general, was able to discover in its own faith a principle of authority that appeared to be as powerful and enduring as the Romans'. The life, death, and resurrection of Jesus became a "decisive and unrepeatable" founding event in the same sense as was the founding of the city of Rome, and the testimony of the apostles became equivalent to that of the Roman *maiores*, the ancestors and greater ones "who had laid the foundations for all things to come." Arendt writes that, "thanks to the fact that the foundation of the city of Rome was repeated in the foundation of the Catholic Church, though, of course, with a radically different content, the Roman trinity of religion, authority, and tradition could be taken over by the Christian era." Thus, in the Christian era, authority came to be located in the church, while political power was located with the princes of the Western world, or in the words of Pope Gelasius I: "Two are the things by which this world is chiefly ruled: the sacred authority of the Popes, and the royal power." It is this separation of power from authority that accounts for the fact that the church has had a career of historical endurance comparable to (and maybe greater than) that of Rome, while political structures in the West have been far more ephemeral.[75]

To a large extent, it was Augustine who performed this transformation of the Christian church.[76] Augustine's transformation was performed through a conceptual articulation that was of a heavily Platonic in character. Because the Romans, due to their general lack of interest in theoretical matters, had always acknowledged the Greeks as their authorities in matters of political theory, Arendt suggests that the Romans had simply "superimposed" the Greek political philosophies on their own "greatly different political experiences."[77] Following a line of argument that appears to have been built on Eric Voegelin's *The New Science of Politics*, Arendt argues that Christianity, in a very surprising way, seems to have allowed the Platonic political concepts to "[unfold] in their fullest political effectiveness."[78] Plato's postulation of the ideas as "spiritual yardsticks, by which the visible, concrete affairs of men were to be measured and judged" was never a fully effective political theory until Christianity, because the measure itself was always an "unseen measure," whose specificity and direct political implications were always in some sense idiosyncratic to the particular philosopher taking the measure. In Christian revelation, "the standards for human conduct and the principle of political communities, intuitively anticipated by Plato, had been finally revealed directly." Arendt quotes Voegelin saying, "in the words of a modern Platonist, it appears as though Plato's early 'orientation toward the unseen measure was now confirmed through the revelation of the measure itself.'" As a result, authority, whose political origin was the concrete political experiences of founding and preserving a sacred order, came to be identified with metaphysical and transcendent standards for human conduct, which provided "for the guidance of all individual judgment."[79] Political judgment in the Christian era revolved around the two conceptual pillars of the tradition of political thought, law and power. The laws of God now served as the evaluative yardstick against which the acts of power were judged. Political judgment thus became more rationalized than the fundamentally political form of judgment found in the Roman era, where the practice of identifying individual political actions with authoritative examples given by tradition did not rob those actions of their *sui generis* character, but instead only provided them with gravitas. The "amalgamation," as Arendt calls it, that merged the Greek political philosophies with the Roman trinity of religion, tradition, and authority thus became the foundation of Western Christian civilization.

After many centuries, however, this foundation began to crumble due to the contingent, historical constellation that eventually led to modernity. At various moments in the early modern period, each of the Roman foundations was challenged. The humanists challenged religion and authority, while

Luther and the Reformation challenged the authority of the church, and, finally, Hobbes and the seventeenth-century political theorists challenged tradition.[80] As each of these pillars of the Western common world was undermined, the public realm increasingly offered less illumination. *On Revolution* is Arendt's story of the women and men who, though only vaguely conscious of it, were responding to this loss of the reality of human freedom by attempting to refound a new public realm.[81] She states that "the revolutions of the modern age appear like gigantic attempts to repair [the Roman] foundations . . . through founding new political bodies."[82] Indeed, the very etymology of the word "revolution," which originally had meant to restore or "revolve back" to a prior order, carried these implications of seeking to reestablish broken political ties.[83] As we've seen, part of the purpose of *The Human Condition* was to show how Greeks—who maintained their public realms tenaciously—went about founding new public realms, since for them founding was an almost commonplace occurrence, as opposed to the Romans who saw their foundation as a monumental and unrepeatable event.[84] Thus, when Arendt pointed out that revolutions always began in a similarly polis-like manner, she was drawing the conclusion that the revolutionary actors seemed to intuit the need to forge a new public realm where action could be recognized and judged intersubjectively.[85]

But through all of this, it was the tradition of political thought that held fast in Western politics. As the various crises arose, Arendt argues, there was a continuous Platonic flavor to the political judgments that informed the responses given to the crises, a Platonism that was the result of the logic of the tradition's conceptual framework. This Platonic flavor consistently tended to introduce elements of violence into the concept of authority, a concept based on an experience, the act of foundation, which in its authentic meaning is devoid of violence. Thus, Arendt argues, Christianity's adoption of the threat of an afterlife with rewards and punishments followed the same tradition and logic as Plato in his political philosophies and, as a result, introduced an element of violence that diluted the Roman concept of authority. This logic played itself out again in the modern revolutions and their theorists, who presumed it was simple common sense that the prospective citizens of their new regimes could not be expected to behave morally without the disincentives involved in eternal punishment.[86] As we will see more fully later, the problem with the revolutionaries' turn to the tradition of political thought, according to Arendt, was that a fundamental kind of violence inherently existed in the logic of the tradition itself. These elements of violence were inherent in the making process that inspired Plato's political theory and arguably structured the conceptual frameworks of all his descendants.

Arendt believed Machiavelli was the first to recognize the incipient decline that was moving just under the surface of Western civilization. This was translated for Machiavelli into a deep contempt for the church, which had introduced the Christian ideal of "goodness"—an ideal that Arendt believed was initially conceived by Plato for purposes specific to the preservation of the philosophical life—into the public realm where it did not belong and could only corrupt the essential nature of politics. She argued that Machiavelli's greatness lay in his ability to unearth fundamental political experiences for which the tradition of political thought had no categories in an effort to provide a new foundation for a unified Italy. The problem for Machiavelli, as it would be for the modern revolutionaries who Arendt believed were his spiritual descendants, was that the act of foundation seems to have eluded them. No event in Western history was truly available on which they could base their political concepts and categories. Even the Romans only understood foundation as an event that occurred in the primordial past; the thought of laying a new foundation would have been the height of hubris to them. As a result, she argues, Machiavelli, like the modern revolutionaries who would come after him, could only turn to the conceptual framework provided by the tradition of political thought. They could only conceive the possibility of foundation in terms of the categories of "making," which had informed the tradition of political thought's basic analogies and which in turn meant that violence was presumed as a necessity of any founding. In order to "make" something new, violence must be done to that which currently exists. According to Arendt, their "justification of violence was guided by and received its inherent plausibility from the underlying argument: You cannot make a table without killing trees, you cannot make an omelet without breaking eggs, you cannot make a republic without killing people. In this respect, which became so fateful for the history of revolutions, Machiavelli and Robespierre were not Romans, and the authority to which they could have appealed would have been rather Plato." There was only one revolution that escaped this logic, the American revolution, and this occurred only because their revolution did not attempt consciously to found a completely new body politic, but instead merely "confirmed and legalized an already existing body politic."[87] But whenever political actors were confronted with the genuine problem of self-consciously founding a completely new body politic, it was invariably to the logic of the tradition of political thought they would turn.

There is more to be said about Arendt's account of revolutionary politics. However, this subject must be set aside for the moment until we have examined Arendt's account of the twin strands of modern necessity: the tradition of political thought and modern science. In Chapter 3, we will examine Arendt's account of philosophy's life of thought, along with its establishment of the tradition of political thought. In Chapter 4, we will examine her account of the role of modern science in the development of modern politics, before returning to the question of modern revolutionary action. As we will see, these two intellectual sources channeled revolutionary politics into patterns of thought that ultimately led to violence and the introduction of necessity into the spaces where human freedom should exist. The crisis and challenge presented by the rise of modernity to its Roman foundations would continue to exist like fault lines in the soil of Western civilization. As modernity's Roman foundations continued to crumble and the landscape continually shifted, political actors again and again attempted to respond, but their responses were channeled into political judgments that could not escape the categories of the tradition of political thought. And this inability of revolutionary politics to escape the logic of the tradition's categories would have fateful consequences for the modern world during the twentieth century.

3 Philosophy and the Tradition of Political Thought

Philosophical *Athanatizein*

I turn now to Arendt's articulation of the philosophical way of life, along with her account of what led it, beginning with Plato, to establish the tradition of political thought. In examining Arendt's thought, Chapters 1 and 2 have necessarily told only one side of her story, the story of men and women of action and their pursuit of political *athanatizein*. But as I argued before, Arendt was not solely concerned with reviving political *athanatizein*: her ultimate goal had been to discover the true relationship between philosophy and politics. There is thus another side of her story to tell, the story of philosophy and the life of thought. Thought has haunted these discussions of action, for while action forms the concrete content of history, the historical reflection that organizes that content into meaningful stories would be impossible without the capacity to think. It is this mutual dependency of thought and action that was ultimately at stake for Arendt.

Generally, both within the literature on Arendt but much more so in the readings of those who do not specialize in Arendt, much more emphasis is placed on her work on politics. This is, of course, understandable given that most of her publications were focused on the political aspect of her thought. But as I argued earlier, the question of what it is to think and the philosophical way of life associated with thinking was of long-standing interest to her, well predating *The Human Condition*'s 1958 publication. One potential objection to this claim is that there is textual evidence suggesting that her interest in thought and the *vita contemplativa* began with the Eichmann trial, which has led several Arendt scholars to suggest that she only became interested in thinking after reporting on Eichmann.[1] In the introduction to the "Thinking" volume of *The Life of the Mind* she seems to suggest as much, saying that "the Eichmann trial, then [which occurred three years after the publication of *The Human Condition*], first prompted my interest in this subject." However, Arendt's previous paragraph indicates that the subject she is referring to in this statement is not *thought* as such but rather the question, "Could the activity of thinking as such . . . be among the conditions that make men abstain from evil-doing or even actually 'condition' them against it." Moreover, the very next sentence after her comment on the Eichmann trial explicitly states that she is referring to "those moral questions."[2] Thus, while the Eichmann trial sparked an idea in Arendt that thought had moral implications, it did not spark Arendt's interest in thought generally. As we've seen, she was interested in thinking well before she wrote even *The Human Condition*, and, in fact, it was the question of the relation of thought and action that initially led to its writing.

Arendt's idea of thinking is a much broader notion than is commonly brought to mind by the idea of the role of "theory" in the commonplace binary of "theory and practice." Theorizing is, of course, a particular type of mental activity, but the thinking activity in general encompasses much more than this, involving such activities as rational deliberation, memory, reflection, and imagination. Arendt claimed that the faculty for thought gave rise to a variety of mental activities, but the highest and purest were the activities of thinking and contemplation. These two activities took place in a space of withdrawal from worldly existence that Arendt called the "thinking ego," located in what she identified as a temporal "gap between past and future."[3] The activity of thinking as such was understood to be the lower of the two, though still of a very high order. It is essentially what we mean when we speak of "reflecting" on a particular topic.[4] It takes the form of a kind of inner dialogue with oneself, which she refers to as the "two-in-one" nature of the thinking ego. Not surprisingly, Socrates is taken as the exemplar of this thinking activity.[5] But the thinking activity is only the handmaiden of an even higher mental activity, contemplation, which thinking has been traditionally understood to have led the way to.[6] Contemplation is not thought but rather the place where thought must break off, where the dialogue of the thinking ego fails to capture the wonder one experiences at the eternal things the thinking activity discovers.

As the highest activity of the thinking ego, Arendt believed contemplation inspired the pursuit of philosophy itself. She argues that the philosophical form of *athanatizein*—"to dwell in the neighborhood of things that are eternal"—was rooted in an experience, accessible and realizable only through thought, which was so profound and awe-inspired that it seemed to demand of those who experienced it that they devote their lives to it. This experience was what the Greek philosophers called *thaumazein*, wonder, and what Arendt calls "contemplation." Given the rather passing references she makes to the activity of contemplation in published work, casual readers of Arendt can be forgiven for failing to recognize the essentialness of this idea to her thought. While she does deal with it to a certain extent in several published works, a number of more direct discussions of contemplation appear in key unpublished pieces she wrote about philosophy and politics. In fact, contemplation seems to function as a kind of implicit center of gravity in her published writings, explaining the authentic motivation behind the philosophical life and, ultimately, the tradition of political thought. Arendt claims that it was this speechlessness of contemplation that ultimately led the philosophers to break with the ancient historians and the political men and women of action; for contemplative experience was so powerful and seemingly so much purer than worldly human life, they concluded that all human things, including politics and its form of *athanatizein*, should be put in its service. While Arendt clearly rejects this, as it were, philosophical coup d'état, she nevertheless considered philosophical experience genuinely authentic.[7]

At this point, it is instructive to note a common misunderstanding of Arendt. Many readers seem to take her Heideggerianism to be essentially a kind of pragmatism. Thus, it is occasionally presumed that Arendt considered thought, its content, and its activities to be simply a matter of practical activity: that is, that what is primordial is action and the *vita activa*, while thought and the *vita contemplativa* can ultimately only find their meaning within our practical life. As an interpretation of Heidegger, this notion probably stretches his thought beyond recognition. Arendt, however, emphatically does not believe this: thought and action are completely distinct activities that occur in completely separate spheres of human experience. Neither the *vita activa* nor the *vita contemplativa* is inauthentic; they simply represent two distinct realms of human experience—one taking place within worldly human existence, the other taking place in a space completely removed from that world, "the gap between past and future."

Arendt argued that this gap between past and future phenomenologically demonstrated that the original experiences of thought were genuinely authentic, but nevertheless—perhaps even understandably—led to the confusions of metaphysical thinking. Her critique of metaphysics was distinct, however, from Heidegger's quasi-religious attack. As we have seen, the philosophers tended to be contemptuous of political *athanatizein*, viewing it as foolhardy and dangerous, but also recognizing it as a necessary evil. Arendt argued that metaphysics provided the conceptual framework that the philosophers drew on to assert an instrumentalized model of politics that idealized the sovereign rule of those with expert political knowledge. As we've seen, this conception of sovereignty remained utopian through much of Western history, whose real politics had been rooted in the Roman political concept of authority. But as the modern age came into its own, Arendt argued that the sovereign model of politics would come to have unfortunate political consequences, the worst of which, of course, the philosophical tradition certainly never intended.

Arendt's fullest discussion of the faculty of thought is found in the "Thinking" volume of *The Life of the Mind*. There she approached the *vita contemplativa* in the same way she approached the *vita activa* in *The Human Condition*: seeking to uncover the authentic experiences behind the philosophical tradition's metaphysically distorted articulations. But, in this case, the task appeared to be more complicated. While in *The Human Condition* Arendt could for the most part ignore the philosophical tradition's articulations of the worldly active life (other than when she was directly attacking it), in the case of the *vita contemplativa* Arendt was forced to confront the philosophical tradition directly. This was because the philosophical tradition was the one tradition that had most intensely and relentlessly engaged in the authentic experiences of the life of the mind.[8] Thus, while it is true that Arendt was attempting to help dismantle the tradition's metaphysical fallacies, such as the distinction between the sensory and the supersensory worlds and the more modern fallacies that unconsciously presuppose it, this was not her ultimate goal.[9] Like Heidegger and Jaspers, she believed that these metaphysical fallacies pointed toward some authentic experience of the life of the mind that led the philosophers into such fallacies, and her task was now to try to understand what kind of experience those fallacies pointed to. In a caustic moment tweaking the analytic philosophy movement of the time, Arendt writes that "it is characteristic of the Oxford school of criticism to understand these [metaphysical] fallacies as logical non sequiturs—as though philosophers throughout the centuries had been, for reasons unknown, just a bit too stupid to discover the elementary flaws in their arguments."[10] The metaphysical history of philosophy could not, in other words, simply be dismissed as "nonsense" as members of the Vienna Circle once claimed. There were authentic experiences that lay behind the distortions they criticized, experiences that were too important to what it means to be human to simply ignore.

The Life of the Mind is what might be called a phenomenology of the experience of "withdrawal." In quotidian terms, it refers to the experience of absent-mindedness that we all have literally every day.[11] But Arendt was in fact making a dramatic claim in this: she was claiming that the theoretical foundations of virtually the entire intellectual history of Western civilization is based on metaphysical fallacies that were inspired and rooted in this prosaic experience. While there are other activities that require this capacity for absent-mindedness to some extent, such as judging and willing, she believed that the activity of thinking is the most worldless, the most withdrawn from worldly involvements. She furthermore believed that thinking is an inherently pleasurable activity, something we like to do, and actually *need* to do in order to live a fully human life. Philosophers seem to experience this need and pleasure in thinking intensely. It has been the philosophers' near obsession with the activity of thinking that led to the two worlds fallacy. Arendt argues that the two worlds fallacy was actually the result of the extraordinarily powerful nature of the thinking activity once it has been adequately discovered and engaged with by a thinking human being. Phenomenological analysis of the thinking activity certainly does not transcendentally justify the idea that there is anything like a supersensible reality; however, Arendt believed that such an analysis does demand some kind of account of "where" exactly we are when we have existentially withdrawn from the world in order to think. The clue that the old postulation of an eternal, supersensible reality points to is that this place, even if it has withdrawn from worldly reality, must still be located somewhere in time, but in a mysterious place in time that escapes the change and contingency of the past and future tenses that we primarily experience either in the context of worldly involvements or in our memories and imaginations.[12] Drawing explicitly on Nietzsche, Heidegger, and Kafka, Arendt asserts that this is the present tense: a tense that is impossible to locate in the mist of our engaged worldly experience and that is only accessible in a space of existential disengagement, which she calls "the gap between past and future."[13] It is only in this space of withdrawal that human beings can think.

The form that the thinking activity takes is dialogical: when we think, it is as if we are "two-in-one," as if we are carrying on a dialogue with ourselves.[14] It is this dialogical form that gives the thinking faculty its inherently critical character. It is another, more modern metaphysical prejudice that this idea of critical thought has come to be identified with the logical structure of the human mind. But Arendt argues that this dialogical structure of thought indicates the authentic nature of critical thinking: the simple capacity to ask questions. The capacity for thought indicates that human beings are critical in an existential sense: we are "question-asking beings." As a result of the existential nature of our critical faculties, we are ultimately led into speculative thinking, into asking ultimate questions.[15] Because there can ultimately be no final answer given to the questions pursued in thought, thinking is an essentially circular and endless activity. Arendt writes that "the business of thinking is like Penelope's web; it undoes every morning what it has finished the night before. For the need to think . . . can be satisfied only through thinking, and the thoughts I had yesterday will satisfy this need today only to the extent that I want and need to think them anew."[16]

This capacity to ask ultimate questions leads to contemplation, where words finally break off in speechless wonder.[17] Unlike the thinking activity, contemplation involved a speechlessness and wonder at the fact of Being as such, which the ancient philosophers had referred to as *thaumazein*, the "pathos of wonder."[18] *Thaumazein* was experienced by the ancients in such a fundamental and profound way that they were inspired to dedicate their lives to it, and they called this pursuit "philosophy."[19] Thus, in *The Human Condition* Arendt writes that "the philosopher's experience of the eternal, which to Plato was *arrheton* ('unspeakable'), and to Aristotle *aneu logon* ('without word'), and which later was conceptualized in the paradoxical *nunc stans* ('the standing now'), can occur only outside the realm of human affairs and outside the plurality of men."[20] There were, furthermore, two directions that contemplation might take. One was that adopted by Aristotle in his scientific works, and it is what is commonly called "metaphysics." It sought to find some kind of theoretical knowledge in the experience of wonder. But the second, earlier, and seemingly more authentic direction it took was to try to stay and dwell in the experience of wonder itself. This was the approach adopted by Parmenides, Plato, and Aristotle in his more ethical articulations of wonder and in his conception of *nous*.[21]

Arendt seemed to believe that this later experience of contemplation had largely disappeared in the modern era but had recently been revived in intellectual life by modern existentialists.[22] In this, as in other instances, Arendt's view of the modern situation was probably too bleak. Contemplative activities such as art and religion have always held a prominent place in modern culture, but even from a scientific perspective, there has been, after all, relatively little economic value derived from *Voyager* space probes and lunar missions. A wonderful example of modern scientific contemplation can be found in the documentary *Particle Fever*, when the physicist David E. Kaplan is challenged by an economist to justify the nearly $10 billion cost of CERN's Large Hadron Collider, the particle accelerator that would soon prove the existence of the Higgs boson. Kaplan simply responded that there was no economic justification for it. Still, Arendt did not believe contemplation had completely disappeared in modernity prior to existentialism. In her 1969 course "Philosophy and Politics: What Is Political Philosophy?" she offered a quote from Coleridge to her students: "Hast thou ever raised thy mind to the consideration of existence, in and by itself, as the mere act of existing? Hast thou ever thought to thyself, It is! Heedless in that moment whether it were a man before thee, or a flower, or a grain of sand, without reference, in short, to this or that particular mode of existence."[23]

According to Arendt, the philosophers took the activities that take place in the gap between past and future and sought to live their lives in that gap and to realize the activities of the gap without reference to human affairs. In this pursuit, she believed the philosophers found a kind of "philosophical freedom."[24] In "The Concept of History," Arendt describes philosophical *athanatizein*, writing that the philosophers

> discovered in the activity of thought itself, a hidden human capacity for turning away from the whole realm of human affairs . . . to "immortalize" meant for the philosopher to dwell in the neighborhood of those things which are forever. . . . Thus the proper attitude of mortals, once they had reached the neighborhood of the immortal, was actionless and even speechless contemplation, the Aristotelian [*nous*], the highest and most human capacity of pure vision, which cannot be translated into words.[25]

This contemplation had no other object or purpose than maintaining this speechless vision, and thus, for philosophers, it was *a-telos*, an activity done for its own sake and for no other end outside itself.[26] As a result, the activity of contemplation, of dwelling in the neighborhood of the things that are eternal, in its truest sense had no relationship with human affairs for the philosophers, not even in providing absolute standards, which Arendt believed Plato only advocated for later for purely political purposes.

However, in *The Life of the Mind*, Arendt argues that one cannot separate thought from human life and action so easily. She argued that, as one of the highest experiences of human existence, one cannot even be considered fully alive if one cannot think, and thus it truly is the case that the unexamined life is not worth living. "To think and to be fully alive are the same," she writes. "[Thinking] is an activity that accompanies living and is concerned with such concepts as justice, happiness, virtue, offered us by language itself as expressing the meaning of whatever happens in life and occurs to us while we are alive."[27] Arendt believed that the original exemplar of thinking in the Western tradition was Socrates, who in fact saw his practice of thinking as a political activity. She describes the function of Socratic thinking as unfreezing "as it were, what language, the medium of thinking, has frozen into thought. . . . These frozen thoughts, Socrates seems to say, come so handily that you can use them in your sleep; but if the wind of thinking, which I shall now stir in you, has shaken you from your sleep and made you fully awake and alive, then you will see that you have nothing in your grasp but perplexities, and the best we can do is share them with each other."[28] Arendt claimed that with the passage of time, words and ideas "such as freedom and justice, authority and reason, responsibility and virtue, power and glory" tend to become "empty shells" that have lost their connection to "their underlying phenomenal reality" and that thought seeks to discover "the real origins" of concepts so that it "can distill from them anew their original spirit."[29] Socrates appeared to see his function in the polis as waking up those that live their lives unconsciously, as if they were asleep, by making them aware of the richness of the experiences behind the language they unconsciously accepted.[30] Socratic thinking allows the thinker to go "through this questioning and answering process, through the dialogue of *dialegesthai*, which actually is a 'traveling through words' . . . whereby we constantly raise the basic Socratic question: *What do you mean when you say . . . ?*"[31]

Yet, the full relevance of the thinking activity to politics derives from the somewhat mysterious way this critical dialogue has the effect of reconciling us to the world by allowing us to understand what is meaningful and significant in our experience. Introducing her notion of thinking at the 1972 conference on her work, she said:

> Reason itself, the thinking ability which we have, has need to actualize itself. The philosophers and the metaphysicians have monopolized this capacity. This has led to very great things. It also has led to rather unpleasant things—we have forgotten that *every* human being has a need to think. . . . Everybody who tells a story of what happened to him half an hour ago on the street has got to put this story into shape. . . . And this is somehow the same sense in which you know it from Hegel, namely where I think the central role is reconciliation.[32]

Thus, Arendt asserts that thought is a continuous process of creating stories and narratives of our experience, because it is fundamentally on a lifelong quest for the meaning and significance of things. Arendt argues that Hegel was certainly correct when he claimed that thought, as our authentic capacity for reflection, is how we reconcile ourselves to our worldly reality. This reconciling activity of thought fundamentally involves recognizing the significance of things in our lives and our world and creating a narrative about them.[33]

Nevertheless, Arendt still believed that there was compelling phenomenal evidence that led the philosophers to conclude that authentic thinking had little relevance to human life and action. At least insofar we have seen her articulate them to this point, there appears to be a vast phenomenal gulf between thought and action. In the 1969 course, she summarizes this phenomenal gulf:

> We started from the analysis of two activities, thinking and acting, which apparently are antagonistic. We enumerated all the properties that separate them. We think by ourselves, but we act together. We look out for the invisible, the non-appearing within the visible [when we think], but [when we act we] are bound to the world of appearance where nothing *is* that does not appear and appear in public. We are immobile and, I should add, age-less when we think; but we constantly move about and [are] subject to time in every respect when we act. [When we think] we are solitary to the point of no longer be[ing] sure of the reality of the exterior world, which we can doubt, including our own reality; and are confirmed in this reality only when joined by other[s] through whom we become one again . . . recognized by them, and assured of reality because of the existence of a common world.[34]

In articulating their true relationship, Arendt will eventually appeal to a third faculty, judgment, which has a unique capacity to bridge this gulf between thought and action. However, Arendt argued that there was a venerable tradition that attempted to reconcile thought and action, not through judgment, which gives each its proper place, but instead by giving thought preeminence over action, arguing that it is the role of thought to guide and rule over action. This was the approach proposed by Plato, and Arendt argued that it ultimately established the conceptual framework in which the entire tradition of political thought would move. As we will see, it became evident to Plato that the goals, ideals, and objectives of philosophy and politics seem to have no obvious connection to one another. They sought forms of realization that had no relation to each other: politics sought realization solely in world of human affairs through action, while philosophy sought realization in an existential position utterly removed from that world, in the activity of thought leading to contemplation. After it became evident that the political world could not be ignored, Plato sought to subordinate politics to philosophy, and this, according to Arendt, was the origin of the tradition of political thought.[35]

Philosophy's Establishment of the Tradition of Political Thought

As we've seen, Arendt believed a primordial conflict existed between philosophy and politics. She believed that an esoteric account of that conflict was written by Plato in his famous allegory of the cave in book 7 of the *Republic*.[36] Her interpretation of the allegory of the cave is a key founding doctrine for Arendt's political thought. She conceived it relatively early in her reflections on political theory, apparently as a direct result of her attempts to understand the extent to which the tradition of political thought had been implicated in the totalitarian terror regimes, especially through the line that proceeded through Marx.[37] In 1954, Heidegger asked for details on the research Arendt was pursuing. Arendt replied that she had been working on a project for "about three years now." As her proposal to the Guggenheim Foundation from 1951 attests, the project she was referring to was what had grown out of a proposed book that would have explained the relationship between Marx, totalitarianism, and the tradition of political thought.[38] The current project she outlined for Heidegger involved three tasks: a distinctive interpretation of the cave allegory; her account of the three activities in the *vita activa*; and her critique of the concept of rulership—all of which play pivotal roles in *The Human Condition*. She suggested that a key element of this project would be a critique of the traditional representation of the relationship of philosophy and politics, which she believed was rooted in "the attitude of Plato and Aristotle toward the polis," an attitude that formed "the basis of all political theories."[39]

Arendt had an ambivalent assessment of the tradition of political thought. She clearly admired the philosophical tradition and philosophical experience,[40] and indeed she considered herself a member of that tradition, at least in practice if not in name, since, as she noted, she still wrote about the *vita activa* from the perspective of the *vita contemplativa*.[41] Moreover, she believed the tradition of political thought had played a venerable role in the history and culture of Western civilization.[42] But she also believed that the tradition of political thought had ignored the true nature of political phenomena and that, as a result, the authentic experiences of freedom that had been lived out by the Greeks, Romans, and modern revolutionaries had been all but lost. She often claimed "that Plato thought that human affairs . . . should not be treated with great seriousness; the actions of men appear like the gestures of puppets led by an invisible hand behind the scene, so that man seems to be a kind of plaything of a god."[43] To illustrate the tendency of the philosophical tradition to demean politics, she often quoted a statement from Pascal that she believed best summarized the tradition of political thought's attitude toward politics. Referring to Plato and Aristotle, Pascal wrote that political philosophy was the "part of their life that was the least philosophic and the least serious. . . . If they wrote about politics, it was as if laying down rules for a lunatic asylum; if they presented the appearance of speaking of great matters, it was because they knew that the madmen, to whom they spoke, thought they were kings and emperors."[44]

Arendt argues that in the cave allegory Plato attempted to capture the philosopher's experience of *thaumazein* in the description of the journey up from the cave into the true light of the sun. This experience is expressed in religious themes by Plato, as a kind of conversion experience: it is a life-changing shock to the identity of the philosopher when he realizes that the mundane world of human affairs in which all his previous life has been spent seems to pale in comparison to the speechless beauty, elegance, and illumination that he discovers in philosophical truth.[45] The problem, however, is that this experience of *thaumazein* has a disorienting effect on the one who experiences it when he returns from contemplation into the world of human affairs. The philosopher returns to the human world unaccustomed to its endless novelty, unpredictability, and heavy reliance on the faculty of speech. As a result, the philosopher's common sense—the sixth sense that should intuitively fit him into the human world—is seriously degraded. According to both Plato and Arendt, this does not simply turn them into harmless oddities, but represents a genuine threat not only to the goals and objectives of the philosopher but to his very life. In the *Republic*, Plato writes:

> And before his eyes had recovered—and the adjustment would not be quick—while his vision was still dim, if he had to compete again with

the perpetual prisoners in recognizing the shadows, wouldn't he invite ridicule? Wouldn't it be said of him that he'd returned from his upward journey with his eyesight ruined and that it isn't worthwhile even to try to travel upward? And, as for anyone who tried to free them and lead them upward, if they could somehow get their hands on him, wouldn't they kill him?[46]

Arendt explicates the problem Plato was pointing to in her 1954 "Philosophy and Politics" manuscript: "Each of these turnings-about had been accompanied by a loss of sense and orientation . . . they can no longer see in the darkness of the cave, they have lost their sense of orientation, they have lost what we would call their common sense. . . . The returning philosopher is in danger because he has lost the common sense needed to orient himself in a world common to all, and, moreover, because what he harbors in his thought contradicts the common sense of the world."[47] Arendt argues that after the death of Socrates Plato concluded that the polis was so corrupt and chaotic that the only way the philosophical way of life could be assured was by establishing philosophically derived rules for the realm of human affairs.

Plato's particular solution was of course built on his philosophical theories, but Arendt argues that Plato's basic approach has essentially structured the presuppositions of the tradition ever since.[48] The philosophers' loss of common sense resulted in their appearing to have no place in the world, and therefore a loss of the ability to exercise judgment appropriately within it. Plato's solution to this problem was to attempt to make philosophy relevant to the world of human affairs in a much more direct and explicit way than Socrates had. To do this, he sought to establish a hierarchical relationship between the *vita activa* and the *vita contemplativa* by claiming that the eternal ideas that the philosophers alone had access to could be a guide to behavior and provide stable measures and standards for judging action.[49] There were at least two key political objectives that this claim was intended to accomplish: it both justified the political rulership of the philosopher, and it made politics predictable to these rulers, thus solving the problem posed by their degraded common sense.

The problem with this approach, however, was that it was rooted in nonpolitical experiences, which lacked an authentic connection to the fundamental political experience of Western civilization. Arendt argues that Plato was searching for a form of political life that only the Romans had experience of: the authentically political authoritarian way of life. "Authority," Arendt writes, "implies an obedience in which men retain their freedom." Authority, in other words, is obedience which is rendered freely out of respect for a sacred source of hierarchy, and thus can involve no coercion or violence.[50] Plato, however, was never able to devise such a hierarchy because, according to Arendt, he had no authentic political experience from which to derive it:

> The grandiose attempts of Greek philosophy to find a concept of authority . . . foundered on the fact that in the realm of Greek political life there was no awareness of authority based on immediate political experience. Hence all prototypes . . . were drawn from specifically unpolitical experiences, stemming either from the sphere of "making" and the arts, where there must be experts and where fitness is the highest criterion, or from the private household community. It is precisely in this politically determined aspect that the philosophy of the Socratic school has exerted its greatest impact upon our tradition.[51]

Arendt points out that the only two viable candidates available, tyranny and generalship, were for various reasons unacceptable to Plato because each in its own way was associated with extralegal circumstances: the tyrant was the "wolf in sheep's clothing" who respected no law, and the general was always a response to exceptional circumstances. Instead, Plato and later Aristotle turned in varying ways to nonpolitical Greek life in order to provide examples and experiences on which to conceptualize this new hierarchy.[52]

In attempting to apply philosophical truth to political affairs, Plato had to reckon with the fact that philosophical truth is "self-evident" and thus has a compelling effect on the mind. The problem was that only philosophers and their political protégés would be able to grasp these truths, and thus some strategy had to be devised to allow the coercion of truth experienced by the philosopher to be accepted by the many who did not directly experience it. Arendt claims that Plato began looking for instances of "glaring inequality" in which "the compelling element lies in the relationship itself," and not by means of "seizure of power and possession of the means of violence." He sought out his analogies in instances of expert knowledge well known to the Greeks, such as the shepherd, the ship's captain, the physician, the master of slaves, and the craftsman, in which rulership was implied in the very relationship itself because the individuals involved "belong to altogether different categories of beings, one of which is already by implication subject to the other."[53]

At this point, Arendt's analysis begins to deepen. She insists that of all these analogies drawn from the realm of expert knowledge it is the craftsman who is the real inspiration of Plato's politics because the craftsman indicates how the doctrine of the ideas relates to human affairs. The textual evidence she gives for this claim is relatively sparse, relying heavily on *Timaeus* and book 10 of the *Republic*.[54] She supplements this evidence with a series of meta-interpretative claims in connection with a strikingly esoteric interpretation of Plato's ultimate purpose for his political dialogues. In the crucial "Reification" chapter (chapter 19) of *The Human Condition*, Arendt argues that the fabrication process is the exemplary instance of all work, that it is this process of making that inspired Plato's particular formulation of the doctrine of ideas as it is commonly understood. The text of the "Reification" chapter suggests that Arendt understood Plato's doctrine solely in the craftsmanship formulation given in *Timaeus* and book 10 of the *Republic*. However, in a footnote she begins to suggest a considerably more subtle understanding of Plato's doctrine. Referencing the work of several classicists, she notes that the common interpretation of Plato's doctrine is borne out by its apparently Socratic and Pythagorean origin. But at the end of the note, she writes, "Needless to say, none of these explanations touches the root of the matter, that is, the specifically philosophic experience underlying the concept of ideas on the one hand, and their most striking quality on the other—their illuminating power, their being *to phanotaton* or *ekphanestaton*."[55]

Arendt is indicating here a line of argument that comes later in *The Human Condition* in chapter 31 ("The Traditional Substitution of Making for Action") and that she repeated in a variety of places both before and after *The Human Condition* was written. In these places, Arendt argues that Plato had two different versions of the doctrine of ideas. One version can be found in dialogues such as *Symposium* and *Phaedrus*, where the essential characteristic of the ideas is their illuminating power and, as a result, the highest idea is always the beautiful. This is the doctrine that most clearly is associated with the experience of *thaumazein* in the activity of contemplation. On the other hand, we find in the political dialogues such as the *Statesman*, *Republic*, and *Laws* Plato claiming that the highest idea is the idea of the good. Arendt surmised that this must have been a conscious decision on the part of Plato: in the Greek language, the word for "good," *agathos*, could carry the meaning of "usefulness" or "fitness for."[56] As a result, if Plato's goal had been to establish the authority of philosophical truth to provide measures and standards for human action and behavior, it was the good that would be the appropriate

highest idea. However, it can serve this purpose only if the relationship between thought and action comes to take the character of the fabrication process involved in work, and thus it is through the analogy of craftsmanship
that the new hierarchical relationship between philosophy and politics is established.[57] Arendt points out in *The Human Condition* that from a phenomenological perspective there is an inner affinity between contemplation and
fabrication, in that both seem to rely on an inner vision in thought, while
action and contemplation seem to stand in "unequivocal opposition to each
other."[58] Arendt thus argues that Plato's true intention in the political dialogues was not to give an authentic account the philosophical experience, but
rather to provide a kind of theoretical coup d'état on behalf of the philosophical way of life over politics. "Even in the first books of the *Republic*," she
writes,

> the philosopher is still defined as a lover of beauty, not of goodness, and
> only in the sixth book is the idea of good as the highest idea introduced.
> For the original function of the ideas was not to rule or otherwise deter-
> mine the chaos of human affairs, but, in "shining brightness," to illumi-
> nate their darkness. As such, the ideas have nothing whatever to do with
> politics, political experience, and the problem of action, but pertain ex-
> clusively to philosophy. . . . It is precisely ruling, measuring, subsuming,
> and regulating that are entirely alien to the experiences underlying the
> doctrine of ideas in its original conception.[59]

Thus, the tradition of political thought was not founded, as most philosophical subject matter had been, in the attempt to contemplate and grasp
the meaning of the phenomena under investigation; rather, it was developed
as an attempt to secure the ability of the philosophers to pursue the philosophical way of life in a hostile polis. Plato's solution was to argue that the
philosopher was the only legitimate ruler of the polis, but in order to do this
Plato was forced to ignore the truly political activities and faculties of human
beings: thought, action, and judgment, all of which essentially involve speech.
Instead, he formulated the structure of the tradition in terms of two activities
that were by their very nature essentially speechless: contemplation and work.
Contemplation supposedly lent the philosopher-king a transcendent source
of authority, because he alone possessed the vision of the idea that was inac-
cessible to those over whom he ruled. But true contemplation had nothing to
do with ruling a polis. It was rather characterized by *thaumazein*, wonder at

being as such, and as a result, Arendt claims, Plato must have consciously chosen to replace the highest idea, which in the nonpolitical dialogues was the beautiful, with the more practically relevant (particularly in the Greek language) idea of the good.[60]

In essence, Arendt's claim is that Plato had to distort authentic philosophical experience and authentic political experience literally beyond recognition in order to establish a relationship between them that allowed philosophy to rule the polis. Politics had been *a-telos*, just as philosophy was: it provided a public realm where acting men and women could perform great deeds. Plato sought to give political action a telos, an end beyond itself, which was to support and protect the contemplative way of life of the philosophers. The analogies Plato drew on in formulating this political ideal were all drawn from nonpolitical elements of Greek life. The idea that rulership reflected the appropriate model of political relationships was a radical argument on Plato's part and would have been perceived as bizarre by his fellow Athenians, who only understood sovereign rule to be appropriate in the context of the private household. This liberation that household rulership achieved was not itself authentic freedom but only a precondition of the political freedom practiced in the public realm. This political freedom was simply ignored by Plato. The entire polis thus became a household that existed to allow the philosophers to pursue what they believed to be the highest activity human beings were capable of, contemplation. Needless to say, Arendt believed Plato was far too keen a thinker to have truly believed all this, and she always maintained that he must have had ulterior motives for doing so, which in all likelihood were a reaction to the execution of Socrates.[61]

Nevertheless, according to Arendt, this introduction of a telos into political action was the origin of the ideal of politics as sovereign rulership, which has dominated the tradition of political thought ever since. In terms of the broader tradition, it would be a tremendous oversimplification to suggest that the hierarchical relationship established between thought and action in the tradition required acceptance of Plato's doctrine of ideas. Plato, rather, established a pattern of thinking about politics that has been tremendously influential in the history of Western political thought, even if most of the specifically Platonic elements of that pattern were eliminated. It resulted in what Arendt called the "two conceptual pillars" of the tradition of political thought: law and rulership. Politics was understood by the tradition to be conducted in the form of a relationship between rulers and the ruled, and this rulership is legitimized to the extent it conforms with just laws.[62] But law can only provide this legitimizing function if it operates in a way similar to Plato's application of the idea of the good to political life, that is, as a "yard-stick by which rule could be measured."[63]

Arendt asserted that this framework was so pervasive in the tradition that it could be observed even in the most insightful theorists of action the tradition offered: Aristotle and Machiavelli.[64] She acknowledged that both Aristotle and Machiavelli had provided powerful articulations of political action and judgment in, respectively, their accounts of *praxis* and *phronēsis* and the relationship between *virtù* and *fortuna*; yet ultimately, they did not escape Plato's framework.[65] Machiavelli, whom Arendt called the "spiritual father of revolution,"[66] developed a theory of action that was accurate until he confronted the problem of founding a regime and was then driven into the fabrication analogy. In her 1955 lectures on Machiavelli, she says that "because Machiavelli had *virtù-fortuna*, he saw action in the light of fabrication only in the predicament of foundation."[67] On the other hand, Aristotle's entanglement with the fabrication analogy was, like Plato's, more or less intentional. Arendt points out that Aristotle was well aware of the distinction between acting and making, and his political philosophy fully reflected this distinction. Nevertheless, Aristotle was in many ways more exemplary of the nature of the tradition. Like Plato, Aristotle was too closely connected to the Greeks' original experiences of political freedom to have failed to recognize these distinctions. She points out that he was "too conscious of the difference between acting and making to draw his examples from the sphere of fabrication,"[68] and that his "whole political philosophy was centered around the problem of *praxis*, action, and had no greater concern than to avoid the interpretation of action in the light of fabrication."[69] Yet, Arendt argues that his two chief examples of action, the benefactor and the legislator, both unreflectively appeal to fabrication. The benefactor loves the one he benefits more because it is something he has made, just as the poet loves his poem. The legislator, on the other hand, is an even more problematic example since, according to Arendt, Aristotle's theory of laws clearly treats them as incidents of fabrication.[70] Moreover, Arendt points out that, even admitting his educational model, Aristotle's concept of political action as ruling and being ruled in turn would have been, from the Greek point of view, in "flagrant contradiction" with his definition of the polis as "a community of equals for the sake of a life which is potentially the best."[71] She thus concludes that Aristotle must have been following in Plato's line of esoterically treating political philosophy, for if he had simply applied his own articulations of *praxis* and *phronēsis*, he could never have arrived at the examples he used, nor could he have adopted Plato's insertion of the notion of rulership—which was always a matter of the private household for the Greeks—into the realm of political action. She writes that "obviously the notion of rule in the polis was for Aristotle himself so far from convincing that he, one the most consistent and least self-contradictory great thinkers, did not feel particularly bound by his own argument."[72] The point is that the principle of rulership by those who know over those who obey, and lawfulness as the criterion of a good regime, had been fully established in Aristotle. Thus, while Aristotle does not rely on the model of the specialized knowledge of the expert, he still nevertheless establishes rulership within the political realm on the basis of an educational model drawn from the "natural" relationships that existed in the household, and lawfulness was the criterion that legitimized these relationships.[73] And it is Aristotle's educational model that, in terms of the tradition of political thought, had perhaps the most direct influence on the history of Western politics.[74]

Summarizing the influence of Greek political philosophy on the history of Western politics, Arendt writes: "This insulation shown by our tradition from its beginning against all political experiences that did not fit into its framework . . . has remained one of its outstanding features. The mere tendency to exclude everything that was not consistent developed into a great power of exclusion, which kept the tradition intact against all new, contradictory, and conflicting experiences."[75] The problem with this conflation of political with unpolitical experiences within the tradition is that it carried within itself latent tendencies and implications of violence, coercion, and indifference to authentic political phenomena that are essential to true human freedom. The consequences of these latent tendencies will be examined in Chapter 4; but for the moment, it is crucial to note that, on the basis of this conflation, political thought came to have what Arendt believed to be a deeply inauthentic understanding of the nature of politics. Political phenomena were now conceptualized not from their own authentic standpoint in the world of human affairs, from the standpoint of philosophy, and as a result, the distinctions within the *vita activa* were either lost or viewed as insignificant.[76] Furthermore, by structuring its conceptual framework in terms of law and rulership, the tradition ultimately came to articulate political experience in a crude and simplistic fashion. Law came to mean measuring, subsuming, and categorizing political action, while political action itself was understood as rulership, the execution of the prescriptions of thought and administration of human activities and behavior.[77] The final result of this view was that in the

Western world politics became instrumentalized: the idea that politics could be a sphere of authentic freedom and self-disclosure has become so foreign that it now seems to defy credulity.

Reflecting on Arendt's Critique

A number of important themes and ideas have been raised in this chapter, and therefore I want to offer some concluding comments. First, in a bit of a digression, I am compelled to point out that Arendt's perspective on nature now seems much less dour than it may first appear in her account of the *vita activa* in *The Human Condition*. It now appears that humans possess two distinct relationships to nature. In the context of the *vita activa*, nature is the ultimate source of necessity, driving human beings to survive in the context of natural biological imperatives. It is this relationship to nature that we share with the animals. However, we can now see that Arendt rightly recognized another relationship to nature, the contemplative relationship, and, arguably, it is this way of relating to nature that may in fact be the purest, most profound experience human beings are capable of. Yet, both relations to nature are in many phenomenological senses similar: they are both essentially speechless and involve an engagement with natural necessity. What allows one relation to express absolute natural slavery to nature and the other to express philosophical freedom is the sphere of human experience it occurs within. Thus, nature—in what is a much more intuitive account of our relationship to it—now seems to bookend the various activities of the human condition.

Second, we can once again observe Arendt's emphasis on action and human agency in her genealogical work, in this case, even in the context of the history of political philosophy. For Arendt, all history must be anchored and have origins in the deeds and events enacted by human beings. Arendt has argued that in the context of the tradition of political thought, its originary founding event occurred with the death of Socrates. Socrates, after all, was no mere victim of the polis; in many ways, he appeared to choose his fate. And in fact, Arendt argues that Socrates chose this fate because he could find no other way to convince his fellow philosophers to take the polis seriously and, in teaching his fellow citizens that only a thoughtful life is a meaningful life, to convince the polis that philosophy could be its "greatest good."[78] As in most instances of action, the results of Socrates' act were other than he expected, but it remains the case that, even at the roots of a tradition that

Arendt believed systematically distorted political phenomena, there was an originary moment of human agency.

Finally, given how broadly Arendt has attacked political philosophy, there will no doubt be many objections to her argument. After all, she has not just attacked one or two thinkers, or even just the ancient philosophers; she has attacked the entire tradition itself for having demonstrably failed to theorize a politics that can account for genuine human agency. Most specialists will no doubt be able to point to aspects of a particular thinker that argue against Arendt's position, and I am largely not interested in disputing these claims. What I want to consider is simply whether she has a point. It seems to me highly likely that she does, and moreover, by the time Arendt's account of authentic political judgment has been examined in Chapter 5, I believe it will achieve even more believability. But presently, consider this current critique, that the tradition misconceived politics in terms of sovereignty, as a practice of lawfulness and rulership. For most of the history of political thought, this perspective seems highly justified. Political philosophy presented itself as the singular arbitrator of the lawful principles of just rulership. What Arendt takes to be the essential characteristics of politics—its conditioning by human plurality, its concern with worldly immortality, its rejection of the idea of the productive paradigm of thought and action—have no place within this framework. Aristotle, for instance, would seem to present the strongest objection to Arendt's argument, for he certainly does recognize Arendt's demand for a return to a noninstrumental conception of political action, and moreover, at least on the surface, her critique of Aristotle is not especially convincing or comprehensive. However, if we take into consideration her broader critique of the tradition of political thought, there may be more to her critique of Aristotle than first appears. While it is true that the *Nicomachean Ethics* amply demonstrates a narrative conception of *praxis*,[79] it remains the case that Aristotle approached human agency from a highly philosophical point of view. The natal and *sui generis* character of action, along with the radical individuality and plurality it entails, are absent, and this is arguably because Aristotle, like the other ancient philosophers, rejected the validity of political *athanatizein* and thus ignored its insights into action. Indeed, when Aristotle does discuss *athanatizein*, it comes near the end of the *Ethics* in a seemingly anomalous discussion of philosophical contemplation.[80] Thus, while Aristotle may not have explicitly given politics a telos in the service of philosophy, he ignored politics' normative bases in its unique form of pursuing immortality—something Arendt believed he would have been well aware of—and instead only indicated philosophy's path to immortality. It is at least arguable, then, that Aristotle did indeed implicitly place philosophy above politics.

Assessing contemporary political philosophy from Arendt's perspective, on the other hand, is a more complicated proposition. Conceptions of political theory such as pluralism, deliberative democracy, and agonistic democracy have suggested an increasing turn away from the idea that philosophy can provide decisive answers to political questions. Indeed, theorists have increasingly presented contemporary accounts of political normative reason that draw strongly on Arendt's own account of political judgment, such as Seyla Benhabib's "interpretive-hermeneutic moral judgment" and Lisa Disch's "situated impartiality."[81] The problem, I believe, is that many of these contemporary theories often still invoke fundamental categories of the tradition of political thought, such as the notion of individual sovereignty and willful freedom, which are still drawn from traditional political conceptions of rulership, even if in this case it is self-rule. The problem is that concepts drawn from the tradition of political thought are bound to lead to muddled and incoherent concepts of political agency, at least from Arendt's perspective. Despite these remainders of the tradition, however, I believe these accounts are a salutary development in political theory and a clear step in the right direction. Indeed, one of the most valuable advances in political theory, in my view, is the growing literature on non-sovereignty, which I discussed in Chapter 1. This literature, inspired by Arendt's original critique of sovereignty, has in a variety of ways attempted to escape the sovereignist model of politics as rulership. But, as we will see in Chapter 4, the most important thing Arendt may have to teach us about non-sovereignty is that rethinking the tradition of political thought may not go far enough. By its very nature, the critique of sovereignty suggests that, as Arendt perhaps most compellingly argued, political phenomena not adequately captured by sovereign conceptual frameworks still go on occurring beyond our sovereignist political theories. In other words, truly escaping the threats to human freedom posed by our world, may involve looking beyond the critique of our tradition and confronting deeper political pathologies. As we will see in Chapter 4, this is what Arendt sought to do in her confrontation with modern politics.

4 | The Origins of Necessity in Human Affairs

Through much of Western history, the tradition of political thought existed at a utopian level, rarely having a concrete impact on Western politics. One of Arendt's most provocative claims was that the tradition of political thought came to have a direct and, in certain cases, virulently dangerous impact on Western politics because of an almost purely coincidental compatibility of modern politics and culture with that tradition. A contingent set of social, intellectual, technological, and economic circumstances emerged in the modern political context, which inverted the *vita activa*, raising labor to a place of political supremacy and rendering action largely politically irrelevant. This modern version of politics oddly turned out to fit like a hand in glove with the tradition of political thought. The reason it was able to do this had to do with the rise of a scientifically conditioned culture that came to view itself, even from a political standpoint, from a distant, theoretical perspective. Thus, Arendt analyzed two distinct sources of necessity in human affairs in her broad critique of modernity: the tradition of political thought and modern scientifically conditioned culture. Together, they both conceptualized and legitimized a mode of political thought that Arendt called ideological thinking. This way of political thinking eventually led to a flawed model of historical and political judgment that justified the worst moments of tyranny in Western politics of the twentieth century and arguably is still present in much contemporary political discourse.

This is a long chapter, containing two parts. The reason for its length is simple: Arendt's account of modern political pathologies is a long, complicated narrative that engages a broad set of historical, philosophical, and intellectual sources. My reconstruction of that narrative began in Chapter 3's account of the development of the tradition of political thought. This chapter will examine how Arendt finished that story. The first part of this chapter will examine the second source of modern necessity, modern scientifically conditioned culture; the second part will then examine how these two elements of necessity interacted to give birth to twentieth-century political tyrannies. At the conclusion of this chapter, we will finally be in a position to understand how and why Arendt understood her theory of political judgment to be a response to this modern predicament.

A short note about Arendt's assessment of the tradition of political thought is in order here. It is important to recognize that Arendt did not believe there was anything necessarily tyrannical about the tradition, at least, not in a pejorative sense. For Arendt, history is a story determined by contingency: because she gives priority to human agency in her historiography, the notion that there is some overdetermining historical essence working behind our backs is far too simplistic a perspective for her. Events could have turned out very differently, but unfortunately they did not, and we must therefore recognize that even venerable institutions and sets of ideas can, under the wrong circumstances, be abused for evil purposes. While the tradition itself probably had good intentions throughout its history, Arendt believed that during the twentieth century it was indeed abused by evil men for sinister purposes. This point still should not lead us to conclude that the tradition was not flawed from the beginning: in Arendt's view, the tradition had always been theoretically crude, failing to adequately theorize authentic political phenomena, and, indeed, this was the very reason it was capable of being abused in the first place. Nevertheless, it would be a pernicious misreading of Arendt to suggest she thought the tradition itself was evil or tyrannical.

A Genealogy of Modern Politics

The final chapter of *The Human Condition* brings the book's many strands together in an unexpected concluding narrative of the origins of modern politics.[1] Prior to the modern age, the idea of changing or altering the human condition had always been conceived of as utopian; yet, the politics of the modern age has been characterized by a wildly successful Promethean project of doing exactly that.[2] The question of what convinced modern people it was even possible to do such a thing haunts Arendt's narrative. Arendt had shown in the preceding chapters of *The Human Condition* that the same human activities have always been employed by human beings. Why did it suddenly occur to humans—almost overnight—that these activities, which had always been done in response to the unchanging givenness of the human condition, could for the first time offer a means of changing or even escaping it? The origins of this revolution in human beings' assessment of their fundamental possibilities is the story Arendt attempts to tell in "The *Vita Activa* and the Modern Age" chapter. She argued that it was the rise of the modern scientific point of view that gave birth to this notion.

The Human Condition and the Discovery of the Archimedean Point

Arendt, as we've seen, argued for the *essentially* conditioned nature of human beings—that attempting to understand our nature without reference to the conditions of our existence would be like attempting to jump over our shadow. The consequence of this observation means that when we ask about the nature of modern science, we cannot appeal to the methodology of modern science, since that would beg the question. As the conditioned beings who perform the activity of modern science, we thus must take into account the conditions of our existence as beings before we can confront our existence as *knowing* beings: ontology, in other words, must precede epistemology. As we saw in Chapter 1, these are conditions such as mortality, embodiment, scarcity, language, plurality, earth-boundedness, historicality, even human life's own technology. These are not objective facts in the conventional sense; they are conditions of our consciousness or subjectivity. On this view, there is no true transcendental subject of knowledge. Even when Arendt moves farthest away from the human condition in her account of the thinking activity, this activity is still "conditioned," in this case by the gap between past and future. Modern science therefore must also be conditioned in some way, and the last chapter of *The Human Condition* seeks both to establish that perspective and to draw out what its political implications have been for the modern era. In attempting to outflank modern science by appealing to the human condition, Arendt was not especially original. But what she did bring to this form of analysis was a distinctive emphasis on its broad political implications for concrete human agency. Thus, when Arendt claims that there are three basic human activities (labor, work, and action) that respond to three basic human conditions (natural necessity, worldliness, and human plurality), this articulation may seem simplistic, but Arendt intends it to be so. She was attempting to achieve a very high level of abstraction in her account of the basic human condition, because she was aware that the story she was about to tell about the relationship between modern science and the human condition becomes very complex very quickly.

Isolating exactly what this scientific point of view is has never been an easy task. Indeed, according to Arendt, science's true point of reference is unique in human history and fundamentally alien to human experience. Because of this inherent alienation from human experience, ambiguity has pervaded attempts to theorize the status of modern science, even among its most brilliant practitioners. With a few significant exceptions,[3] scientists have for the most part ignored this question, and left the problem to philosophers. The philosophical position most often used for the analysis of science—particularly in the period since Kant—has suggested that a "view from nowhere" (Thomas Nagel) or "a God's eye view" (Hilary Putnam) is most appropriate, that is, that, at least as a methodological presumption, science seeks to find a point outside of space and time and causal sequence, since this would ultimately be the only way to fully understand "how the universe works," which in terms of modern science's methodology is the basis of all explanation.[4] This is the presumption at the heart of Kant's faculty of reason: that certain "regulative ideas," which can in principle never be attained, nevertheless structure our epistemological presuppositions.[5] In "The *Vita Activa* and the Modern Age," Arendt seems to be arguing that this "regulative" account of scientific methodology is not quite correct. She refers to the point of view of modern science as an "Archimedean point," and it does not seem to mean quite the same thing as a "God's eye view" or a "view from nowhere." She seems to believe that a point of reference that fully transcended the conditions of our universe, even as a conditioning regulative idea, would fail to offer intelligibility to human knowledge.[6] The Archimedean point for scientists is located either outside or beneath the earthbound conditions of human life: anywhere in the cosmos, in fact, that is most convenient for a particular scientific undertaking—anywhere, that is, *except* from within the human condition.[7]

Modern science represents what Arendt believed was a kind of secret human wish for "rebellion against" the human condition, which for virtually all of human history until the dawn of the modern age was thought to be a mere fantasy—"like the fulfillment of wishes in fairy tales."[8] Though an extension of it, this "Archimedean wish" is profoundly different from the condition of "worldliness" established through the human activity of work, which had always represented the uniquely human aspiration of transcending natural necessity.[9] In her critique of human rights in *The Origins of Totalitarianism*, Arendt argues that it has always been this "deep resentment against" the "mere givenness" of the human condition that provided the urge to develop highly political societies.[10] However, political societies did not seek to escape the human condition as such, but instead sought to establish a human artifice as a bulwark against the natural necessity that was an unavoidable condition of human life on earth. This perspective of "political resentment" against the human condition never sought to escape it, but only sought to establish a space for human political freedom. The "political" perspective is— and always will be—embedded in the human condition. As she noted in her critique of imperialism in *Origins*, "the concept of unlimited expansion" pre-supposed by imperialism can only lead to "the destruction of all living com-munities. . . . For every political structure, new or old, left to itself develops stabilizing forces which stand in the way of constant transformation and ex-pansion."[11] The "Archimedean wish," however, aspires to escape the human condition completely by finding a point outside the earth and the human condition that could allow it to move or alter the world and human life as such.[12] The Archimedean point seeks to escape even those worldly conditions that establish a space for human freedom and thus, if this wish were ever fulfilled, would be far more radical than the mere establishment of a worldly regime of human artifice.

No doubt this wish would have remained pure fantasy but for the occur-rence of a completely unexpected event in human history, whose political ramifications, according to Arendt, were from the perspective of the premod-ern world almost unbelievable. This was the invention of the telescope. The telescope (to use a much overused and abused concept) introduced a new paradigm into human history. This was not mere skepticism, which had been a topic of philosophical debate since pre-Socratic philosophy. The invention of the telescope was a "demonstrable fact," and as such, it had ramifications that went far beyond the mere idea of skepticism toward the human sense apparatus.[13] Arendt writes that "the modern age began when man, with the help of the telescope . . . learned that his senses were not fitted for the uni-verse, that his everyday experience, far from being able to constitute the model for the reception of truth and the acquisition of knowledge, was a constant source of error and delusion."[14] As a result of this experience, hu-manity learned a lesson that fundamentally changed the way it viewed and interacted with the world.[15] It recognized that truth—at least, that is, truth as defined by modern scientific methodology as the absence of error and illusion—could not be achieved in the context of the simple givenness of the human condition.[16] Therefore, that givenness had to be escaped, so that a point of reference could be established outside it.[17] As luck would have it, humanity already had at its disposal an activity that it had long used to escape certain aspects of the human condition. This was the activity of work, which humanity has always used to establish a human artifice to escape, to a limited degree, the natural necessity of earthbound existence. While human beings will probably always be terrestrial creatures, it became apparent that a perspective outside terrestrial life could be achieved, an "Archimedean point," and this point was achieved not solely through humanity's natural knowing capacities, but only after these knowing capacities had been augmented, altered, or even rendered irrelevant by the tools humanity was about to build through work. This Archimedean point, it was discovered, could be used to realize unheard of possibilities that could "increase man's power of making and acting, even of creating a world, far beyond what any previous age dared to imagine in dream and phantasy."[18]

The invention of the telescope was a definitive instance of Arendt's attempt to give human agency a central place in historical reflection. The discovery of the telescope was what she calls in *The Human Condition* an "event."[19] An event, for Arendt, is sharply distinguished from an idea.[20] The idea of the Archimedean point had existed in the imagination of Western humanity for a very long time, but only as a kind of thought experiment. No idea could ever exert an objective and concrete influence on the history of mankind in the way an event could. As an event, the invention of the telescope was, according to Arendt, an eruption of genuine novelty in the apparently eternal natural time sequence.[21] It is crucial to recognize the implications of the move Arendt is making here. By claiming that the modern scientific worldview, that is, the Archimedean point, is the result of the human act of inventing the telescope, it can justifiably be argued that Arendt successfully outflanked modern science. If modern scientific methodology, which on its own terms would reject the possibility of authentic events, is itself the result of an event, Arendt can then plausibly claim that human deeds, events, and history have a form of reality that the explanatory models of modern science cannot account for. Human agency must then be understood to be more primordial than modern science's methodology, since such an event brought modern science into being and is thus a necessary element in any attempt to explain the meaning of modern science itself.

What is of immediate interest for Arendt's story, however, is that the invention of the telescope did not simply reintroduce an old idea into the intellectual discourse of Western civilization. As an "event," it instead demonstrated in concrete reality that escape from the human condition was an objective human possibility and, furthermore, exemplified the strategies that would need to be employed in order to do it.[22] Of course, escaping and eventually altering the human condition was a project that could not have immediately been given concrete reality. Nevertheless, the genuine possibility of making such a circumstance an actual, concrete reality was almost immediately realized by those who recognized Galileo's discovery for what it was. Arendt writes: "While the new science, the science of the Archimedean point, needed centuries and generations to develop its full potentialities . . . it took no more than a few decades, hardly one generation, for the human mind to draw certain conclusions from Galileo's discoveries . . . ; and while this change naturally remained restricted to the few . . . [it foreshadowed] the radical change of mind of all modern men which became a politically demonstrable reality only in our own time."[23] Descartes arguably articulated the definitive instance of this realization in his *Discourse on Method*:

> But as soon as I had acquired some general notions regarding physics . . . [and] I had noticed where they could lead . . . I believed I could not keep them hidden away without sinning grievously against the law that obliges us to procure, as much as is in our power, the common good of all men. . . . For these notions made me see that it is possible to arrive at knowledge that would be very useful in life . . . and thus render ourselves, as it were, masters and possessors of nature. This is desirable not only for the invention of an infinity of devices that would enable one to enjoy trouble-free the fruits of the earth and all the goods found there, but also principally for the maintenance of health . . . and that one could rid oneself of an infinity of maladies.[24]

The visionary—even prophetic—modern Prometheanism of Descartes's statement here is striking. No doubt a more deeply Archimedean viewpoint on the human condition, and the possibilities of transcending it afforded by modern science, can scarcely be imagined. One might, for instance, juxtapose this formulation with the incredulity and contempt that the Greeks directed toward Xerxes' insolence toward the earth's chthonic powers in building his marvelous bridge of boats across the Hellespont, expressed most famously in Aeschylus's *Persians*.[25] The most radical moment in Descartes's formulation is his contemplation of a new kind of philosophy, a "practical" philosophy that was to challenge the "speculative" philosophy of "the schools." Practical philosophy, of course, had existed at least since Plato and Aristotle, but what was meant by this term was very different from what Descartes envisioned.

This older practical tradition would have balked at Descartes's vision, since even philosophical accounts of human action argued that the objectives and ideals that it should pursue were above the mere "welfare of mankind" that Descartes now believed was the highest objective of philosophy. Thus, the fundamental difference between the old practical philosophies and Descartes's new practical philosophy is that philosophy itself—and not just a rather questionable and specific branch of it—now comes to be defined and have meaning only insofar as it furthers the welfare of mankind. In other words, the end and telos of philosophy is no longer located in the life-changing experience of contemplation, but instead is in bringing about the "common good" of mankind. Thus, ultimately, though it is true that many of the natural sciences still retain in certain respects the old contemplative ethos, it can hardly be denied that the enormous prestige modern science holds in our society is due to its wildly successful fulfillment of the promise of the practical philosophy envisioned by Descartes.

This shift in the meaning of philosophy was not, however, simply some haphazard development in the history of ideas. Arendt argues that it was instead a justifiable and even logical response to the discovery of the Archimedean point. Western civilization, according to Arendt, had traditionally understood there to be a hierarchy between the two ways of life, where the *vita contemplativa* was recognized to represent human possibilities that were of a higher order than the *vita activa*.[26] This hierarchy was primarily a result of the Romans' embrace of the ancient Greek philosophers as their authorities in matters of theory and was established firmly after the Platonic reaffirmation of Western civilization was articulated by Augustine and the Christian church.[27] This hierarchy, it should be noted, is not identical with the tradition of political thought. The tradition of political thought had sought to understand and establish a relationship between the two ways of life in order to secure the way of life of the philosophers. The hierarchy of the two ways of life, on the other hand, was simply a function of how the inhabitants of the West understood the essential human possibilities available in the human condition. In a world where the human condition was simply given and unchanging, the life of the mind was conceived to be higher than the life of action because it represented the only genuine possibility of leaving the human condition behind. As Aristotle writes, "the wise man can practice contemplation by himself [as opposed to needing other men to perform noble deeds before] . . . he is the most self-sufficient of all men," and "it follows, then, that the activity of the gods, which is supremely happy, must be a form of contemplation. . . . Happiness, then, is co-extensive with contemplation, and the more people contemplate, the happier they are."[28]

According to Arendt, the profound impact of the discovery of the Archimedean point can be grasped most fully by understanding how its clear implications for human possibilities within the human condition completely altered the preeminence awarded both among and within the *vitas*—a shift in preeminence, moreover, that would appear to those experiencing it to have been completely merited. The telescope conclusively demonstrated that the human sense apparatus, which had developed in response to the human condition, was incapable of knowing the universe. Instead, it was revealed that humans had to develop tools and experimental techniques that escaped the human condition and allowed them to study the universe from the Archimedean point. In other words, while humans would always have a need and desire to understand the world in which they lived, they realized that they could never arrive at this knowledge through their given knowing capacities, but instead could arrive at it only through their capacities for making. As a result, a double reversal occurred in the *vitas*: within the *vita activa* preeminence was justifiably given to the goals and standards of the activity of work, while at the same time the traditional hierarchy among the *vitas* was inverted.[29] Thus, for the first time in Western civilization, doing came to carry greater prestige than contemplating. According to Arendt, "man's thirst for knowledge could be assuaged only after he had put his trust into the ingenuity of his hands. The point was not that truth and knowledge were no longer important, but that they could be won only by 'action' and not by contemplation. It was an instrument, the telescope, a work of man's hands, which finally forced nature, or rather the universe, to yield its secrets."[30] The hierarchy between the *vitas* in the modern age was inverted because human beings concluded, based on the discovery of the Archimedean point, that "one can only know what he has made himself."[31] In this phrase, Arendt is pointing out that prior to the modern age, knowing something meant knowing "what" or "why" it was, while understanding the natural processes that determined "how" it worked had always been a concern of the fabrication process's technical apparatus. In the modern age, this question of "how" became the defining characteristic of knowledge because it allowed for a level of certainty previously unavailable to humans' knowing capacities—but only on the condition that what was known was something in a certain sense "made" by the knower through the technique of experiment. Arendt writes that the experiment allows humans, instead of only being conditioned by nature, to prescribe conditions to nature that would not have occurred otherwise than as a result of human thought.[32] And, of course, none of this would have been imaginable without the discovery of the Archimedean point.

But it was not only the newly revealed truth-generating capacities of the work activity that gave birth to these reversals. In fact, it was the practical implications that drove this reversal: for if there is such a thing as a profound existential resentment against the human condition, then work had clearly demonstrated that humanity now had the capacity to grant the age-old utopian fantasy of escaping and altering the human condition. Within a century and a half, these new conditions would come to be a reality that would define the political circumstances of the modern age.[33] Western civilization would see a previously unimaginable level of abundance that placed increasing pressure on political institutions to realize "unheard of conditions of universal equality" in concrete social life for all of its citizens.[34] Yet, for all of the deservedly prestigious accomplishments that modern society has achieved with the help of the Archimedean point, Arendt insists that they have not come without costs. According to Arendt, this vast expansion of human welfare only came as a consequence of a deep, unrecognized darkening of the human world and an alienation of human judgment that would have profound and, at times, catastrophic consequences for Western civilization.

The Rise of Modern Politics

Arendt concludes *The Human Condition* by expressing what she believed was the Faustian bargain entailed in the discovery of the Archimedean point. "If, in concluding," she writes, "we return once more to the discovery of the Archimedean point and apply it, as Kafka warned us not to do, to man himself and to what he is doing on this earth, it at once becomes manifest that all his activities, watched from a sufficiently removed vantage point in the universe, would appear not as activities of any kind but as processes."[35] Arendt was here expressing a long-standing observation about the nihilistic tendencies inherent in modern liberal politics and linking it to modern science's Archimedean perspective. To view humans beings from the position of the Archimedean point robs them of their dignity; it makes them, in principle, nothing more than worldless though highly intelligent animals—*animal laborans*. The debate over the existence of modern nihilism is of course long-standing, going back centuries.[36] Though it certainly cannot be resolved here, Arendt's intervention into this debate is a powerful one, one that is instructive and informing, not to mention in many ways highly persuasive, especially if we admit that her distinctions among the *vita activa* have validity. In what follows, I will try to show why I believe it is a perspective that demands to be taken seriously and, indeed, that it is possibly even dangerous not to.

In *The Human Condition*, Arendt argues that our modern world is "a society of laborers."[37] By this Arendt means that the hierarchies within the *vitas* have been completely inverted. Action and work have become ambiguously indistinct activities that are performed for the sake of labor, that is, for the right of all human beings to perform their part in the increasing abundance and consumption of human welfare (126, 130–135, 236). Thought and the *vita contemplativa*, to the extent it is pursued for its own sake as an authentically theoretical activity, are viewed at best with indulgence and mild contempt by the *vita activa*, which now has difficulty appreciating the purpose of a thoughtful activity that does not ultimately somehow contribute to greater abundance and consumption (289ff., 297). In other words, it is labor and the society it has produced that now give meaning to all other human activities. The problem with this state of affairs is that labor can never be a meaning-generating activity in the same way that thought and action are; labor, no matter how effortless it may become, will always be driven by the necessity of the life process. Thus, according to Arendt, in the very structure of its active life, modern society is fundamentally nihilistic, perversely making the one activity that is most futile, labor, the purpose of the activities humans possess that can produce the meaningfulness that could justify their existence. But this radical change in the conditions of human life was no mere happenstance. Arendt believed that beneath the surface the discovery of the Archimedean point drove the process.

Arendt uses the term "world alienation" to characterize this dark side of the discovery of the Archimedean point (253–257, 261–268).[38] It signifies the relation of modern individuals to their worldly conditions in the modern era. As we've seen, Arendt understands human activity to center around the fact that human beings are always already conditioned by a common world that separates and relates them and a public realm that provides a sphere for humans to gain immortality. Modern world alienation means that the common world and public realm have ceased to perform these functions in an unambiguous way, and, as a result, its inhabitants have increasingly lost their common sense, the intuitive feeling or sixth sense that fits them into the common world. The Archimedean point has altered the conditions of human life in ways that are virtually unintelligible in terms of the traditional world of Western civilization and, in the process, replaced the common world as the reference point of Western politics.

However, the discovery of the Archimedean point, though by far the most significant, was not the only factor that brought modernity into existence (264). There were at least two other elements involved. One of these elements was Western civilization's Christian tradition, which asserted life as the highest good (313–314). This element provided a kind of hidden center of gravity in the chain of events that would lead to the full flowering of modernity, in that at key moments the modern age of the older traditional Western world could have chosen to move in different directions than it eventually did. For Arendt, the influence of Christianity's emphasis on life seems to be the underlying factor that pulled the modern age toward the modern world it eventually became (314, 318–319). The second element is the expropriation process that began in the Reformation but that, unintentionally, led to the end of feudalism and the expropriation of the peasantry (251–252). The significance of this element lies chiefly in its involvement in a fundamental shift in the notion of property in the Western world, which had far-reaching consequences for the conditions of life in the modern age. Prior to the expropriation begun during the Reformation, property had always been understood as a sine qua non condition of citizens' activities: not something that fundamentally involves politics itself, but something that had to be in place as a shelter from the necessities of life and the public gaze (34–36, 61–64, 186–187). Arendt writes that "property, as distinguished from wealth and appropriation, indicates the privately owned share of a common world and therefore is the most elementary political condition for man's worldliness" (253). When expropriation brought the end of feudalism, the peasants lost their private places in the world, and as a result, were the first definite strata of the inhabitants of Western civilization to experience world alienation. "The new laboring class, which literally lived from hand to mouth, stood not only directly under the compelling urgency of life's necessity but was at the same time alienated from all cares and worries which did not immediately follow from the life process itself" (254–255). Expropriation began a process that would lead to a radical redefinition of property, particularly by classical political economists such as Locke, Smith, and Marx, whose work was so central for laying down the principles of modern interpretations of the tradition of political thought (101–109). In the modern age, property was redefined in terms of wealth, a commodity that was amenable to accumulation and appropriation but that in concrete reality had little relationship to the older ideal of privacy—indeed, in many ways actually worked against it (61–62, 110–111, 253–256). Arendt points out, however, that what was unique about the process begun by the Reformation expropriation was that it was not like previous instances of this process, in that "expropriation and wealth accumulation did not simply result in new property or lead to a new redistribution of wealth, but were fed back into the process to generate further expropriations, greater productivity, and more appropriation" (255).

These three key elements—the discovery of the Archimedean point, the Christian emphasis on life as the highest good, and the expropriation process leading to the industrial revolution—provided the historical transformation that would eventually result in the modern age's central political obsession, universal equality, and the society of laborers that is above all animated by this politics. Nevertheless, there is no question that the Archimedean point was the dominant variable, for without the pattern of thinking that arose from it, a pattern of thinking that focused on the concept of "process" rather than the traditional idea of "being," the other two elements might have remained unremarkable (296–297). The fact that process thinking would come to dominate the modern world with the kind of absoluteness it has was at first glance not necessarily obvious, according to Arendt. The discovery of the Archimedean point initially seemed to lead to a world dominated by *homo faber*: a world where work was the highest activity of human beings (294–296). This conclusion seemed unavoidable because, since human knowledge was now recognized to depend on the capacity to develop tools and instruments that allow us to escape the human condition, all activity was now interpreted from the viewpoint of work. Arendt points out that the structure of the fabrication process always leads to an objective, finished product, and, as a result, it was at first not obvious that the modern world would lose confidence in the objective world in the drastic way it has (296–297). Initially, the modern age

> found its most plausible theory in the famous analogy of the relationship between nature and God with the relationship between the watch and the watchmaker. The point in our context is . . . that in this instance the process character of nature was still limited. Although all particular natural things had already been engulfed in the process from which they had come into being, nature as a whole was not yet a process but the more or less stable end product of a divine maker. (297)

Thus, for a time in the early modern age it appeared that *homo faber* would establish a new world built on the idea of work as the highest activity. Human beings, made in the image of God, were simply taking the standpoint of the One who made nature (295–296). The activity of work, to the extent it was an activity that responded to the condition of worldliness, tended to judge itself—along with its own internal standards of "creativity and productivity"—according to objective worldly standards such as "utility and beauty," and idealized the objective, expressive activities of the artist (152, 167ff., 296). There is even an authentic public realm associated with *homo faber*, the exchange market (159ff.).

However, this politics of *homo faber* was fundamentally unstable due to its origins in the experience of the Archimedean point. To the extent the Archimedean point was its basic, authoritative point of reference, there was ultimately no fixed point of reference *homo faber* could appeal to. Those who utilize the Archimedean point "move freely" through the universe; yet, if one does so, this would therefore imply that there is no stable way to orient one's self to worldly existence (263–264, 284). Consequently, a world based around the standards of *homo faber* turned out to be analogously unstable. By its own internal logic, the instrumental standards of the work activity eventually drive it to seek out authoritative standards beyond itself (165–166, 284, 304–308). Arendt argues that the means/end category, which is central to the utilitarian logic of work, is trapped in an infinite regress: when restricted to its own standards, it does not have some deeper meaning beyond that category to appeal to (154–155).

Politically, this meant that, since the modern age, action and work have become ambiguously associated with one another (228–230). Action has consistently been interpreted in terms of the means/end category, with the result that when humans sought to reestablish an authentic political realm in the modern age through the novel phenomenon of revolution, they naturally sought to reject the laboring and consuming activity that characterized modern politics and recurred back to the slightly older interpretation of political action interpreted in terms of *homo faber*, since on the basis of the Archimedean point, any other interpretation was nearly inconceivable (157–158, 207, 228–230, 236–238). Prior to the modern age, such exogenous standards were provided by the activity of contemplation in the form of Christianity, which having reinterpreted and co-opted the Roman foundations of tradition, religion, and authority, provided standards and goals for the work of *homo faber* (302–304). However, as the logic of the Archimedean point became more apparent, it increasingly became the case that this traditional way of arriving at exogenous standards was implausible to the inhabitants of the modern age.

Arendt points out that, unlike traditional philosophy, which was based on the primordial experience of *thaumazein*, or wonder, the primordial experience of modern philosophy is doubt (273–274). "Just as from Plato and Aristotle to the modern age conceptual philosophy, in its greatest and most authentic representatives, had been the articulation of wonder, so modern philosophy since Descartes has consisted in the articulations and ramifications of doubting." Summarizing the unprecedented and radical nature of modern scientifically informed doubt, Arendt writes:

> Cartesian doubt, in its radical and universal significance, was originally the response to a new reality. . . . The old opposition of sensual and rational truth, of the inferior truth capacity of the senses and the superior truth capacity of reason, paled beside this challenge, beside the obvious implication that neither truth nor reality is given, that neither of them appears as it is, and that only interference with appearance, doing away with appearances, can hold out a hope for true knowledge. (274)

This new experience of doubt became a primordial experience because it was far more radical than the ancient skeptical doubts about the human sense apparatus. To the extent doubt now became the driving force in the human pursuit of knowledge, certainty became the ultimate standard of knowledge, and certainty of knowledge, it appeared, could only be gained by escaping the human condition and by "making sure" through the use of tools (290). Thus, it was demonstrated that neither human sense faculties nor even human reason could be trusted, because the substantive or conceptual reason that philosophers prior to the modern age had employed had ultimately always depended on an original relationship with human common sense (274–275). Once common sense was called into question, substantive conceptions of reason, even while they intended to criticize common sense, had no place to begin.

Thus, a profound skepticism toward given human experience lies at the roots of modern science. This radical skepticism is the source of modern "world alienation," because now a wedge has been driven between our worldly experience and our beliefs and confidence in the way things truly are. The Roman trinity that underpinned the Western world was for the first time regarded with suspicion—which in a political sense amounted to its virtual destruction—and common sense, as the sixth sense humans possess that fits their other five senses meaningfully into the world, had now been shown to be intuitively oriented toward a world that, from the perspective of modern science, was ultimately only a source of illusion (275). This realization was greeted with horror by anyone not dazzled by modern science's Promethean possibilities: "the feeling of suspicion, outrage, and despair . . . was the first, and spiritually is still the most lasting consequence of the discovery that the 'Archimedean point was no vain dream of idle speculation'" (267). In other words, the price humans paid for the unheard of capacities given to them by the discovery of the Archimedean point was the loss of confidence in their common sense, along with all it allowed them to hold dear. "It is as if Galileo's discovery proved in demonstrable fact that both the worst fear and the most presumptuous hope of human speculation . . . could only come true together, as though the wish would be granted only provided that we lost reality and the fear was to be consummated only if compensated by the acquisition of supramundane powers" (262).

Be that as it may, humans still experienced life within the human condition. If their common sense had been delegitimized, then some new way of politically organizing themselves would be needed. The beginnings of the solution to this problem that would eventually be devised began when modern philosophy, starting with Descartes, turned inward and discovered that if we can no longer trust our common sense, there were at least certain processes and structures of the mind that we all shared. Arendt argues that common sense was thus replaced by what Hobbes had called "reckoning with consequences," or, in Arendt's terms, "common sense reasoning" (282–284). Since modern humans were increasingly alienated from "given reality," the only reality humans in the modern era felt they could be certain of was the reality that they produced on the basis of an introspective examination of the structure of the human mind, exemplified by mathematical knowledge, since "neither God nor an evil spirit can change the fact that two plus two equals four" (284). Thus, Arendt argues that it was Descartes's ingenuous solution that eventually solved the problem of the political instability of the Archimedean point: while scientists could always move the Archimedean point where they needed to for research purposes, practical problems could be solved by locating the Archimedean point within the human mind. But when this shift toward process thinking occurred, the old early modern idea of a universe based on the model of the watch and the watchmaker became untenable: reality was no longer interpreted in terms of the thing observed, but instead in terms of the forces and processes that underlay it (296–297). That which appeared was now only an incidental indication of the invisible forces or processes that constitute actual physical reality, and thus the criteria for knowledge in modern science became "whether or not it will work," that is, whether the experiment produces the result that had been predicted in the hypothesis. Arendt argues that, as a result of this, the standard of success became the singular criterion of judgment of modern scientific knowledge (278). And as we will see, this standard has become, if not the only practical standard of judgment in the modern world, at least the preeminent one.

On the basis of this notion of thinking in terms of processes, humans began to look for processes outside the direct confines of philosophical intro-spection and experimental science. They began to see processes in places they had never before thought to look: the realm of human affairs. In *The Human Condition*, Arendt argues that process thinking interacted with expropriation and the Christian emphasis on life as the highest good to give birth to the modern age's politics of universal equality and its corresponding society of laborers. The classical political economists exemplified this approach when they developed their theories about the origins and development of property. Process thinking drew their attention to the fact that expropriation had started off "a hither-to unheard of process of growing wealth, growing property, and growing acquisition" (105). Locke clearly seems to have interpreted property in terms of the traditional idea of maintaining a privately owned piece of the world (105–106, 115). Yet, he located the origin of property not in the objective worldly structure of the human artifice but instead in human "labor power," which according to Arendt can never be the origin of property, since labor is our response to the natural necessity of the biological process that our privately owned share of the world is intended to be a bulwark against.

While from a phenomenological perspective this was a contradiction, Arendt argues that political economists had discovered a powerful phenomenon, one that would profoundly and irrevocably transform the Western world. They discovered that human labor power has an essential fertility: it always creates more than is necessary for its own maintenance. And furthermore, the accumulation of human wealth, demonstrated in their time in this novel process of expropriation, was somehow the result of human labor power (101–106, 111–112). It is ultimately, therefore, this labor power that is the source of the abundance that the modern world has seen, and only incidentally the result of the explosive growth and development of our society's technology (118–126). Since tools and technology are always characterized by instrumentality, by the category of means and ends, they may just as well be directed toward creating a stable world as they may be toward increasing the natural fertility of human labor (121–122, 308). Our world would certainly have nothing like the abundance it has now if it were not for the tools and implements of modern labor power, but it is always labor, as the source of wealth, that is being accentuated and strengthened. Without it, our modern technology would be meaningless.

Like Descartes's realization of the tremendous possibilities at stake in the development of modern science, the political economists recognized that if expropriation was generalized to society as a whole, humans could expect great improvement in their material conditions. But Arendt points out that since this process had actually been the result of the end of feudalism and the worldless condition of these new workers in the emergent industrial revolution, this condition of worldlessness would also have to be generalized in order for the process to be applied to the whole of society. This meant that the inhabitants of the modern age would have to come to interpret themselves and their politics as a society of worldless laborers. She believed that theoretically this articulation had been persuasively performed by Locke, Smith, and, most comprehensively, Marx (101ff.). Nevertheless, some higher standard had to be in place in order to animate and bring into concrete existence this society of laborers. Her solution was to argue that the Christian notion of life as the highest good is the element that provided this animating principle (313ff.). Christian theology tended to place the life of the individual at the center of its outlook. Unlike the political societies, such as the Greeks or Romans, that preceded it—for whom immortality was achieved through *athanatizein* in an enduring common world—Christianity understood immortality to be bound up with the fate of each individual believer in the afterlife (314–315).[39] In *The Human Condition*, Arendt writes that "the Christian 'glad tidings' of the immortality of individual human life . . . reversed the ancient relationship between man and world and promoted the most mortal thing, human life, to the position of immortality, which up to then the cosmos had held" (314). Thus, what was sacred was the life of each believer, since this was the condition of their immortality, and not free political action in the company of their peers. And this belief in the sacredness of life has remained one of the great commitments of Western civilization, remaining surprisingly "unshaken by . . . secularization and the general decline of the Christian faith" (314).

However, the modern version of this belief in the sacredness of life is arguably far less elevated. In the modern world, for the first time people began to abandon the category of the immortal altogether (74). Thus, the elevated ideal of Christian beatitude was replaced by what Arendt considers a far more bovine kind of value for life: modern "happiness" (133–135, 308–311). In terms of the concrete organization of modern society, life had to be articulated from the standpoint of the Archimedean point, and this meant understanding the processes that made for a modern good or "happy" life (307–309). Arendt argues that modern happiness was most thoroughly articulated by utilitarian philosophy, which understood happiness as simply when pleasure outweighs pain in the utilitarian's pleasure/pain calculus. In that sense, utilitarian philosophy was simply the logical extension of Descartes's turn toward introspection and common sense reasoning (309). From this perspective, all human activity is reduced to "behavior": the predictable responses of human animals to pleasurable or painful stimuli (40–46, 322). As a result, the ideal of modern politics—especially from the utilitarian tradition, which still heavily influences modern public policy—has become essentially herdlike. Political judgment is thus reduced to commonsense reasoning. Far from the *doxa* we all as citizens in a common world are entitled and obligated to render, in a mass society the goal of politics is conformity: we would ideally all think essentially the same way about everything because our pleasure/pain calculus allows us to replicate the same perspective infinitely many times. Speaking of individuals in mass society, Arendt writes that "men have become entirely private, that is, they have been deprived of seeing and hearing others, of being seen and being heard by them . . . they are all imprisoned in the subjectivity of their own singular experience, which does not cease to be singular if the same experience is multiplied innumerable times" (58).

Of course, beyond the political articulations of happiness in modern society, many people may have in mind more elevated notions, but generally these are idiosyncratic, or at best limited to traditional views that have long since lost their concrete relevance and effectualness to our world. In political terms—in terms of how we organize our world—they should be irrelevant from the viewpoint of modern liberal politics. This is most evident in the very language modern society uses to describe its standards as "values" (162ff., 213–214, 235n, 307–308). This language is drawn directly from the language of sociology and political economy, and thus analyzes standards of judgment from an Archimedean perspective as social processes. As a result, standards are by their very nature understood as "relative," in the sense that they only represent the relative value given them by a given society (163–165, 307). As a result of all of this, the only "value" that ever gained genuine authority in modern society was the idea of "universal equality" (32–33, 39–41, 130).[40] But this is only a logical extension of the fact that a politics conditioned by the perspective of the Archimedean point must necessarily level out anything that would distinguish us from each other.

Thus, Arendt argues in *The Human Condition* that the modern age saw the raise what Marx called "socialized man" (321) and what she referred to as the "society of laborers" (5, 31, 46). It is tempting to focus on the fact that modern society is a "consumer society," for that is certainly an apt description (126ff.). Nevertheless, Arendt considers the idea that we are a society of laborers a more authentic description of our society, since in her view it reaches deeper into the meaning of what our society actually is and how it came to be. From the perspective of the Archimedean point, once life and modern happiness were asserted as the highest goals and ideals of modern politics, it was unavoidable that labor would be raised to the highest position in the *vita activa*, because labor is the activity associated with the maintenance of life. In modernity, biological necessity—to the extent it is concerned with laboring and consuming the products of that labor—essentially characterizes how we organize and interpret our world and ourselves. The political ideal of the modern world is a kind of laborer's utopia (131–133, 322). The ideals of modern politics are chiefly concerned with ensuring that all citizens are jobholders (since without an "occupation" *animal laborans* loses his or her identity), that these jobs involve relatively easy labor, and, above all, that each inhabitant of our society is entitled to a substantial share in the consumption of its ever increasing abundance (46, 117, 126, 131–132, 319, 322). No doubt Marx's communist utopia was the clearest articulation of this ideal, but Arendt argues that it is just as much the underlying outlook of capitalist societies, at least to the extent that it is the initial presumption of our politics (133–135). Thus, it is true that we are a consumer society, but this is only because a consumer society would necessarily be the ultimate objective of a society of laborers. Consumption is inevitably entailed in the laboring activity: they are like two sides of the same coin (99–100, 108, 124–126, 131–138). Modern politics, therefore, is the era where *animal laborans* has occupied the public realm (134). The public realm of modern society is the social realm, where humans are expected to behave as docile, domesticated animals who quietly and predictably perform their jobs and conform to the expectations of society (40–47, 130ff., 322). Thus, the social realm does not provide a space of self-disclosure for men and women of action to reveal themselves; instead, it is a realm of conformity, hypocrisy, and corruption, where the uniqueness and plurality of humans get reduced to our basic commonalities as human animals (40ff.).

Arendt and the Question of Modern Justice

Manifestly, the most consequential political question posed by Arendt's analysis of modernity concerns the origins and status of the singularly modern value of universal human equality. It is important to understand exactly what Arendt believes about this value and where she fits into the long-standing discussion over its significance. To the extent liberal notions of human rights and human equality claim to assert a kind of infinite distinctiveness and priority for the individuality of each human being, Arendt would certainly have no problem with this. It is, after all, the fundamental assertion of the condition of plurality. Instead, the worry Arendt seems to be raising is whether modernity's formulations and concrete realizations of human rights and universal equality may somehow systematically undermine this infinite human worth it has arrogated as distinctively its own. In other words, is modernity's interpretation of human political equality fundamentally implicated in modernity's presumed nihilistic tendencies? In recent years, major works of philosophy and intellectual history have challenged this notion.[41] The upshot of these works would be to sever the link writers such as Tocqueville, Nietzsche, Heidegger, and Arendt drew from liberal Enlightenment ideals of human rights and individual equality to modern nihilism by arguing that liberalism was not inherently nihilistic, but instead was motivated by certain aspirations and a substantive conception of the good. While these arguments appear to be successful in turning aside Heidegger's and Nietzsche's more historically essentialist attacks, I believe they are less so against Arendt's more concrete argument, which, dominated by her concern with discovering the elements of human agency in historical narrative, tends to emphasize the sheer contingency of historical events. To point out that liberalism was animated by certain substantive moral ideals and patterns of thought that preceded the modern era does not necessarily imply that Arendt's narrative of modernity is wrong. Arendt is not disputing that liberal individualism was motivated by certain preexisting ideals, but rather she is attempting to explain why that particular ideology, among other potential competitors, became so incredibly successful as modernity consolidated itself. In her notion of world alienation, Arendt was arguing that a common *world* had arisen—a result of specific moments of human agency—which was inherently nihilistic, and liberal idealism happened to be the most compatible ideology available with that world. The problem this poses to liberal idealism is that whatever aspirations it may have, those aspirations will inevitably be thwarted so long as this nihilistic common world persists.

Still, there is little point sidestepping the withering scorn Arendt directs toward prominent contemporary political categories such as social justice and public policy, particularly in *The Human Condition*.[42] This contempt is real, and any attempt to explain it away would risk losing the force of Arendt's critique of modern society. However, it is important to be clear about exactly why Arendt regarded these standards and practices with such scorn. It is not that social justice or public policy is in any sense the source of the problems Arendt was attacking. Rather, what Arendt found objectionable about them has to do with the fact that she is convinced they could only have gained the prominence they have in a society where human beings interpret themselves politically as laboring animals. She believed that public policy could only have become as successful and effective as it has been over the last century if the humans in the society it is applied to have been rendered more or less predictable, and such predictability can only be found in humans insofar as they are responding to natural necessity. To the extent public policy is more or less highly effective in modern society, this suggests that our worldly human artifice has ceased to be a bulwark against natural necessity and instead has come to channel natural necessity into the human world.[43] Similarly, Arendt believes that social justice, as the political ideal that seeks universal equality above all, could only have become the highest ideal of a society of laboring animals that views all distinctions among its members with suspicion, envy, and hostility. And, moreover, the seriousness of this critique cannot be overstated. Arendt believes that humans, as essentially conditioned beings, to the extent they engage in politics, can create new conditions for themselves.[44] But as a result of this, the society of *animal laborans* is trapped in a vicious circle. To the extent they view themselves politically as nothing more than laboring and consuming animals, they will increasingly create a world that matches this self-interpretation, and thus make this self-interpretation more and more of a reality; and therefore all human beings' higher capacities, such as action, thought, and work, stand in great danger in the modern world.

Arendt's tone softens somewhat in her writings after *The Human Condition*. Prior to the twentieth century, the modern demand for universal equality had meant that any attempt to found a political realm that could support political action was doomed to be thwarted by the hopelessness of ever totally escaping poverty. If all citizens were entitled to true freedom, then they must all first be freed from the yoke of natural necessity, and this seemed unimaginable. However, we have now reached an era where this is no longer inconceivable. Arendt writes:

> The advancement of the natural sciences and their technology has opened possibilities which make it very likely that, in the not too distant future, we shall be able to deal with all economic matters on technical and scientific grounds, outside political considerations. . . . Our present technical means . . . [suggest that] the wreckage of freedom on the rock of necessity which we have witnessed over and over again since Robespierre's "despotism of liberty" is no longer unavoidable.[45]

What we cannot conclude, however, is that these new possibilities for liberation from necessity automatically guarantee that freedom will follow. We may just as likely (perhaps more than likely) go on living as laboring and consuming animals. Liberation is not freedom, according to Arendt, and the tendency to conflate the two was the fatal flaw of the modern age. Fully understanding why this mistake seemed so unavoidable and what it has meant for the world we live in will take us to the end of Arendt's story with the emergence of the modern world, a story that ends by crystallizing the problem of the oblivion of political judgment in modernity and setting the stage for the attempt to answer the question that absorbed the remainder of Arendt's life after *The Human Condition* of how political judgment and agency could be revived.

The Failure to Refound Freedom and Its Consequences

With the arrival of the modern era, Arendt argued that political actors would again and again futilely attempt to reestablish a space for authentic freedom. As we will see, what thwarted these attempts was a failure of political judgment. When the problem of foundation was posed to the revolutionary actors, they had no access to the fundamental political experiences of the Western world. They did, however, have access to the tradition of political thought and its fabricative model of the relation between thought and action, and, in the unique circumstances of revolutionary politics, the appeal to this model of political judgment turned out to have dangerous tendencies and, occasionally, disastrous consequences.

Revolution and the Modern Failure of Political Judgment

As we have seen, Arendt claimed that modern society is a society of laboring animals. In such a society, human activity is oriented not toward action but by behavior, so that it can ensure the conformity and predictability necessary for its smooth functioning. But this smooth functioning cannot happen spontaneously; it requires political action in the form of public policy and legislation to ensure this smooth functioning. Arendt argues that in the modern era, authentic political action and the work activity have been ambiguously associated with one another.[46] Of course, as we've seen, the idea that political action could be conceptualized in terms of the fabrication analogy was ancient. But until the modern era, much like the idea of the Archimedean point itself, the notion that politics could fully become a matter of making and be determined according to the means/ends category of instrumentality had for the most part remained utopian.[47] The possibility that political action could be conducted in any consistent fashion in the mode of the fabrication analogy only became a realistic possibility in the modern era. The old traditional worldly conditions of freedom that revolved around the Roman trinity were politically and intellectually undermined by modern science. After this, all that remained of traditional Western politics was the tradition of political thought, whose actual relation to Western politics had been ambiguous, representing an inauthentic understanding of political life.

In the modern era, however, the tradition of political thought—almost as a matter of coincidence—became much more relevant to Western politics, because the interests and activities of the inhabitants of the Western political world had been reduced to the kind of predictable consumption and behavior that is found in the society of *animal laborans*. On that basis, it was for the first time possible to assume an Archimedean perspective in relation to political society, much like the old utopian thought experiments. It would be possible to look at human activities in terms of predictable and manipulable processes that could be structured and restructured according to the findings of empirical research into human biology and society. All of this was predicated on the idea that humans are driven by the necessity to consume, that at least in terms of their social/political existence this is their chief function and goal in life, and to the extent they behave otherwise, they are acting "irrationally." Thus, Arendt argues, political action in the modern era is conceptualized from the perspective of *homo faber's* attitude of "sovereignty."[48] As we've noted, while the tradition of political thought had always theorized political action in this way, the actual implementation of sovereignty had always been resisted by the "non-sovereign" elements of Roman tradition and civilization. It is only in the modern era that these non-sovereign elements were, at least as a political factor, eroded enough by modernity to allow for any actual attempt to implement true political sovereignty. Arendt points out that Descartes and Hobbes, as the thinkers who most made use of the discovery of the Archimedean point to reshape politics, discovered their respective theories of sovereignty at virtually the same time, Hobbes in particular exemplifying how the modern era would come to think about political action as "reckoning with consequences."[49]

According to Arendt, the legitimacy of this model of political action was established by drawing on the two conceptual pillars of the tradition of political thought: law and rule.[50] These two pillars were all that remained of the old Roman political world on which the authority and legitimacy of Western politics had been based. On the modern interpretation of political action, an act of coercion and manipulation of a given political society could be justifiable only so long as it could be subsumed under a legitimate legal order. Traditionally, the source of the legal order was conceived to be derived through the contemplation of a transcendent or metaphysical source.[51] In the modern era, such a transcendent appeal was no longer believable, and various forms of natural law theory, which had their source in modern process thinking, came to predominate. The problem with this was that the status of natural law remained ambiguous. In the old traditional order, there was an objective world of laws and tradition that restricted the sovereignty of political actors. Now that all that was left of traditional Western politics was the tradition of political thought, the inadequacy of the tradition increasingly became clear. The tradition of political thought had always presumed a distinction between human-made positive laws, which provided the human world with stability, and their source of authority in a higher order. So long as the old metaphysical political tradition at least buttressed the idea of a separation between the imperfect human world and an ideal political world, Arendt argues, there remained certain built-in limitations on any attempt to do away with the distinction between positive and natural law. However, by the time of Kant, the goal became to completely subsume all positive laws under universal natural law. The problem with this move to eliminate the gulf between positive and natural law, Arendt argues, was that the modern age had come to understand the laws of nature through the lens of modern science, as laws of movement. As various modern ideologies emerged, it became increasingly apparent that almost any process could be identified in history and asserted to be the law of historical movement. As a result, anyone who claimed to understand such natural laws of movement in human history or politics could feel justified in ignoring or changing at will any positive law.[52] Thus, the flaws in the sovereignty model of modern politics are evident in a kind of crystallized purity right from the beginning with Hobbes, who understood political action in the mode of instrumentality as "reckoning with consequences," and who argued that the sovereign was only limited by his or her ability to interpret of the law of nature.[53] However, in themselves, none of these political categories and concepts necessarily had to lead to the tyranny and violence that they would eventually be used to justify. If, as Arendt claimed, the goal of sovereignty was ultimately to ensure the smooth functioning of the worldless society of *animal laborans*, there seems no obvious culprit within this framework of sovereignty that would necessarily lead to such tyranny.[54] Arendt argues that in all likelihood, the worst abuses of the sovereignty model of modern political action would not have happened if it had not been for a novel phenomenon that arose toward the end of the eighteenth century: revolution.[55]

The rise of revolution was related to the emergence of sovereign politics in that they can both be tied back to shifts in Western civilization toward modernity, but they are not the same phenomenon and do not spring from the same human impulses. To state the distinction most succinctly, sovereignty sprang from the human impulse toward liberation, the desire to escape natural necessity, while revolution sprang from the human impulse for freedom, the desire to achieve immortality through political action, and in Arendt's view any attempt to understand the political history of the modern Western world demands an understanding of this distinction. She notes that prior to the modern age, the distinction between the rich and poor was believed to be natural, and that poverty constituted a fundamental aspect of the human condition. However, modern people began to doubt that this was the case, and, as a result, it was believed that any new political order demanded universal equality and emancipation. Thus, revolution, beginning with the later stages of the French Revolution, came to be identified with what Arendt calls the "social question." "The social question," she writes, "began to play a revolutionary role only when, in the modern age . . . men began to doubt that the distinction between the few, who through circumstances or strength or fraud had succeeded in liberating themselves from the shackles of poverty, and the labouring poverty-stricken multitude was inevitable and eternal."[56]

A common misinterpretation of Arendt is that she is claiming in *On*

Revolution that all political action can only occur after liberation has been achieved. I have already argued that Arendt's notion of political action, once properly understood, transcends this understanding. Indeed, any attempt to pursue political liberation would itself presuppose an originating political action. Yet, there appears to be textual evidence in *On Revolution* that would lead us to suppose otherwise. I believe this can be explained by recognizing that Arendt is referring to a very specific kind of political action in *On Revolution*, a political action specifically concerning the problem of founding new public realms. To a perhaps surprising degree, the textual foundation of the prominent interpretations of Arendtian political action is based in a particular reading of *On Revolution*. Generally, scholars take *The Human Condition* to be Arendt's statement of her political philosophy; but in fact the interpretation of political action that anchors the interpretations I have been arguing against draw significantly on *On Revolution* and would not be nearly as persuasive without various statements made by Arendt there.[57]

The two original modern revolutions, the American and the French, began as vaguely articulated rebellions against what they considered "tyranny." But once the "tyranny" was overthrown, the revolutionaries were confronted by a task the magnitude of which was breathtakingly unexpected. The revolutionaries, in overthrowing political orders that stretched back to the traditional era, were at the same time overthrowing the last vestiges of the old Roman civilization, and, as a result, stumbled into historical forces and circumstances that they had been at best only vaguely aware of.[58] Thus, politically speaking, the revolutionaries were confronted not just by the prospect of reviving a human faculty of political action that had atrophied in the preceding millennium, but also with the massively more daunting prospect of having to found a new political order to replace the now defunct Roman order where they could practice this revival of political action. "What the revolutions brought to the fore," Arendt writes,

> was this experience of being free, and this was a new experience, not, to be sure, in the history of Western mankind—it was common enough in both Greek and Roman antiquity—but with regard to the centuries which separate the downfall of the Roman empire from the rise of the modern age. And this relatively new experience . . . [was] at the root of the enormous pathos which we find in both the American and French Revolutions, this ever-repeated insistence that nothing comparable in grandeur and significance had ever happen in the whole recorded history

of mankind, and which, if we had to account for it in terms of successful reclamation of civil rights, would sound entirely out of place.[59]

Indeed, Arendt argues that even the very etymology of the word "revolution," which originally had meant to restore or "revolve back" to a prior order, carried these implications of seeking to reestablish broken political ties.[60]

Arendt claimed that what thwarted these attempts to refound a new public realm in the modern era was the "social question," the fact that modern revolutions became mired in attempts to solve problems related to poverty and other social ills. But the mistake many of her interpreters have made is that they take her to be claiming in *On Revolution* that any concern over social questions is corrosive of any kind of political action whatever. This assumption misses the specific point she was making about the nature of the phenomenon of revolution and the problem of founding new political realms. Since modernity and its scientifically conditioned perspective tended so inexorably toward the social and the politics of consumption as an end in itself, Arendt believed that any attempt to refound a political realm needed to focus solely nonsocial and fundamentally political concerns.[61] The occasional places in the text where Arendt makes comments that seem to support the received interpretations are almost always addressed to the specific context of revolutionary activities, of why they succeed or fail. She writes for instance that "the whole record of past revolutions demonstrates beyond doubt that every attempt to solve the social question with political means leads into terror . . . which sends revolutions to their doom."[62] While this statement might be read in a number of ways, I would argue that it is not claiming that all political interventions in the social question necessarily lead to terror, but only that it does so in the context of revolutions. Thus, when Arendt argued that concern with the social question undermined the goals of the revolutionaries, she was not making a claim about political action in general, but rather a specific point about what kind of character political action must have if actors want to refound a true public realm in the modern context.

Arendt argues that the sole exceptional case of successful revolution was found in America. Indeed, the idea of revolving back seemed surprisingly apt for the American founding experience in that many of the Roman staples of political life and action seemed to reappear in America, such as, for instance, the Supreme Court, which she argues bears the same function as the Roman Senate of augmenting political action with authority derived from a foundational event—in this case, the ratifying of the Constitution. The reason for this American exceptionalism, she claims, was that there already existed conditions of more or less equality of social conditions, at least among those who would be counted in the citizenry. And, moreover, the act of founding was not an act of complete novelty, as in the European revolutions, but instead only ratified practices that had already grown up organically. Arendt's unusual America exceptionalism was likely informed by her biographical experience as a refugee from revolutionary politics, which seemed to lead her, perhaps understandably, toward a distinctive immigrant's patriotic fervor. What she appears to have had in mind was the civically active America that Tocqueville had described.[63] In the last fifteen years, political science research has at least to some degree borne out some of Arendt's claims about American exceptionalism. Robert Putnam and Theda Skocpol have shown that most of American history was characterized by a relatively high degree of civic engagement that has only in the last forty or so years given way to a much more bureaucratic and centralized form of civic life. In fact, Skocpol shows that in *On Revolution* Arendt actually seems to underestimate the amount of civic engagement that took place in America throughout the nineteenth and twentieth centuries.[64]

In contrast to America, the European revolutionary tradition has had a very different experience. Because they had no predeveloped political practices comparable to those of America, and therefore needed to theorize how to found a completely new body politic, the European revolutions turned to categories derived from the tradition of political thought, and this had fateful consequences. The tradition had theorized the idea of founding in terms of the fabrication analogy: in order to bring into existence something new, violence had to be done to what already existed.[65] For Arendt, who argued that the foundation of a public realm emerges from the power generated by people acting together, this was one of the tradition of political thought's greatest errors.[66] Yet, the tradition of political thought could not itself be blamed for the violent forces that were released by the European revolutions. This came from the new Promethean prospects modernity seemed to offer to the common people. These prospects introduced powerful forces of natural necessity into a problem—the problem of founding—which she believed required the total absence of necessity. As a result of this, liberation became the predominate issue of the European revolutionary tradition and overwhelmed the original impulse toward freedom that had initially instigated the French Revolution.[67]

According to Arendt, the French Revolution was a fundamental experience for those who observed it, an experience so profound and novel, it seemed to demand that any political thought that came after it somehow account for that experience. What shocked the revolutionaries and their observers was the fact that the revolutions, beginning most famously with the French, gave birth to bizarre disparities between causes and effects, between the intentions of the actors and the eventual outcomes of the revolutions. These outcomes seemed to render almost absurd the framework of political action as sovereignty and the notion that the fabrication analogy could be a model for founding new political orders.[68] Each time they were attempted, the revolutions twisted out of control and made the revolutionary actors "the fools of history."[69] The observers of the French Revolution literally marveled at what they saw. They were treated to a spectacle that demonstrated events of obviously enormous historical import. These events seemed ultimately to be controlled by no one's obvious intentions, to set off chains of violent events that went in completely unexpected directions. And when the events had finally run their course, it was clear that the meaning of the events was far different from what the actors had intended. Writing of Kant's reaction to the French Revolution, Arendt says that his reaction was "by no means unequivocal . . . he never wavered in his estimation of the grandeur of what he called the 'recent event,' and he hardly ever wavered in his condemnation of all those who had prepared it."[70] She quotes Kant saying:

> The revolution of a gifted people which we have seen unfold in our day may succeed or miscarry; it may be filled with misery and atrocities to the point that a sensible man, were he boldly to hope to execute it successfully the second time, would never resolve to make the experiment at such a cost—this revolution, I say, nonetheless finds in the hearts of all spectators (who are not engaged in this game themselves) a wishful participation that borders closely on enthusiasm, the very expression of which is fraught with danger.[71]

For the generation that followed Kant, the revolution was, if possible, even more significant. Arendt asserts that for Hegel the French Revolution was the central disclosive event of world history (and therefore philosophy and politics), and, as a result, history had to be taken as serious as philosophy or politics: "Hegel opened the dimension of time—the past tells a meaningful story, it unfolds the only true meaning . . . we did not know this before the French Revolution disclosed it . . . [in the] French Revolution, truth bec[ame a] reality: visible [and] concrete."[72]

As a result of all of this, the idea of history came to be seen as a powerful new political category.[73] Utilizing process thinking, spectators of the French Revolution such as Kant, Hegel, and Marx came to believe that, much like the process of expropriation, which has led through human misery to the possibility of unheard of abundance, history in general must contain processes that work behind the backs of humans. Of course, the progressive idea of history well predated the French Revolution. What the French Revolution did, according to Arendt, was to make this idea of progress a fundamental experience, not just for philosophers of history but for the masses who would increasingly become more and more engaged in revolutionary politics. Moreover, Marx and the ideological political movements of the nineteenth century that would follow in his pattern of thought came to believe that if these processes could be identified and harnessed by revolutionary actors, the revolutions might finally be successful and end in the establishment of the long-sought-after freedom. History, it was thought, might be the missing element in the revolutionary dream that squared the circle, allowing liberation to dialectically transform into freedom.[74]

Arendt argues that this solution to the problem of refounding freedom for the modern era was based on Hegel's development of dialectical argumentation.[75] Using dialectical reason, Hegel discovered that the notion that freedom and necessity must necessarily conflict may only be valid in abstraction.[76] When their concrete content is dialectically worked out, however, we see that they can be reconciled in the historical process of freedom. In her course on Marx in 1966, Arendt says that for Hegel "the power of the negative is in all becoming: only because something dies is something else born . . . truth is never contained in a single statement but only in a movement. [Thus], the axiom of contradiction is no longer right . . . in the life process A was non-A and becomes non-A again."[77] She argues that because he accepted contemplation as the highest activity, Hegel's philosophy of history remained within the tradition of political thought's contemplative distance from the political realm. Asserting that contemplation was identical with freedom, he thus argued that freedom was found in recognizing our practical activity as a realization of this freedom.[78] According to Arendt, Hegel incorporated "the two 'worlds' of Plato into one moving whole. The traditional turning from the world of appearance to the world of ideas . . . [or back] takes place in the historical motion itself."[79] As a result of his traditional idealization of contemplation, to the extent he saw his philosophy as a philosophy of history, he was ultimately bound to idealize the existing political circumstances of his era.[80]

Hegel scholars have noted for a number of years now that there is no "method" in Hegel's system, and that his philosophy is inseparable from the concrete content of his substantive philosophical and political traditions.[81] Arendt agreed with this interpretation; however, she argued that Hegel did establish a certain framework of political thinking that turned out to be amenable to a much more politically activist application. Arendt argues that Hegel essentially eliminated completely the distinction between natural law, as the law of historical motion, and positive law. To the extent the modern state had come to be the realization of Absolute Spirit in history, according to Hegel, all its positive laws were fully legitimized by natural law through the realization of the Absolute in history. Arendt believes that Marx, however, sought to "formalize" a method from Hegel's work and, in doing so, attempted to point a natural law of historical motion into the future, as opposed to using it simply to the justify the present.[82] "Hegel's error," Arendt writes, "was that he took account only of the past. Action concerns the future."[83] In doing so, Marx provided the model of the ideological movements that would follow in his wake, eventually resulting in totalitarian politics. According to Arendt,

> dialectic only first developed as a method once Marx deprived it of its actual substantive content. Nowhere has the acceptance of tradition with a concomitant loss of its substantial authority proved more costly than in Marx's adoption of the Hegelian dialectic. By turning dialectic into a method, Marx liberated it from those contents that had held it within limits and bound it to substantial reality. And in doing so, he made possible the kind of process-thinking so characteristic of nineteenth-century ideologies, ending in the devastating logic of those totalitarian regimes whose apparatus of violence is subject to no constraints of reality.[84]

Yet, Arendt believed Marx came far closer than Hegel to recognizing the new political realities of the modern era, and the result was an attempt to solve the problem of liberation and freedom in a manner that did not explain away these new realities in the way that Hegel had. But that attempt would still ultimately remain doomed to failure, because it could not escape the structure of the tradition of political thought.

Arendt argues that Marx recognized that the demand for universal equality in the modern age meant that the solutions Hegel and other representatives of the tradition offered were "only superficially posed in the idealistic assertions of the equality of man, the inborn dignity of every human being, and only superficially answered by giving laborers the right to vote."[85] She claims that Marx recognized that the only human activity in which all human beings, as individuals, were most fundamentally equal was in their capacity to labor as *animal laborans*.[86] Thus, when Marx argues that equality had to be realized in concrete social conditions, and humans had to become "socialized men," this only meant actualizing the condition of modern consumer society as fully as possible.[87] To the extent this consumer society was not as fully realized as Hegel had thought, Marx therefore insisted that philosophy could no longer be concerned with merely "interpreting the world"; it now must change the world.[88] Arendt concludes that this apparent contradiction stems from his belief in the dialectical structure of history. "Marx's own hope, nourished by his belief in the dialectical structure of everything that happens, was that somehow this absolute rule of necessity would result in, or resolve itself into, an equally absolute rule of freedom."[89] Thus, in formalizing Hegel's dialectic, Marx posited that the dialectic was not simply a way of grasping how philosophy realizes itself in our existing daily life, but in fact represented a deep insight—inspired by the modern ideal of process thinking—into the processes at work in history, which could guide political action to bring about conditions that could not be made sense of based on existing circumstances.[90] Marx thus believed that if we allow our revolutionary action to be guided by the laws of history without reference to any clearly defined end goal (what essentially amounts to a kind of historicized deontological account of action), then the liberation that can only come from the abundance of labor and work will somehow allow the circle to be dialectically squared, and revolutionary liberation will finally result in a freedom, the nature of which will only become clear after the dialectic has completed. As a result, Arendt argues, this formalization of Hegel's dialectic in Marx's thought is what led to the well-documented "flagrant contradictions" that arise in his work when he discusses the eventual communist utopia. She points out that almost all Marx scholars have noted the nonsensical nature of the utopia.[91] If labor is humanity's most productive and essential human activity, and labor power the source of human equality, what activity would be performed in the communist utopia when labor was abolished? Similarly, if revolutionary violence was the highest form of political action, what sort of meaningful free action would exist when history had concluded and there was no more need for violence in the utopia?

These contradictions were symptomatic of the unique form of theorizing that followed Hegel, which Arendt calls "turning operations," and which were exemplified in Kierkegaard, Marx, and Nietzsche.[92] The turning operations were pursued because the traditional foundations of Western civilization had been undermined by modern science.[93] They were the last attempts of the tradition of political thought to reconstitute the Western world: they had intuited that in the modern era the old hierarchy of the activities had been inverted by the Archimedean point, and that if the old civilization was to survive, it would have to somehow account for this politically. Yet, each attempt ended in self-defeat. Of the three thinkers, Nietzsche was perhaps the most clear-sighted—the only one who eventually recognized the inevitability of this self-defeat so long as they stayed within the traditional framework, eventually concluding that "together with the true world we abolish the world of appearances."[94] Marx's turning operation involved inverting the traditional hierarchy of activities: where Hegel held to the old assumption that contemplation was the highest human activity, Marx asserted labor as the highest activity. But Marx, like the tradition he still belonged to, degraded action and politics by idealizing an activity (labor instead of contemplation as in Hegel's case), which was essentially speechless.[95] And also like Hegel, Marx asserted that historical necessity was associated with the highest activity, which was now labor; as a result, all politics and philosophy, and thus all action and thought, were asserted to be mere "ideologies"—nothing more than superstructural functions of the society and means of production.[96]

The Emergence of the Modern World

At the height of the modern era of politics, the model of political judgment inherited from the tradition of political thought had thus become what Arendt called "ideological thinking." This, she believed, was Marx's legacy to the question of the relation of thought and action. It is difficult to exaggerate the impact of Marx's work on the nineteenth- and early twentieth-century political scene. Of course, Marxism became one of the major challengers to Western liberal and social democracy. But Marx's influence, particularly his formalizing of Hegel's dialectical reason, arguably had a more enduring formative influence on all modern political thinking after him. Arendt had argued that in modern political thought it was the process, not the thing, that was believed to be real.[97] Thus, even in Western liberal democracies the political options available tend to be understood in "ideological" terms, that is, in terms of certain historical processes dominated by the ebbing and flowing of the "progress" of a certain idea. The left side of the political spectrum tends to be dominated by the idea of the progressing or regressing of the idea of freedom, while the right of side of the political spectrum is dominated by the idea of authority.[98] For Arendt, the reason these ideas have become ideologies understood to operate in opposition to one another is because they have lost their substantive grounding in a common world; in the old Roman world, these two ideas, far from being opposed, would have been thought to be preconditions of one another.

Of course, the assertion that all modern political thinking, even in Western democracies, is essentially ideological carries some highly controversial implications. What *exactly* is an ideology? What role did it play in totalitarian politics and political regimes, and how does ideological politics differ from totalitarianism? Finally, what shifted in the twentieth century that allowed ideologies—which had existed for quite a while before totalitarian politics came into existence—to play the role they came to play in totalitarian political movements and regimes? And, moreover, if, as Arendt suggests, ideologies still play a central role in modern politics, why—other than in the rather watered-down communist versions that existed after Stalin—has ideology not given birth to new brands of totalitarian politics in the postwar era? These are complex political questions for us, and while Arendt did have answers, those answers were at best rather impressionistic.

According to Arendt, after Marx the notion that there are historical processes or laws of historical motion that can guide political action metastasized into a variety of what she calls "isms": nationalism, liberalism, conservatism, imperialism, socialism, capitalism, communism, or racism.[99] These ideologies, in a way similar to Marxism, claimed to be able to offer a "total explanation" of history.[100] Yet, for all the overconfidence they seemed to project, the ideologies were actually a response to a sense of profound insecurity. With the failure to refound Western politics in the radically changed circumstances of the modern era, Arendt argues that the Western world entered a period of historical crisis in the twentieth century.[101] In historical crises, Arendt argues that the "prejudices" that once reliably oriented the inhabitants of a particular world begin to "crumble." But instead of attempting to pass new "judgments," which could establish new prejudices, modern political actors thought to radicalize the now defunct prejudices and instead turn them into "pseudo-theories" or ideologies. Thus, while prejudices were effective in sparing the individual from having to constantly pass judgments on everything he or she encounters, ideologies went much further, claiming to explain all occurrences and thus shield the individual from ever having to pass judgment again.[102] Ideology, in other words, replaced what Arendt had called common sense. Ideology, as she sees it, claims to be a kind of scientifically achieved "super-sense" that is far superior to the old, and now quite unreliable, common sense.[103] As we've seen, the political inspiration for ideologies has its roots in the ancient distinction between *nómos* and *physis*, between the positive laws that give human societies stability and the law of nature that provides the authority of those laws.[104] What Marx achieved, according to Arendt, was to draw out the implications of this idea of natural law if it were actually applied to concrete politics through modern theories of history.[105] If history is governed by certain natural laws, this suggests that positive laws, as stabilizing forces, may in fact come into conflict with the natural law, and since natural law is the source of the authority and legitimacy of those positive laws, the positive laws should lose out in any conflict.[106] But in order to perform such a role, the natural law had to be articulated in a much more historically concrete manner than the earlier modern political philosophers had articulated it. The problem was that virtually any idea could serve as the premise of a natural law of history, and this is what allowed ideological politics to proliferate in the way it did.[107]

Nevertheless, Arendt insists that, though ideologies certainly formed crucial elements of totalitarian politics, they were not identical with totalitarian politics.[108] She argues that for the most part, the abuses ideologies were put to by totalitarian regimes were resisted by the remaining elements of the old world, particularly by the class structure of the modern party system in the nineteenth century. Parties during this period represented certain interests that effectively tied them to a common world, since, for Arendt, to have self-interest implied having a stake in a deeper *inter-est*, an in-between that separates and relates the individuals in the groups. As we will see, totalitarian politics was oddly characterized by a distinctive lack of self-interest and utilitarian calculation.[109] But ideologies turned out to be relatively ineffective at agenda setting in the context of the old class-based party system. Arendt argues that this was because ideologies, as attempts at total explanation, can consistently organize any set of facts in a way that is explained by their idea of historical process. But as a result, the ideologies tended to end up disconnected from the concrete facts of the political situation.[110] This tendency was famously criticized by Eduard Bernstein, the closest associate and protégé of Marx and Engels. Bernstein, after spending several years in labor politics in Germany eventually broke with Marx and Engels after their deaths and suggested that Marxist ideology was having a counterproductive impact on the social democratic parties. He argued that Marx would have never submitted to having his work turned into a kind of political theological dogma, and thus Marxists needed to reembrace "critique," to replace the "cant" in their ideology with "Kant."[111]

The question we are unavoidably left with—indeed, one of the major theoretical lacunae in *The Origins of Totalitarianism*—is why did ideologies begin to have actual political effectiveness in the world during the twentieth century, most catastrophically exemplified in totalitarian politics? The answer Arendt appears to have proposed to this question was that this new effectualness of ideologies did not derive from some shift in the worldly conditions of the nineteenth century, but rather that an entirely new world had emerged in the twentieth century, what she called the "modern world."[112] It was this new world—replacing the modern age of the old Western world—and the strange, unexpected political possibilities it offered, that allowed ideologies, and therefore by extension the tradition of political thought, to have for the first time a genuine political effectiveness and agenda-setting relevance.[113] Though the idea of this new modern world seems to be a highly significant point for her, she seems to have had difficulty formulating and explaining it. She mentions it briefly in the prologue to *The Human Condition*, though, as in other instances, her language is rather oblique and impressionistic, linking it to "the first atomic explosions."[114] Elsewhere in *The Human Condition*, she refers to it as "our technically conditioned world,"[115] while in *Between Past and Future* she calls it a "technological world"[116] and refers to "a chaos of mass perplexities on the political scene and of mass opinions in the spiritual sphere."[117] Beyond these statements, there is not a great deal of detailed theory in her published work. In the following, however, I want to try to flesh out the concept with a somewhat inferential approach, based on some unpublished source material.

In late 1951, Arendt wrote a proposal to the Guggenheim Foundation for support for a projected sequel to *The Origins of Totalitarianism*.[118] One of the major flaws in *Origins* was that the bulk of the evidence it offered concerned the Nazis. Yet, the key claim of the book was that totalitarianism represented a form of government that was not captured in terms of the traditional left-right political spectrum, applying equally to the Soviets and the Nazis whatever their ostensible ideological claims might have been. Because of the lack of evidence concerning the Soviets, *Origins* could not substantiate this central claim and thus seemed to have failed to have convincingly demonstrated the essential commonality of the totalitarian regimes. The Guggenheim proposal is one of the few places where Arendt explicitly recognized this problem. In the proposal, Arendt suggested that the major obstacle in relation to the Soviets was that, unlike the Nazis, Soviet ideology was directly rooted in the tradition of political thought. She believed this presented conceptual perplexities that did not apply in the Nazi case and that made it more difficult to substantiate her claims about the fundamental political commonalities that existed between the Soviets and the Nazis. However, as Arendt worked on the project, she came to believe that the tradition of political thought itself had to be dealt with directly, and most of the early to mid-1950s saw her engaging not just with Marx but with the tradition as a whole.[119] It is often thought that Arendt eventually gave up on the projected Marx book, or at least became more interested in the larger political concerns that resulted in *The Human Condition*. This is true in certain broad terms, but it does not recognize how deeply intertwined the two projects remained for Arendt. It seems that at some point in the process of researching the Marx book Arendt discovered what she came to call the modern world, and she realized that it provided the missing link between the Nazis and the Soviets that allowed their respective and seemingly disparate ideologies to mutate into what amounted to fundamentally similar totalitarian regimes.

The first place the notion of the modern world appears is in a 1953 article called "Ideology and Terror: A Novel Form of Government,"[120] which she eventually edited into the final chapter of *The Origins of Totalitarianism* in the 1966 edition.[121] At this point, the concept of the modern world did not appear to be explicitly formulated yet, but instead seemed to be implicated in her articulation of the phenomenon of totalitarian politics. This is because Arendt seems not yet to have fully developed her crucial political concept of "worldliness," though a close of reading of *Origins* and "Ideology and Terror" shows that it seemed to exist in an inchoate form. While there are moments in the 1966 edition of *Origins* where Arendt does mention the existence of the "common world,"[122] a comparison with the first edition shows that these were additions made to the text after its first publication.[123] Instead, the notion of the common world seemed to run as a kind of undercurrent in the original edition of *Origins*, in such passages as her discussion of the Boers' degeneration from the civilized world,[124] in T. E. Lawrence's attempt to lose himself in the "Great Game" of imperialism and the stream of history,[125] and in her critique of imperialism.[126] By the time of "Ideology and Terror," however, the notion of the common world seems to have gained some significant purchase on her thought, though it was still not given the kind of prominence it would later have. It mainly operates as a kind of implicit explanatory vehicle for accounting for the existence of the political experience of "loneliness" in the twentieth century, which she believed was what allowed totalitarian politics to come to power. The loss of a common world meant that human beings, even though they lived together in a mass society, no longer had a world to separate and relate them. Thus, Arendt argues that totalitarian politics were able to seize upon these masses and move them politically through the internal application of ideology and the external application of terror. While her treatment is highly impressionistic, we can note at least three novel elements of what would eventually come to be called the modern world: the loss of the common world and emergence of mass society; the use of ideology, which Arendt claims was a replacement for common sense; and finally, the ability to apply terror in an extremely effective manner.[127]

When Arendt speaks offhand of the modern world, she tends to suggest that it came into existence with the development of nuclear weapons and the advent of totalitarianism, writing that both the bomb and totalitarianism were "the fundamental experiences of our age, and if we ignore them, it is as if we never lived in the world that is our world."[128] What Arendt seems to have meant by this was that these two experiences were in some way revelatory of the new world we have come to inhabit. It stands to reason that the modern world is constituted by a much broader array of political experiences than these two singular and highly revealing occurrences. Her 1968 lecture course "Political Experiences in the Twentieth Century" appears to demonstrate this by outlining a broad array of political experiences from the twentieth century that begin with the First World War and proceed through the emergence of totalitarianism and the advent of the bomb. The course outline projected that they would discuss nine political experiences: World War I, its aftermath on Western Europe, the Russian Revolution, the broader left-wing search for a new political order, the 1930s consolidation of the totalitarian regimes, World War II, the French Resistance, the Nazi death factories, and Hiroshima.[129] The text of the course suggests that Arendt understood all of these experiences to depict how humans in the first part of the twentieth century perceived the emergence of this new modern world.

Most of the typed sections of the course focus heavily on the meaning of the post–World War I era. The initiation of World War I shocked the world, resulting in an unexpectedly bloody and prolonged affair, and left the participants asking why it had been fought in the first place.[130] The aftermath of the war saw the coming to consciousness of the "Lost Generation," and Arendt believes that few generational nicknames have ever been as apt.[131] The First World War saw the breakdown of the class system, when many of the old social distinctions got lost through postwar economic upheaval and the fact that elites and the lower classes were forced to work and fight shoulder to shoulder during the war. "The most important result," Arendt writes, "the slate was swept clean, [and we saw] the terrible freshness (Sartre) that descended upon the world."[132] She claims that especially among the intellectual and social elites, the war left an unforgettable mark on their consciousness: "war as [a] liberating catastrophe from [the] bourgeois world of security . . . [the] sacrifice [of war allowed one] to show something for one's life."[133] Arendt believed that the war had somehow brought the old world to its conclusive end, and the members of the Lost Generation somehow sensed that they existed in an odd in-between period before a new world had fully come into existence but after the old world had passed. This is the explanation for what she believed was a general trend in the early twentieth-century politics of ideology: the loss of self at the core of self-interest and desire to give oneself over to the movement of history in a mass movement. What the members of the Lost Generation were sensing was the coming of a new world: "nobody seemed sorry for the old world. Everybody seemed eager to build a new one . . . and those that wanted to go back to the old world . . . it was no longer there or they [no longer] fit into it."[134]

Since *The Origins of Totalitarianism*, Arendt had been fascinated by the life of T. E. Lawrence, and there are several pages in the lecture course that are nothing but excerpts from his collected letters. Noting his loss of self-interest, she quotes him saying that he had been "cured of any desire to do anything for himself."[135] Summarizing the ethos of the era as Lawrence exemplified it, she wrote in *Origins* that "the story of T. E. Lawrence in all its moving bitterness and greatness was not simply the story of a paid official or a hired spy, but precisely the story of a real agent or functionary, of somebody who actually believed he had entered—or been driven into—the stream of historical necessity and become a functionary or agent of the secret forces which rule the world."[136] "'I had pushed my go-cart into the eternal stream,'" she quotes him saying,

> "and so it went faster than the ones that are pushed cross-stream or up-stream. I did not believe finally in the Arab movement: but thought it necessary in its time and place." . . . Although Lawrence had not yet been seized by the fanaticism of an ideology of movement, probably because he was too well educated for the superstitions of his time, he had already

experienced that fascination, based on despair of all possible human re-sponsibility, which the eternal stream and its eternal movement exert.[137]

And this became the surprising pathos of the era, according to Arendt, which understood its agency no longer as doing "'a thing for himself nor a thing so clean as to be his own' by giving laws to the world, but has a chance only 'if he pushes the right way,' in alliance with the secret forces of history and necessity—of which he is but a function."[138] In *Origins*, Arendt outlines how this ethos was embraced by the social castoffs and members of the criminal underground, whom she refers to as the mob and who would eventually be-come the fanatical leaders of the mass movements of the era and ultimately of the totalitarian regimes that came to power in the 1930s.[139] Richard Overy, in agreement with Arendt, writes in his 2004 study *The Dictators: Hitler's Ger-many, Stalin's Russia* that

> Hitler, like Stalin, did not pursue power simply for its own sake. The trappings of power seemed to have meant very little . . . but it was power for a particular purpose. Hitler regarded the power he enjoyed as a gift of providence for the German people . . . his personal power was a power assigned by world history. . . . [Hitler and Stalin] were driven in each case by a profound commitment to a single cause, and for differing rea-sons they saw themselves as the historical executors.[140]

Just as Lawrence had, they saw themselves as executors of historical forces whose end results could not be predicted but that had nevertheless filled them with a profound sense of selfless purpose. And these "functionaries" of history were perfectly situated to inspire the masses of the early twentieth century who had lost their world and been financially ruined by the economic and political catastrophes that followed the war. Arendt thus suggested that there was some kind of deep connection between the ideological politics of the era and a growing sense of nihilism that caught hold of the Western world in the early twentieth century.

This connection between ideology, totalitarianism, and nihilism was the-orized in more depth in 1955, when Arendt gave a research seminar at Berke-ley where she presented a revised and expanded version of the argument of *The Origins of Totalitarianism*.[141] This seems to be the closest Arendt ever came to providing a statement of her solution to the problem that the Marx book was intended to solve. Virtually all of the elements found in the original theory of *Origins* are found in 1955 course: anti-Semitism; imperialism and the decay of the nation-state; the political constellation formed between the elites, the mob, and the masses; the ideological political movements; and so on. However, now the nihilistic underpinnings of Arendt's post-*Origins* theory of ideology and terror in totalitarian mass politics are accounted for. Referencing Nietzsche heavily, Arendt asserts that nihilism is the fundamental experience behind all ideologies.[142] The modern world is characterized by a profound "relativism,"[143] and the result has been the chaos of opinions that is modern ideological politics. In this situation where consistency is what defines the truth of an ideology, just as in the case of modern science in general, success is the criterion that defines the truth of a theory or ideology.[144] But it is at this point that the peculiar traits of the modern world take their revenge. Arendt outlines a theory of the history of modern nihilism that proceeds in three stages. The first stage corresponds to the emergence of the modern age, where political action is undertaken within the framework of the means/end category, or in Arendt's words: "Everything is permitted for the sake of something else, but only for this sake. . . . This from Machiavelli to Marx." The second stage is characterized by the shift toward historical movement and ideological politics, as we saw in the case of T. E. Lawrence, and thus, according to Arendt, "everything is permitted, period." In this stage, the idea of a justifying end was effectively abandoned, even in the very obscure senses given by Marx's communist utopia or Nietzsche's superman. But the third stage is the most disturbing and problematic: it is the stage where not just anything is permitted, but where anything is *possible*. She writes that "[previously, what was] permitted was limited by possibilities which were in the human condition on the one hand and nature on the other. This is no longer [the case.] Everything is possible: the change of nature as well as the nature of man."[145] This third stage of nihilism seems to be an early formation of what Arendt means by the modern world.

By the time of *The Human Condition*, Arendt had begun to formulate this final stage of nihilism, that is, the modern world, in terms of what she called "acting into."[146] This was the ideal implied in the notion of the Archimedean point from the very moment it became a concrete possibility with the invention of the telescope, but which she believes has only been fully realized with the coming of the modern world. In this new world, humans could act—and not just think or make—from a truly universal standpoint. In "The Concept of History," Arendt argues that the history of the West can be broken down into eras dominated by certain self-interpretations of the essential faculty of human beings. Since the beginning of the modern age, the faculties of work and labor have successively been used to define the essential characteristic of human beings. The coming of the modern world has signaled, she believed, a new conviction that action was the essential characteristic of human beings. But unlike previous eras, where action's natality was contained by the essential limitations inherent in the human condition, we now have discovered the ability to act from a position outside the human condition and to begin processes that could never have naturally occurred in the context of the facts of human life as it was originally always given to human beings.[147] This is an unnerving proposition. With such potential historical and technological capacities, what in principle is the limit of our human possibilities, and, if we do not know, how could we propose to find them and thus take responsibility for them?

Humanism and Human Limits After the Archimedean Point

Today, it seems that Arendt's worst fears no longer threaten us. In the time since she wrote about totalitarianism and the human condition we have seen Western politics appear to return to a much less ambitious and more stable politics. Arendt might say that Western politics—particularly, after the collapse of the Soviet Union—has abandoned history and the hope of human freedom it was once believed to offer, and has settled for the politics of the *animal laborans* and the quiet, if less than elevated, joys of private life. But the question remains: What is the nature of this stability? Is it real, or is it merely a temporary historical reprieve, rooted in exhaustion at two world wars and the Cold War? Is there still something profoundly dangerous in the way modern politics thinks and judges? Clearly from Arendt's perspective, so long as we do not truly understand what it is we are doing, the existence of the modern world guarantees that, just as the inhabitants of the Western world never imagined the possibility and consequences of the Great War, we will remain in the grip of perils that we may not fully comprehend.

When Arendt suggested that the final stage of nihilism meant that anything was possible, she was, of course, speaking hyperbolically. *The Human Condition* was after all written primarily to explain the worldly conditions of human life, whether the Archimedean point is taken into account or not. The problem is that modern science's Archimedean point has made it much more difficult than it once was to determine human limitations and capabilities, and thus to pass judgment and decide on courses of action. What can be done and what cannot be done, and what the implications are of our doing or not doing them have become ambiguous. In a 1968 lecture on the Archimedean point, Arendt says:

> In other words, what I am pleading for here is a new realization of the factually existing limitations of human beings. To be sure, these limitations can be transcended up to a point, and men have always transcended them—in imagination, in philosophical speculation, in religious faith, in scientific discoveries. Only by transcending limits, moreover, can we become aware of them. . . . [But] the Archimedean point which actually would permit man to know all and to do all can never be reached . . . man can only get lost in the immensity of the universe.[148]

Thus, judgment, if it is to be reliably discovered once again, will require somehow disentangling all of these ambiguities. Is this possible? In a variety of places, Arendt argues that we must learn once again to be humanists.[149] This means that we must learn to be cultivated citizens. Of course, as citizens we cannot know everything, but we can become literate and cultivated enough to make good judgments through dialogue with other literate and cultivated citizens. And in this process of debate and deliberation, Arendt seemed to believe we could come to have a highly developed commonsense connection for the world we live in, even if it is a "technically conditioned world."

However, this humanist ideal is not as easy to attain as it sounds. There are a variety of unfortunate and inappropriate ways of thinking about the world that we have inherited from our modern history that make doing this highly problematic. We have to, in a certain sense, filter out thinking constructed on the basis of modern science from the authentic human activities. Arendt's solution to this problem was to provide authentic articulations of the basic human activities. But these articulations will be pointless if we are not capable of employing the judgment necessary to apply them. Thus, a way of relating thought and action must be discovered that does not fall back into ideological thinking and the tradition's fabricative model of political judgment. In other words, we need an authentic political philosophy. Thus, we now turn to the solution to the problem of thought and action developed by Arendt: her theory of judgment.

5 | Arendt's Theory of Judgment

In Chapter 4, I explored Arendt's account of the formidable political pathologies inherent in modernity. I now want to argue that she understood her theory of judgment to be her fundamental response to this modern predicament. As I have been claiming throughout this study, Arendt believed the modern situation required an authentic form of political philosophy. How does her theory of judgment make this authentic political philosophy possible? The core of Arendt's account of judgment revolved around an attempt to clarify the nature of the phenomenon of common sense and to understand the fundamental role it has in political reflection. The notion of common sense is ancient, extending at least as far back as Aristotle, and probably even further to the Greek sophists. As a widespread colloquial expression, one naturally assumes its meaning is vacuous; yet, the concept has been widely used in numerous languages both past and present, and in nearly all cases indicates a similar phenomenon, one taken seriously by philosophers and statesmen alike in the history of Western political thought. Almost always associated with what Aristotle called "prudence," it seems to denote a kind of worldly wisdom cultivated through natural insight, practical experience, and humanistic education. Arendt virtually always described common sense the same way: It was an intuitive feeling for worldliness, a "sixth sense . . . that fits us into, and thereby makes possible, a common world."[1]

The question of common sense runs like a red thread throughout her mature writings. What defined political and non-sovereign forms of existence for Arendt had to do with whether a functioning common sense related the individuals of a particular world together. The modern failure of common sense dominates *The Origins of Totalitarianism*, providing its central explanatory element.[2] While less often explicitly discussed in *The Human Condition*, it remained pivotal to the book's ultimate argument, which revolved around

Arendt's account of the modern turn from common sense toward technical rationality, or "common-sense reasoning," as she called it, leading to a politics of the human animal species that prioritized labor and hyperconsumption.[3] This attempt to replace common sense with "common-sense reasoning" is her central explanation for the introduction of elements of necessity into politics. We saw in the Chapter 4 how the rise of process thinking and the undermining of the traditional Western world led to an erosion of common sense and the appeal to commonsense reasoning, while in Chapter 3, we saw that it was the philosophers' alienation from common sense that led them to establish the tradition of political thought on the model of a sovereign form of political judgment.[4]

As we've seen, the inability of the revolutionaries to escape the tradition of political thought's sovereign model of judgment was a necessary ingredient in the worst instances of modern tyranny. The tradition of political thought had been unable to offer the revolutionaries what they were truly seeking: a renewal of human freedom in the modern world. Instead, it led to a conception of political action that theorized the act of founding as an instance of fabrication and to a conception of history that justified ideological politics. Arendt believed that what the revolutionaries needed was a more authentic understanding of the relation of thought and action, an authentic political philosophy, which was practiced on the basis of not commonsense reasoning but common sense. Given that philosophy has historically had something of an uneasy relationship with common sense, how could common sense offer philosophy the rationality and universal standards it demands for its practice? This was the deep problem Arendt believed her theory of judgment solved.

Scholars typically focus on several texts in order to reconstruct her theory of judgment: the two essays in *Between Past and Future* dealing with the question of judgment and her lectures on Kant's political philosophy.[5] In her theory, Arendt argues that what is commonly understood as Kantian political philosophy was not very well developed and possibly not even seriously believed by Kant himself.[6] Arendt claims that Kant's authentic political philosophy can only be found in the *Critique of Judgment*, even though he may not have recognized this fact. While this claim at first seemed somewhat outlandish, it has increasingly gained credibility, and not just among Arendt's contemporary proponents but also among philosophers who are interested in using the third *Critique* for moral and political philosophies that are not directly related to Arendt's thought.[7] The basic outlines of her theory are as follows: Taking as her starting point the fact that each of us exists in different locations in the common world and therefore has unique perspectives on it, she argues that any discussion we have about the world and appearances in the world can only take the form of opinion. However, this appeal to opinion does not imply that our judgments are purely subjective. She argues that in the *Critique of Aesthetic Judgment*, Kant articulated the unique form of inter-subjective validity political opinion appeals to, which he called "enlarged mentality." This means that whenever we judge, we implicitly take into account the perspectives of other actors through an act of reproductive imagination, and indeed that the best political judgment is capable of taking in the widest variety of perspectives. Kant argues that enlarged mentality is a kind of hidden faculty implicitly anchored in what we prosaically call common sense, which he refers to by the Latin *sensus communis*.

This theory of judgment has been the subject of numerous attacks. George Kateb and Seyla Benhabib have criticized her theory for an apparent amorality. Kateb argues that her theory was motivated by her "aestheticiza-tion of politics." He believes she was driven to aestheticize politics because she sought to distinguish political phenomena from "the practical, the moral, and the universally truthful."[8] Kateb does not recognize any other possible form of evaluative activity, and so he argues that she must have believed that political evaluations are simply aesthetic evaluations. As a result, Arendtian judgment places too much weight on what amounts to existential standards of judgment, thus becoming dangerously amoral in his view. Benhabib echoes this concern.[9] Arendt draws a strict distinction between morality and politics: morality is a concern with the integrity of the self, while politics is a concern with the world we have in common. Benhabib denies that this separation is possible, for this would mean that political institutions would not be open to criticism from the perspective of universal human rights. She therefore finds Arendt guilty of relativism and irrationality in normative contexts, arguing that there is a "normative lacuna" in Arendt's thought, and "a resistance on her part to justificatory political discourse, to the attempt to establish the rationality and validity of our beliefs in human rights, human equality."[10]

Jürgen Habermas, Ronald Beiner, and Peter J. Steinberger focus on a related problem in Arendt's claim that political judgments are noncognitive and that politics demands that we maintain a strict distinction between truth claims and political opinions.[11] They find this distinction problematic be-cause her account of judgment would then appear to be irrational. Without a cognitive relationship between the competing arguments, they argue, there can be no way of deciding which argument is right. By drawing a distinction between truth and political opinion, Habermas, for instance, believes that Arendt creates a rational gap between differing political opinions, which, he argues, must necessarily involve some kind of truthful relationship between those involved in the debate. Arendt, he argues, has an "antiquated concept of theoretical knowledge" leading to "a yawning abyss between knowledge and opinion that cannot be closed with arguments."[12] Ronald Beiner raises similar worries, arguing that political opinions must appeal to at least some version of truth.

A different line of criticism comes from Beiner and Richard Bernstein, who argue that there appears to be a fundamental contradiction in Arendt's theory of judgment.[13] Bernstein argues that there is a tension between two different contexts in which judgment seems to appear in her work: politics and intellectual life.[14] He argues that in essays such as "The Crisis in Culture," judgment seems to appear in a more deliberative capacity, as a kind of practical wisdom like *virtù* or *phronēsis*. But later in *The Life of the Mind*, judgment seems to take on a different sense, according to Bernstein. Arendt places much less emphasis on its prospective qualities and much more on its retrospective qualities. In the later works, judgment seems to become a matter of contemplation, of passing judgment on what has already happened. In his "Interpretive Essay" to *Lectures on Kant's Political Philosophy*, Beiner agrees with Bernstein's position, arguing that there is no other conclusion to be drawn than that Arendt simply had two different theories of judgment: an earlier, more political and practical one, and a later contemplative and retrospective one.[15] Bernstein, for his part sees in this "a deep tension between acting and thinking," evident throughout her work, which she never reconciled.[16]

This apparent duality in Arendt's theory of judgment led Beiner to another line of criticism.[17] He argued that Kant's account of judgment in the *Critique of Aesthetic Judgment* is an explicitly reflective activity, and thus has no structural capacity to accommodate teleological judgments. While it is, of course, perfectly appropriate to articulate a nonteleological account of judgment in the context of the human capacity to reflect on the beautiful, politics inevitably involves purposes. As a result, Arendt's account of political judgment, particularly in the Kant lectures, appears to be inadequate or, at best, incomplete.

Finally, other critics also have problems with the basic project of reappropriating Kant's aesthetics for politics.[18] Andrew Norris focuses on the notion of *sensus communis* that Arendt borrows from Kant. Relying heavily on the version of *sensus communis* Kant provides in the deduction section, he argues that Arendt misinterprets Kant's account of *sensus communis*. When this misinterpretation is recognized, any philosophical a priori justification for applying Kantian *sensus communis* to politics becomes untenable. Arendt's theory, he argues, may therefore be "suggestive," but it lacks any true philosophical standing.[19] Peter Steinberger, working along similar lines, is even more critical, claiming that Arendt's use of the third *Critique* in this way ultimately ends in the very real potential for "nihilism" in her politics.[20]

Clearly, Arendt's theory of judgment seems to have had an unusual capacity to capture intelligent people's interest; but it has also, however, seemed to leaving them unsatisfied. In the following, I am going to try to explain how these worries can be addressed. I believe that none of these attacks, in fact, are finally justified. Benhabib and Kateb do not recognize how far Arendt expands the scope of political judgment. While Benhabib, for instance, is correct that Arendt does define morality as a concern with the self and politics as a concern with the world, her critique fails to recognize that in doing this Arendt dramatically expanded the purview of political judgment, so that many of the elements we associate with moral judgment now appear in the realm of political judgment. What Benhabib considers a normative lacuna is simply Arendt's aversion to rationalist justifications of universal norms. As for Habermas and others' worries about the distinction Arendt draws between truth and political opinion, Arendt is on much firmer ground than they think. To draw a distinction between truth and political opinion does not necessarily indicate an "abyss" between them. Arendt is only arguing that these are two different activities that complement one another but that still must be sharply distinguished. Beiner and Bernstein's concerns with the apparent conflict between the judgment of the actor and the spectator in Arendt's work is similarly unfounded. While their recognition of the conflict between thought and action in Arendt indicates a subtle engagement with her work, as we have seen, Arendt was well aware of this conflict and was pursuing a resolution to the problem in her work on judgment. The fact that for Arendt politics and history were essentially the same activity indicates that there were not two different theories of judgment in her thought. Rather, it only indicates two different perspectives on judgment: one anchored in the *vita activa*'s worldly engagement and one anchored in the *vita contemplativa*'s gap between past and future. Moreover, more recent literature on the third *Critique* shows that, contra Beiner, there likely is a place for interested elements in Kant's account of aesthetic judgment and that the pure judgments of taste Beiner has in mind in his teleological critique were introduced by Kant mainly for purposes of transcendental deduction. Finally, critics such as Norris who suggest that Arendt's use of Kantian *sensus communis* is flawed have a point to a certain extent. Nevertheless, their conclusions go too far: even if the initial deduction of *sensus communis* in SS20-21 cannot be directly applied to politics as Norris probably rightly claims, this does not necessarily mean that Arendt cannot appeal to the same phenomenological validity she appeals to in other aspects of her work, such as her various articulations of the *vita activa* or *vita contemplativa*. In other words, even if Arendt abandoned the formal deduction—and it appears she did sometime after 1964—she could still claim that any possible political experience demands a capacity for common sense in terms that closely resemble Kantian *sensus communis* as it is articulated in the rest of the third *Critique*. Such a claim is not merely "suggestive," at least not in the sense Norris seems to mean it. Indeed, in his view any phenomenological argument would then have to be considered merely suggestive.

Understanding Arendt's theory of judgment first requires understanding the theoretical problems that she believed it solved. We will see that what led to her theory of judgment was an ongoing research agenda concerned with clarifying the nature of common sense and its relationship to politics. What led her to Kant's account of judgment was her apparent recognition of a long-standing inability of traditional practical philosophy to account for the rationality of judgment. In the lead up to her turn to Kantian judgment, Arendt appears to have recognized that the concept of common sense, which had anchored so much of the history of reflection on practical reason and which also had been so central to her work to that point, appeared to be rationally ambiguous. What she discovered in Kant was an account of how common sense could truly offer a unique source of rationality. This hidden faculty of "enlarged mentality" that Kant articulated appeared to offer a genuine account of the unique rationality of judgment and, as a result, to perhaps offer the key to an authentic form of political philosophy.

The Validity of Common Sense

Like many other aspects of her thought, Arendt's theory of judgment developed over time. Unfortunately, as in these other aspects, much of the development of her ideas occurred only in her mind and, indeed, possibly only at a rather intuitive level. Thus, we occasionally see her articulate an idea and then several years later return to the idea, having developed it far beyond what it had previously been. As a result, reconstructing the rational development of Arendt's ideas often requires quite a bit of inference. This is perhaps most dramatically the case in the context of her theory of judgment: initially, it is so highly Heideggerian that it anticipates crucial ideas in Gadamer's *Truth and Method*; yet, it eventually concludes in a quite significant break from the earlier Heideggerian theory in her turn to Kantian judgment. Because Arendt never explains exactly why she made this turn, reconstructing her theory of judgment will require a broader contextual analysis of her theory and some well-informed inference.

Arendt's formulation of common sense as a sixth sense that fits us into the common world is strikingly, if unsurprisingly, Aristotelian, linking together Aristotle's two conceptions of common sense.[21] Aristotle's comments on common sense are sporadic and fragmentary, and reconstructing his account of it involves a certain degree of hermeneutic license. The first idea is *koinē aísthēsis*.[22] A highly subjectivist and psychological formulation, it posited that in order for the five senses to be useful, there must be some intuitive sixth sense that synthesizes the data of our senses and fits it into experience, thus enabling us to practically engage with our environment. The second idea—found in the *Rhetoric*—he calls *endoxa*: an understanding of the implicitly shared opinions of one's political community.[23] While Aristotle never explicitly links *endoxa* with *koinē aísthēsis*, David Summers argues that there are strong indications that Aristotle believed they were.[24] Aristotle also never explicitly refers to either term in his discussion of practical reason in the *Nicomachean Ethics*,[25] but it has traditionally been surmised that *phronēsis* was reliant on both common senses. When Roman humanists considered the education and culture necessary to instill political judgment and virtue in Roman citizens, they linked the two terms under the Latin word for *koinē aísthēsis*: *sensus communis*. This practice continued in Renaissance era humanism and went on to strongly influence eighteenth-century commonsense philosophers and, indeed, Kant himself in the *Critique of Aesthetic Judgment*.[26]

Arendt's Aristotelian definition of common sense no doubt came from her Heideggerian philosophical background; indeed, her initial pre-Kantian accounts of judgment are highly reliant on Heidegger. This is evident in her initial engagement with the question of philosophy and politics in 1954. There she attacks, as a philosophical prejudice, Aristotle's limitation of *phronēsis*, or practical reason, to solely a faculty of action, arguing that outside the philosophical tradition Greek common opinion understood thought and action both to be relevant to *phronēsis*.[27] She argues that the current Greek opinion, exemplified in Sophocles' *Antigone*, understood *phronēsis* as "understanding and this on its highest level." In *Antigone* "action and thought are almost one and same, summed up as it were and bound together in the great words with which man meets his destiny and asserts himself in his essentially human condition . . . this insight is finally *eudaimonia* . . . the state in which the meaningfulness of the human condition as a whole is revealed at every single moment to one particular human being."[28] There can be little doubt that this existentialist revision of *phronēsis* was inspired by Heidegger. As we saw in Chapter 1, Heidegger's philosophy was an existentialist rearticulation of Aristotelian practical reason; Heideggerian *phronēsis* asserted that true action was only possible after it was given meaning by authentic thought in a confrontation with mortality.[29] As a result, Heidegger understood thought to be a form of action, and indeed the highest kind of action. But this apparent identity of thought and action in Heidegger's *phronēsis*, not to mention Arendt's own early theory of judgment, seems increasingly to have nagged Arendt. In her later Kant-inspired theory of judgment, she would seek to make clear distinctions between the activities of thought, action, and judgment.

This initial attempt to theorize judgment was not coincidentally her most Heideggerian attempt; indeed, it was so Heideggerian that it anticipated many of Gadamer's ideas in *Truth and Method* (1960). Both the early Arendt and Gadamer rely heavily on *Being and Time*'s book 5. As we have seen, the two parts of *Being and Time* are organized around Aristotle's two forms of practical reason: *techne* dominates the first part, while the second part outlines Heidegger's contemplative and existentialist version of *phronēsis*. *Being and Time*'s arguably most important philosophical contribution is the idea of "being-in-the-world," and Heidegger spends the pivotal and highly influential book 5 analyzing its constitutive concept "being-in." Arendt's Aristotelian formulation of common sense appears to be simply a more accessible phrasing of Heidegger's "being-in." Being-in incorporates both Aristotelian versions of common sense: the practical, utilitarian know-how of *koinē aísthēsis*, along with the capacity for cultural and historical evaluation of *endoxa*.[30] This initial account of judgment comes in her 1954 essay "Understanding and Politics." Like Gadamer in *Truth and Method*, Arendt's argument is framed in classic hermeneutic terms of the interpretative circle's virtuous circulation between knowledge and understanding. Understanding is our precognitive ability to deliberate and act practically, a kind of contextual intelligence of our human world's structures and cultural meanings. Knowledge gives us a clearer understanding of our context, helping us to improve our practical deliberations. Understanding precedes and succeeds cognition, providing the contextual framing that our pursuits of knowledge must always start off from and return to. In the article, "understanding" combines elements of the faculties Arendt would later distinguish as thought and judgment. She describes understanding as "a process which never produces unequivocal results"; that it is "an unending activity, by which . . . we come to terms with and reconcile ourselves to reality, that is, try to be at home in the world."[31] These are all descriptions we find Arendt later using with reference to thinking in works such as "Thinking and Moral Considerations" and *The Life of the Mind*. On the other hand, other elements of Arendt's discussion of understanding would later characterize her account of the faculty of judgment. In the early essay, she links judgment to the final conclusion of the interrelationship of knowledge and understanding, calling it "true understanding."[32] As with Gadamer, this true understanding "always returns to the judgments and prejudices which preceded and guided the strictly scientific inquiry" in order to give it a more profound meaning, and thus start the process over again. The faculty that allows this circular process of understanding is "common sense." She calls common sense the "Ariadne thread" that ties the results of research back to the origins of the inquiry in lived experience.[33]

However, three years later Arendt significantly altered her views on judgment. Her thought journal shows that she took extensive notes on Kant's *Critique of Judgment* in August of 1957.[34] In a letter to Jaspers dated August 29, 1957, Arendt wrote that she had been "reading the *Kritik der Urteilskraft* with increasing fascination. There, and not in Kant's *Kritik der praktischen Vernunft*, is where Kant's real political philosophy is hidden."[35] From that point forward, her discussions of judgment would be expressed in Kantian aesthetic terms, such as impartiality, representative thought, enlarged mentality, and *sensus communis*.[36] This move represents an arguably surprising shift for someone with her philosophical background, particularly given that the logic of his Heidegger-inspired account of judgment led Gadamer in *Truth and Method* to attack Kant for formalizing *sensus communis* by situating it as a faculty of the subject, thus dislodging it from its substantive cultural background.[37] If that is so, it raises a number of puzzling questions: What did Arendt find unsatisfactory in the earlier, hermeneutic theory that demanded the introduction of Kant's *Critique of Aesthetic Judgment*? What did she discover in the third *Critique* that resolved those inadequacies? Why did she ultimately side with Kant's formal and subjectivist account of *sensus communis* over Heidegger and Gadamer's more substantive and communitarian version?

Arendt's thought journal indicates that Kant appeared to resolve at least two problems in the earlier hermeneutic theory. First, it explained the relationship between judgment and the radically potent version of action she had recently theorized in the just completed manuscript of *The Human Condition*. Her notes show that she recognized this relationship to have been implicitly theorized by Kant in his discussion of taste and genius. She writes in note 34, August 1957, "Auch verhält sich Urteil und Tat in der Politik genau wie Geschmack und Genie" (Also, in politics judgment and action behave like taste and genius).[38] This recognition would become the pivotal moment of her most important account of judgment in the 1970 version of her *Lectures on Kant's Political Philosophy*. Second, it offered a crucial refinement to her earlier hermeneutic account of *sensus communis*. Writing mainly in German, she notes that the *Critique of Aesthetic Judgment* appealed to an unusual kind of *Gültigkeit*, or validity, different from the universal validity of the first *Critique*, a validity that she finds Kant calling a *subjektive Allgemeingültigkeit*, a subjective general validity.[39] She argues that when Kant uses the German word for "universality," *Allgemein*, in the *Critique of Aesthetic Judgment* he actually means "generality," since in German *Allgemein* can mean either. Arendt notes that this is explicitly opposed to the universal validity of the first *Critique* ("im Gegensatz zu universaler Geltung").[40] In contrast to the compelling effect the first *Critique's* universal validity has on the mind, this subjective general validity "lays claim to validity but without compelling in the least."[41] This concern with finding a kind of validity that does not compel the mind but that still may be considered legitimate remained the central concern in her ensuing accounts of judgment.[42] Indeed, in her first version of lectures on Kant's political philosophy in 1964, Arendt repeatedly asserts that she is seeking an "a priori principle"[43] that will prove "that man is essentially a political being."[44] Though it is not clear that she proves this, the principle she believes can do this is common sense. "The question is: Is common sense a constitutive principle of experience, something without which experience would not be possible . . . ?"[45] It seems likely that this would have remained the central focus of her unwritten "Judging" section in *The Life of the Mind*, since she appears to have held to it well into her research on the *vita contemplativa*. As late as the 1972 conference on her work, Arendt continued to characterize her work on judgment as centrally concerned with discovering a kind of "validity" in judgment that was unique to the political sphere.[46]

To my knowledge, Arendt never explicitly stated what she found problematic in the earlier Heideggerian theory of judgment that would have motivated this turn to Kant; thus, it is at this point that we must draw some inferences. Based on her comments in the thought journal, I believe we can be confident in surmising that the problem she saw in the earlier theory must have taken something like the following argument: Arendt appears to have concluded that hermeneutic theories of judgment are rationally incomplete because they contain a practical aporia rooted in the ambiguous status of common sense, which dates all the way back to Aristotle's original failure to account for the relation between *koinē aísthēsis* and *endoxa*. Hermeneutic theories of judgment ultimately cannot explain how common sense can be the source of better or worse judgments—why given similar knowledge, a better judge should consistently make better decisions than poorer judges—because they merely force the two concepts together without truly explaining how they provide standards to each other. Without an account of their relation to each other, any account of practical reason is conceptually driven to accept one or the other version of common sense as the default standard, that is, it must either accept a standard that is idiosyncratic to the individual or one based on the absolute authority of the community. While empiricists are ultimately driven to the former, phronetic theories such as Heidegger's, Gadamer's, and the early Arendt's must adopt the *endoxa* of the individual's community as their default standard. But when such a highly communitarian standard of common sense is accepted, we are logically unable to explain how there could be rational deviations in the behavior of individuals taking part in a particular *endoxa*. The only way to escape this trap is to find an experience one could appeal to outside its framework, such as Heidegger's concept of authenticity rooted in a confrontation with one's mortality or Gadamer's later apparent turn to Platonic metaphysics. In Heidegger's case, this led back to a profoundly private articulation of phronetic judgment, one that has no validity beyond the individual's life story. In order for there to be an appropriate standard located directly in the phenomenon of common sense, what is needed is an account of common sense that is more intersubjective than *koinē aísthēsis* but that does not lose itself in the absolute authority of community's *endoxa*. Arendt believed that with his notion of a "subjective general validity," Kant was the first to give a genuine account of how this was possible.[47] The problem was that Kant understood this validity to be limited to aesthetic judgment. Arendt therefore would have to show that it could be applied to her own concerns with politics and practical reason and, moreover, explain why Kant did not do so himself.

The Political Elements of the Third *Critique*

I want now to examine the elements of the *Critique of Judgment*[48] on which Arendt based her theory of political judgment. As is well known, Arendt died before she was able to write the "Judging" section of *The Life of the Mind*, and thus we do not know for certain how she would have articulated that faculty within her most comprehensive account of the *vita contemplativa*. Nevertheless, there should be little doubt that Arendt's interpreters, since Ronald Beiner's editing of the 1970 Kant lectures, have been correct to assume the "Judging" section would be drawn in some way from the Kant lectures. All of her statements about judgment in *The Life of the Mind* suggest that she would have drawn on Kant's *Critique of Aesthetic Judgment* in her articulation of the faculty of judgment and furthermore suggest that she would have appealed to her unique interpretation of Kant's political philosophy in formulating this account of judging.[49] The problem, or perhaps rather the limitation, involved in relying on the 1970 lectures is that of the thirteen lectures in the course, only the last four are directly concerned with Kant's account of the faculty of judgment in the *Critique of Aesthetic Judgment*. The preceding nine lectures are concerned with justifying her claim that the *Critique of Aesthetic Judgment* should have been part of Kant's political philosophy and with showing how this reinterpretation of Kant's political and aesthetic work fits into her own ideas. Arendt's description of judgment in these last four lectures was somewhat perfunctory and truncated, and therefore many of the ideas discussed have a rather suggestive quality. However, there is an earlier version of her lectures on Kant's political philosophy from 1964 that deals with the *Critique of Aesthetic Judgment* far more substantially. Adding the 1964 version to 1970 version, together with her notes from the *Denktagebuch* and Kant's *Critique of Judgment* itself, allows us to arrive at a fairly clear picture of her theory of political judgment. However, before turning to the third *Critique* it will be helpful to briefly discuss its philosophical context.

Eighteenth-century accounts of practical reason carried remarkably analogous problems to those Arendt was confronting in her own work on judgment. Indeed, it appears that given the era's philosophical milieu, the notion of applying the third *Critique* to moral and ethical judgment almost certainly occurred to Kant, and the more interesting question may in fact be why he himself did not. When the *Critique of Pure Reason* appeared, Kant was well aware of its epochal significance. He quickly recognized, however, that his peers did not appreciate this, largely due to its distance from the era's mainstream thinking.[50] Kant believed the Enlightenment's central commitment should be to the ideal of rational individual autonomy and felt he had provided a superior foundation for this. However, he had also placed a paradigmatically vast gulf between himself and his contemporaries. Eighteenth-century philosophers were fascinated by aesthetic experience, widely speculating on its link to practical reason, including the precritical Kant himself.[51] With his deontological and rationalist account of moral reasoning, Kant essentially asserted that his contemporaries' ideas were outmoded. As a result, the third *Critique's* major professional motivation became to show how Kant's critical philosophy addressed the significant ideas of that period.

The major competitor to the Enlightenment in Germany was the Sturm und Drang movement led by Johann Georg Hamann, Johann Wolfgang von Goethe, and Kant's former student Johann Gottfried Herder. The Sturm und Drang had a strong affinity toward romantic nationalism and was an outlet for impulses that challenged the Enlightenment's emphasis on reason, individual autonomy, and cosmopolitanism. Herder developed highly communitarian theories of language, interpretation, historical culture, and aesthetics, which strongly influenced many of the thinkers that led to Heidegger. By the 1770s, a rivalry had developed between Kant and Herder. Kant seemed to view Herder as representative of dangerous tendencies in the Sturm und Drang toward irrationalism, often caricaturing Herder's actual opinions (to be fair, these were not always easy to discern). Herder had begun associating himself with what Kant called the movement's "cult of genius," which challenged the Enlightenment by arguing that the pure originality of true genius expressed the spirit of a culture and land, transcending rules and rationality. Kant viewed this as the intellectual legitimation of impulses that led to "enthusiasms" and fanaticism and was determined to show that even these experiences were governed by rationally autonomous principles.[52]

However, Kant also wanted to connect his critical philosophy with the earlier language of the Enlightenment. British empiricists, such as Shaftesbury, Burke, Hutcheson, Kames, and Hume, and German Enlightenment thinkers, such as Baumgarten, Meier, and Mendelssohn had speculated about the relation between moral and aesthetic judgment, linking both to certain feelings or "sentiments."[53] Common sense was often invoked, though how it functioned and the way it provided standards for particular judgments widely varied.[54] Greatly influencing Kant had been Hume's distinction between moral and aesthetic sense, which asserted that moral sentiments are based on interests properly understood and therefore on reason, but that taste was based in common sense.[55] But Hume had observed a paradox in aesthetic judgment, in that while such judgments are inevitably subjective they must somehow not be *fully* subjective, since then it would be impossible to criticize them.[56] He eventually concluded that only an empirical consensus among qualified critics could be appealed to, one that was bound by "the different humours of particular men," and "the particular manners and opinions of our age and country."[57]

By the 1760s, Kant had absorbed most of the significant British literature, whether through secondary sources or translations.[58] Prior to beginning work on his critical philosophy, Kant appeared to have a similar sentiment-based approach to morality and aesthetics. Although his eventual universalist ethics can be detected, it was connected to moral feeling concerning the dignity of mankind.[59] As for taste, he agreed with his British contemporaries that its standard must be an empirical consensus. After the *Critique of Pure Reason* appeared, Kant argued for the categorical imperative as the a priori principle of morality, while continuing to suspect that the standard of aesthetic judgment could only be a posteriori.[60] But by 1787 Kant had changed his mind, indicating in a letter that he had only recently worked out an a priori principle of taste.[61] The establishment of such a principle would have been highly significant to his goals for the Enlightenment. It would have brought clarity to the Enlightenment's disparate speculations on the relationship between moral and aesthetic judgment, while also damaging the German Enlightenment's main competitor, the Sturm und Drang.

As in the first two *Critiques*, Kant illustrated the problem with an antinomy: The feeling of pleasure in the beautiful is subjective, thus leading me to assert that my claim of beauty is only valid for myself; yet, when I claim something is beautiful, I am asserting that *everyone* should also find it beautiful. [62] This recalls Hume's paradox, but it also echoes the practical aporia of hermeneutic theories of judgment: Is there a principle of judgment that is able to account for the possibility of legitimate differences of opinion and better or worse judgments? If I find a poem profound while you find it clichéd, is it possible that *both* our opinions might be valid, but also possible for one of our opinions to be better than the other? This is the question Kant attempts to answer in the third *Critique*.

Kant locates the domain of judgment in the faculty of "the feeling of pleasure and displeasure;"[63] judgment, therefore, in some sense is a feeling.[64] But Kantian judgment is a very complex feeling, a feeling that reflexively interacts with a variety of mental faculties, thus making it a kind of *intelligent* feeling.[65] In the 1964 lectures, Arendt points out in the course of her discussion of the feeling of the sublime that Kant had a long-standing and wide-ranging interest in such complex and intelligent feelings. She points out that two different intelligent feelings are indicated—the feeling of respect and the feeling of the sublime—when, at his most lyrical, Kant wrote at the end of the second *Critique*, "Two things fill the mind with ever new and increasing admiration and wonder, the more frequently and persistently one's mediation deals with them: *the starry sky above me and the moral law within me.*"[66] These two feelings are indicative of the philosophical tradition's contemplative experience of *thaumazein*, "the speechless wonder before the whole of Being."[67] Judgment was yet another complex feeling, but in this case Arendt believed it was a much more political feeling than these earlier philosophical feelings.

Kant opens the third *Critique* with an introduction that is interesting for several reasons. He is attempting to explain the role of judgment within the constructive epistemology of his critical philosophy, and in order to do this he is led for the first time to provide the entire framework of his constructive epistemology. In the first *Critique*, Kant somewhat cursorily presents judgment as a rather mysterious faculty. In an early version of Wittgenstein's rule-following argument, he points out that in the context of cognition, where judgment's function is to subsume particulars under given universals, any rule we establish for this process requires yet another rule for its application, and so on indefinitely.[68] Judgment in the first *Critique* is simply the faculty that puts an end to this indefinite application of rules: "And thus we find that, whereas understanding is capable of being taught and equipped by rules, the power of judgment is a particular talent that cannot be taught at all but can only be practiced."[69] The reason for this cursory treatment seems to have had to do with the nature of transcendental argumentation. It is only possible to identify a faculty's a priori principles if it can be shown that the faculty is in some respect autonomous. For Kant, the various faculties of the human mind (understanding, reason, imagination, judgment, and so on) interact differently depending on the context of experience or "domain," as he calls it. In each domain, one faculty is legislative, providing the essential principles of that domain, while the other faculties support it. In the theoretical domain understanding is the legislative faculty, while in the practical domain reason is legislative.[70] To the extent understanding and reason are not determined by other faculties within their respective domains but instead legislate to those faculties, they are autonomous in those domains, and this is what allows us to search for their a priori principles. Thus, in order to show that this mysterious faculty of judgment had a genuine rationality of its own, Kant needed to find a realm of experience where judgment was autonomous, where its functioning was not determined by another faculty but where it legislated to itself.[71] If he could find this, it could then be possible to identify and justify a priori the structure of judgment, and he believed he had found this in aesthetic experience. Thus, in the first introduction, he writes that "it is actually only in taste . . . that judgment reveals itself as a [faculty] that has its own principle and hence is justified."[72]

The rather loose tie that binds the two parts of the *Critique of Judgment* together is the concept of purposiveness. Kant believes that judgments of taste involve what he calls a "merely formal purposiveness."[73] We find an object beautiful, according to Kant, when its form seems to have been purposively made to appeal to the way our cognitive powers are made.[74] This is crucial because Kant must establish that what is being judged is not the object itself, but rather the response of the subject's cognitive faculties to the beautiful form of the object, which is itself largely produced by the subject's faculties."[75] Since it would be "ridiculous" for someone with taste to claim that his pleasure in the beautiful is idiosyncratic to himself,[76] Kant reasons that beauty cannot be something perceived directly through sense data. We may experience gratification or agreeableness in an attractive object, but the feeling of pleasure we experience in this case has no claim to validity on other human beings, since it is unavoidably idiosyncratic to our interests. In other words, in order for the feeling of pleasure to be universally communicable to other subjects, we must not have an interest in it, because interest is always particular to who we are as individuals.[77] The pleasure in the beautiful, according to Kant, is a "disinterested delight," a pleasure that is "disinterested and free," since "all interest either presupposes a need or gives rise to one."[78] He argues that the form of the beautiful object sets off a spontaneous interaction of our faculties of cognition and imagination, what he calls a harmonious "free play" among them, and since the domain of cognition is universally communicable this means that the pleasure experienced in their free play is also universally communicable.[79]

To this point, however, no aesthetic judgment has been passed, though some form of cognitive empirical judgment has been, according to Kant.

Kant has only shown that the pleasure in the form of the beautiful object is disinterested and universally communicable. There is still no explanation and justification for judgments of taste, and therefore no account of how aesthetic experience gives insight about the faculty of judgment. A second moment must now take place where I must judge my feeling of disinterested delight. This decision is not based on my own personal inclinations, but by an appeal to an essential structure of judgment that allows me to take a perspective that stretches far beyond my own inclinations. Kant calls this essential structure of judgment *sensus communis*. In her interpretation of Kant, Arendt insists that it is only in this second moment that aesthetic judgment occurs.[80] Kant's appeal to *sensus communis* is clearly the most important concept in the third *Critique* to Arendt. In the 1964 lectures she not only examines Kant's account but also discusses precursors who likely influenced Kant, such as Dubos, Muratori, Gracian, Gottsched, Baumgarten, and Cicero.

Kant first describes *sensus communis* in *S*20 of the third *Critique*, as an implicit sense that must be presupposed so that there can be an "attunement" between the mental faculties.[81] As noted earlier, Norris has argued with some justification that this initial account of *sensus communis* cannot be convincingly applied to nonaesthetic phenomena. However, in *S*40 Kant's account of common sense becomes much more intuitive, and so much so that it is hard to see how the accounts from *S*20 and *S*40 are even the same phenomenon. In *S*40, he explains how *sensus communis* draws on the faculty of reproductive imagination, stating that "we must here take *sensus communis* to mean the idea of a sense *shared* by all of us, i.e., a power to judge, that in reflecting takes account (a priori), in our thought, of everyone else's way of presenting something, in order *as it were* to compare our own judgment with human reason in general."[82] Kant's name for this process is "enlarged mentality," to which he gives the following definition: "Now we do this as follows: we compare our judgment not so much with the actual as rather with the merely possible judgments of others, and thus put ourselves in the position of everyone else, merely by abstracting from the limitations that may happen to attach to our own judging."[83] In other words, when we decide if our pleasure in the beautiful should be approved or disapproved of, the appeal to *sensus communis* is not to our own idiosyncratic judgments but rather to an imagined standpoint that takes into account how other judges would judge our feeling. It is crucial to understand, however, that this appeal to common sense is not a decision procedure. In the moment of judging, I do not try to think up different standpoints, as Kant's initial formulation here might suggest. Kant almost immediately qualifies his description: "Now perhaps this operation of reflection will seem too artful to be attributed to the ability we call *common* sense. But in fact it only looks this way when expressed in abstract formulas."[84] Enlarged mentality is not a procedure of thought, but a standpoint I cultivate removed from my private point of view, which takes in others' points of view, and it is from this broader standpoint that I pass judgment. Arendt quotes Kant saying: "However small may be the area or the degree to which a man's natural gifts reach, yet it indicates a man of *enlarged thought* if he disregards the subjective private conditions of his own judgment, by which so many others are confined, and reflects upon it from a *general standpoint*."[85] In other words, someone with common sense always, of course, has her own partial point of view; but she also has a kind of second point of view, a more expansive viewpoint that by its very nature is political in the broadest sense.

At this point, however, Kant's analysis leaves some things to be desired, in that several implicit features of his account of taste should have been better fleshed out. First, there is, at least prima facie, an ambiguity concerning the relationship between the pure judgments of taste and the aesthetic object. This, of course, recalls a general question of Kantian epistemology (i.e., the status of noumena and phenomena), but it is clearly relevant to the specific nature of Kant's aesthetics: to wit, does the actual object of taste—or, in Arendt's case, politics—have any causal relation to a judgment of taste. This is perhaps more damaging to Arendt than to Kant: one of the objections to Arendt's use of Kant is that in order to be truly disinterested pure judgments of taste seem to be limited to a very small category of phenomena, and it is unclear how political judgments could ever be truly free of interest.[86] However, as both John Zammito and Henry Allison note, there appear to be two forms of aesthetic judgments in the *Critique of Aesthetic Judgment*: what we might call pure and impure judgments of taste.[87] Kant's chief interest in pure judgments of taste appears to have been related to the specific argument of the transcendental deduction. Though Kant does not state it explicitly enough, any attentive reading shows he clearly understands that the vast majority of aesthetic judgments have some kind of interested element, such as books, poems, songs, or physical human beauty. Obviously, these are the kinds of judgments that dominate the section concerned with fine art and genius and would also, if Arendt is right, then be the kind of judgments involved in political and ethical questions. Norris's critique of Arendt's use of Kant is mainly directed at the deduction's pure judgments of taste and does not appear to recognize that Kant understood most judgments of taste to involve at least some elements of interest.

Second, Kant only implicitly deals with the reflexive, ongoing effect of taste on the feeling of pleasure in the beautiful, that is, judgment's capacity over time to develop and cultivate this feeling in more subtle and sensitive ways. The fact that he assumes this reflexive capacity for cultivation is evident in any of Kant's comments and articulations of artistic and critical experience. Kant, for instance, argues that aesthetic and artistic judgment is best culti-vated by judging other exemplary instances of fine art. He writes that "for all fine art, insofar as we aim at its highest degree of perfection, the propaedeu-tic does not consist in following precepts, but in cultivating our mental pow-ers by exposing ourselves beforehand to what we call [the humanities]." It is also, moreover, implicit throughout his extended discussion of the relation-ship between taste and genius, especially in his comments on artistic training and cultivation. Kant points out that a young poet cannot be brought to abandon his belief that his poem is beautiful, despite the critical comments of others. To the extent he does this, in other words, the young poet is refusing to partake in the *sensus communis* of his audience. "Only later on," says Kant, "when his power of judgment has been sharpened by practice, will he volun-tarily depart from his earlier judgment."[88]

Finally, there are several key terms still left unspecified in Kant's formula-tion of *sensus communis*: who is the "everyone" to which we refer, and to what community do I appeal in seeking this general standpoint? In principle, since the faculties in question are present in all human beings, the "everyone" I refer to and the community I take part in are potentially the entire human race.[89] However, this principle of the universality of judgment is delimited by the fact that, as both Kant and Arendt repeatedly emphasize, the *sensus com-munis* is only valid for all *judging* subjects.[90] They both insist that we take into account the views of everyone's "*possible* judgments," that is, their point of view *only under the hypothetical condition that they had judged*, even if in actu-ality they have not cultivated taste and cannot judge. When we claim that something is beautiful, we are not appealing to the unreflective pleasure in the beautiful that any human being is capable of; rather, we are appealing to what their feeling of the beautiful *should* be *if* they had cultivated a sense of taste. Moreover, in practice, this community I appeal to is significantly de-limited by the practical considerations involved in the cultivation of taste. Kant points out that each subject has to start from "crude dispositions given by nature," and individuals begin cultivating their taste through the examples of judgment and artistic taste provided by those who influence and train them, through the exemplary works of the humanities and through reciprocally communicating their pleasure to others who also have cultivated a sense of taste.[91] This is a key point for Arendt. She repeatedly emphasizes that judgment is cultivated above all by the "company" we choose: the examples of judgment we rely on and appeal to in cultivating our common sense.[92] Thus, while in principle I could appeal to all judging subjects, in point of fact, my *sensus communis* is by far more influenced and cultivated by those whose judgment I trust, whom I take to be examples of good judgment and taste, and those with whom I spend my time reciprocally communicating my judgments. Thus, both for practical considerations and in principle, Arendt asserts that the proper translation of Kant's *Allgemeingültigkeit* in the *Critique of Aesthetic Judgment* is not "universal validity," because in actual fact it is not truly universally valid; the proper translation is "intersubjectively" or "generally" valid.[93] It is generally valid because the validity it appeals to is hypothetical: it asserts a claim on all subjects not categorically but only insofar as they have developed a capacity to judge by participating in *sensus communis*.

The upshot of this is a kind of oblique rejection of cultural relativism. Kant, and Arendt following him, draws a distinction between what he calls *sensus communis*, or true common sense, and "community sense," the unreflective prejudices I grow up with in my community and culture, which presumably—fairly or not—Kant had in mind when he thought of the Sturm und Drang.[94] According to Kant, "community sense" is common sense at its lowest common denominator: it is literally "common," denoting a kind of vulgarity and lack of cultivation. *Sensus communis* implies a sense of civilization—a certain cultivation, humaneness, and sensitivity—irrespective of whatever culture or community I happen to grow up with and live in.[95] As a result, there are in principle no exceptions made for cultural differences in these judgments: to the extent judging subjects participate in *sensus communis*—no matter what their cultural backgrounds and practices may be—as they "quarrel" or debate about objects of taste, they will over time move toward consensus as they cultivate more sensitivity in their *sensus communis*.

With all this in place, Kant could now deal his blow to the Sturm und Drang's challenge to the Enlightenment. In a scathing section drenched in irony and contempt, Kant explains how genius and taste remain governed by rationally autonomous laws. He begins by acknowledging that the production of great art requires more than taste alone, but must also have what he calls "spirit" [*Geist*]: "Of certain products that are expected to reveal themselves at least in part to be fine art, we say that they have no *spirit*, even though we find nothing to censure in them as far as taste is concerned. A poem may be quite nice and elegant and yet have no spirit. A story may be precise and orderly and yet have no spirit."[96] Kant argues that spirit is a unique endowment of talent and originality, which "cannot be communicated but must be conferred directly on each person by the hand of nature. And so it dies with him, until some day nature again endows someone else in the same way." However, Kant then argues that of the two faculties necessary for great art, it is taste, and not genius, that is the higher and more important faculty. He argues that only "charlatans" with "shallow minds" believe that they can display genius by ignoring standards of taste.[97] Whatever inherent brilliance an artist may have, it is futile, according to Kant, without the element of taste, "for if the imagination is left in lawless freedom, all its riches in ideas produce nothing but nonsense." Taste, he says, "consists in disciplining (or training) genius. It severely clips its wings, and makes it civilized, or polished; but at the same time it gives it guidance as to how far and over what it may spread while still remaining purposive. It introduces clarity and order into a wealth of thoughts, and hence makes the ideas durable, fit for approval that is both lasting and universal, and hence fit for being followed by others."[98] In other words, whatever fundamental human freedom is registered in artistic genius, it is futile without a form that is "communicable" to those who constitute its community of judges. This description is all-important to Arendt. She believes Kant's description of the faculty of genius clearly expresses many of the same characteristics Arendt associates with action, and, indeed, we will see that both are rooted in essentially the same faculty for spontaneous natality, though they are expressed in different areas of human experience. She believes that Kant formulated the relationship between action and judgment by analogy when he formulated the relationship between taste and genius: the same capacity for natality that characterizes action can be found in artistic genius, and, indeed, so much so that in the modern age, with its limited possibilities for true action, Arendt asserts, "the work of genius . . . appears to have absorbed those elements of distinctness and uniqueness which find their immediate expression only in action and speech."[99]

In conclusion, it is worth considering whether Arendt achieved her goal of establishing the intersubjective validity, as opposed to universal validity, of political judgment? Given that the deduction itself remains controversial, it would appear that she did not, at least from a strictly Kantian point of view, which is wholly reliant on the deduction's success. Arendt herself gives no real direct assessment of the deduction, though she does devote a few pages to it in the 1964 course. Critics, such as Paul Guyer and Anthony Savile,

argue that it was not successful, while sympathetic interpreters, such as
Henry Allison, argue that these critics have understood the scope of Kant's
deduction too expansively and once this more limited scope is taken into
consideration, Kant is shown to have been successful.[100] Andrew Norris is
therefore probably correct in his observation that the formal deduction of
sensus communis in SS20-21 cannot be convincingly applied to politics.[101]
Nevertheless, Arendt's claims still have quite a bit of theoretical power. Kant's
phenomenological articulation of *sensus communis* has little intuitive connection to the articulation of SS20-21, and it might be suspected that we could
dispense with the deduction version if we do not fully accept the entire critical framework, which Arendt, of course, did not. Beyond the formal deduction, Kant's articulation of *sensus communis* arguably still has a
phenomenological validity. Specifically, it does appear that some kind of faculty of enlarged mentality must be presupposed in any "reflective" activity of
judgment, that is, any activity not determined by pre-given rules.

Applying the Third *Critique* to Politics

Arendt presented her argument that the *Critique of Aesthetic Judgment*
should have been applied to politics in her 1970 lectures on Kant's political
philosophy, where she claims that Kant had all the pieces in place to discover
the idea himself if he had had more time. Kant, she argues, became aware of
authentic political phenomena late in life and only after he had committed to
the system of his critical philosophy. She argues that what led him to the
discovery of the political was the rise of modern revolutionary activity in the
French Revolution.[102] The revolution seemed to indicate certain phenomena,
distinct to the political realm, which did not fit easily into Kant's critical system. She argues that this led to what appears to be a flagrant contradiction in
Kant's practical philosophy. Politically, Kant could not bring himself to deny
the tremendous significance of "the recent event," as he called the revolution;
yet, from the standpoint of his moral philosophy, he was bound to condemn
the actions of the revolutionary actors. Arendt quotes Kant stating that despite all the French Revolution's "miseries and atrocities [it still] nonetheless
finds in the hearts of all spectators . . . a wishful participation that borders
closely on enthusiasm. . . . For that event is too important, too much inter-
woven with the interest of humanity."[103] Arendt thus proposes that when
political and historical phenomena were finally taken seriously by Kant, two
principles appeared that seemed to be in direct conflict: a principle by which

an actor should act and a principle by which a spectator judges the meaning and outcome of those acts.[104]

Arendt believed that flagrant contradictions in the writings of great thinkers indicated the deepest meaning of their thought, elements that point to their deepest concerns and most potent ideas,[105] and this is exactly what she believes occurred when Kant became aware of authentic political phenomena. Kant's solution to this contradiction was to replace political theory with philosophy of history, postulating that the principle of politics and history centered on the progress of the human species. Kant asserted that an event was great to the extent it demonstrated the work of nature operating behind the backs of human beings, allowing them to develop into fully free, rational, and moral beings.[106] In the 1964 course, Arendt argues that this teleological conception of politics and history is predicated on conflating nature with history and fabrication with action: nature works like an artist through the process of history to bring about an ideally moral human species. The political problem, she argues, is that by treating history and politics as natural, human plurality, the central condition of politics, is ignored, and humans are treated as members of species who are conceived as expendable in the ultimate progress toward moral perfection.[107] In the 1970 lectures, Arendt turns to an immanent critique of Kant's political thought in order to explain why he arrived at this error. According to Arendt, there are three different conceptions of humanity in Kant's thought corresponding to three different aspects of his system.[108] The first conception is the intelligible, rational, and moral humanity articulated in the first and second *Critiques*. The second is the notion of humanity as a species found in his historical and political writings, drawing its conception of judgment from the second part of the third *Critique*, concerned with teleological judgment. The third conception corresponds to the first part of the third *Critique*, concerned with aesthetic judgment, and, Arendt argues, to the very idea of critical thought in general, which animated and motivated Kant's philosophy as a whole.[109] This third conception is concerned with humanity as what Kant calls "sociable" beings. Arendt argues that in this third conception Kant understood human beings as political beings, conditioned by plurality and living in communities together on the basis of common sense. The crucial mistake Kant made in his political philosophy, she argues, was that he located political action in the sphere of morality and political judgment in the sphere of nature, which led him to employ the teleological judgment of the third *Critique* rather than the judgment of appearances that could be found in the *Critique of Aesthetic*

Judgment.[110] In other words, since aesthetic judgment is the only aspect of Kant's critical philosophy that appealed to the authentically political conditions of the human condition, he should have employed some kind of political version of aesthetic judgment rather than a historically applied version of teleological judgment when attempting to judge and grasp the meaning of political phenomena.

According to Arendt, Kantian aesthetics is uniquely capable of addressing itself to her own political conditions of human life such as worldliness, plurality, and natality, and when these conditions are taken into account, they resolve the conflict in Kant's practical philosophy. She argues that the solution to the apparently paradoxical relationship between the actor and spectator in Kant can be found in his analysis of the relationship between taste and genius. This is this clearly the key moment in the 1970 lectures: all of her argument about the conflict between the actor and spectator in Kant's practical philosophy had led up to this moment, and when she finally turns directly to the *Critique of Aesthetic Judgment*, she begins by pointing to the "analogous" relationship between taste and genius.[111] Arendt's reference to taste and genius as "an analogous problem" in the 1970 lectures is something of a misformulation, however. It is not that taste and genius are analogous to action and judgment; rather, it would be more accurate to say that both relationships draw on the same fundamental human capacities, and thus virtually anything said in the *Critique of Aesthetic Judgment* can generally be applied in some sense to action and judgment. Just as taste does, political and historical judgment takes its bearing from our common sense, the sixth sense that intuitively orients us to a common world. This common sense happens by escaping our "subjective private conditions" and "putting ourselves in the place of everyone else" through the development of "enlarged mentality."[112] But this only applies to "everyone else" insofar as they are human beings endowed with a faculty of judgment, even if they fail to use that faculty. Political *sensus communis*, according to Arendt, "extends over 'the whole sphere of judging subjects' but not further."[113] In her essay "The Crisis in Culture" Arendt writes: "Judgment, Kant says, is valid 'for every single judging person,' but the emphasis in the sentence is on 'judging'; it is not valid for those who do not judge or for those who are not members of the public realm where objects of judgment appear."[114] This does not mean that it is not valid for all human beings: indeed it is, but only generally, only under the hypothetical condition that all humans had cultivated a *sensus communis*.

Thus, there appear to be structures built into the very nature of judgment that resist relativism and solipsism: judging subjects will increasingly become sensitive, civilized, and sophisticated in their exercise of judgment because of their participation in the political *sensus communis*, and this will increasingly bring their judgment into consensus with other cultivated judges. Arendt writes that "what Kant calls taste, Cicero called *cultura animi*, a mind so trained and cultivated that it can be trusted with judging and taking care of the world."[115] In this, Arendt was evoking the Roman notion of *humanitas*, which claimed that judgment is cultivated by "choosing our company."[116] When we begin to concern ourselves with the world, our sense of judgment is likely to be crude, simplistic, and parochial. Enlarged mentality is cultivated by carefully considering exemplary instances of judgment and by participating in a community of citizens who are willing to offer their *doxa*, their judgment of the world and the events that occur there.[117] As we participate in this process of, in Kant's words, "reciprocal communication," we develop a more sophisticated and subtle sense of judgment and thus become truly broad-minded, possessing an "enlarged mentality."[118] Because of this, Arendt writes at the end of her "Crisis in Culture" essay that "even if all criticism of Plato is right, Plato may still be better company than his critics. . . . We may remember what the Romans . . . thought a cultivated person ought to be: one who knows how to choose his company among men, among things, among thoughts, in the present as well as the past.[119] The process is something like climbing high hill. We begin at the bottom with an uncultivated and crude understanding that is trapped in our individual private conditions and our community's prejudices and unreflective understandings, what Kant had called "common human understanding." But as we cultivate our judgment, we, so to speak, climb up the mountain and as we get higher our perspective can take in more and more of the landscape, we can take in the viewpoint of more and more perspectives. The essential point, however, is that this is still my own perspective. I have two different vantage points, one that is based in my subjective private conditions, and one that takes in a broader political landscape of perspectives. I have not left the world in search of the objectivity of the Archimedean point; instead, I have gained another "impartial standpoint," a standpoint that sees more broadly than that of a private individual. As Walt Whitman says, it is as if I am "both in and out of the game."

Arendt's account of judgment has been highly contemplative to this point. The challenge she faced was to understand how it incorporated deliberative elements. She notes in the 1970 Kant lectures that action would be sheer "lawless freedom" and "nothing but nonsense" without a sense of taste or political judgment that cultivates the skill and genius of the actor by providing "the discipline (or training) of genius; it clips its wings . . . gives guidance . . . brings clearness and order."[120] But action seems to carry a separate deliberative and prospective faculty that she consistently associates with the idea of the "virtuosity" of genius. Genius, as we've seen, draws on the same human faculties of spontaneity and natality as action. Both faculties involve what Kant called "spirit": the unique talent or natural endowment to bring something meaningful into existence that did not exist before. In "What Is Freedom?" Arendt notes that action and art are similar in that, while both the actor and the genius have certain motives and aims, the result of their activity is only free and meaningful to the extent it "transcends" those aims: as with art, action comes to have a meaning and significance that the actor could not have predicted when he or she first undertook the action.[121] When a musician gives a brilliant rendition of a piece of music, clearly having the "aim or objective" of playing the song is not what makes the performance great; rather, it is, as Machiavelli would say, the musician's *virtù*, or virtuosity, the musician's naturally endowed talent and skill that allow the performance to "transcend" the sheer aim of playing a tune.[122] Machiavelli's concept of *virtù*, in fact, appears to have been Arendt's inspiration when she imagined the way this dynamic concept of action related to judgment. Indeed, it is evident that Machiavellian *virtù* was, along with Aristotelian *praxis*, one of the key influences on her theory of action in *The Human Condition*. In her 1955 lectures on Machiavelli, she anticipates the relationship between worldliness and action in Machiavelli's concepts of *virtù* and *fortuna*:

> Greatness as greatness of this world is constituted through *virtù* and *fortuna*. *Fortuna* is a constellation in the world which is visible only for *virtù*; *fortuna* is the appearing of the world, the shining up of the world, the smiling of the world. It invites man to show his excellence. . . . But only together can greatness come into being. But the true *fortuna* which is more than chance sleeps unless *virtù* wakes her up. World and man are bound together like man and wife: action fits man into the world like eyes fit us to see the sun. . . . Action shows the world's *fortuna* and man's *virtù* at one and the same time.[123]

Moreover, while *The Human Condition*'s treatment of action almost completely ignores the dimension of deliberative judgment, virtually any other time Arendt deals directly with action, she associates it with Machiavellian *virtù*. Many of the formulations from the 1955 course are reproduced in *Between Past and Future*, where Arendt states that "freedom as inherent in action is perhaps best illustrated by Machiavelli's concept of *virtù*, the excellence with which man answers the opportunities the world opens up before him," that it is "the response, summoned up by man to the world," and therefore is "the specifically political human quality."[124]

But how, finally, does thought, whose nature is so clearly opposed to this dynamic relation of action and judgment, play into this relationship. Thought, according to Arendt, gives what she calls "depth" to judgment, allowing it to have a concrete historical meaning uniquely its own that is achieved through thought's ability to reflect on and frame narratives and stories.[125] Because there is potentially no end to our ability to reflect, the activity of thinking tends to leave the thinker in a state of paralysis. We cannot carry our thoughts into the world of everyday life because we do not have time to think there. "Practically," she writes, "thinking means that each time you are confronted with some difficulty in life you have to make up your mind anew."[126] What is needed, according to Arendt, is some kind of faculty that can, in a sense, refreeze the concepts and meanings thinking has unfrozen in its reflections, by giving them a decisive form again after they have been reflected on, so they can again serve the same function in common sense that the previously frozen concepts and meanings had served. Comparing the thinking activity to Penelope's endless weaving and unweaving of her web, Arendt claims that judgment allows the thinker to come to a conclusion on his potentially endless reflections.

> The faculty of judging particulars (as brought to light by Kant), the ability to say "this is wrong," "this is beautiful," and so on, is not the same as the faculty of thinking. Thinking deals with invisibles, with representations of things that are absent; judging always concerns particulars and things close at hand. But the two are interrelated . . . judging, the by-product of the liberating effect of thinking, realizes thinking, makes it manifest in the world of appearances, where I am never alone and always too busy to be able to think. The manifestation of the wind of thought [i.e., judgment] . . . is the ability to tell right from wrong, beautiful from ugly.[127]

Thus, in the context of history and politics, what judgment provides is a decision—an ability of the storyteller, historian, judge, politician, or citizen to conclusively decide about which narrative most fully and authentically captures the meaning of the deeds that he or she has observed. Arendt illustrates this by pointing to the occasion of Odysseus's visit to the court of the Phaeacians. Upon hearing the bards tell his story, "Odysseus, listening, covers his face and weeps, though he has never wept before, and certainly not when what he is now hearing actually happened. Only when he hears the story does he become fully aware of its meaning."[128] Arendt believed this capacity of the historical observer to finally "set [the story] right" demonstrates the authentic relationship between thought and judgment.[129] The political question that thought must always pose has to do with the fact that our own individual stories are not the only stories in the world; there are a multitude of other stories, all of which must find their place in the common world. In essence, by making reference to a cultivated *sensus communis*, judgment allows us to bring our stories together into the common world.

This brings us to the controversial question of Arendt's distinction between morality and politics. Arendt argued that the concerns of politics and morality were distinctly different: morality concerned the basic integrity of the self, while politics was concerned with action in and maintenance of the common world.[130] According to Arendt, morality was a kind of by-product of the thinking activity that goes on as a dialogue one has with oneself: people who fail to be moral are those who seem to have an inability to think, and she pointed to Adolf Eichmann as an exemplary instance of this phenomenon.[131] There are some actions we will not be willing to take simply because we value the ability to think, because if we did so we could not face the prospect of having to live together and carry on an ongoing dialogue with, for instance, a murderer, thief, or rapist. Arendt believed that such people are thoughtless people, because if they could think they would not be able to commit the deeds they did, in fact, commit. However, when we engage in political activity, we orient ourselves not on the basis of such moral phenomena but on the basis of political judgment. As I noted earlier, this distinction is not as disconcerting as it might appear, because Arendt in fact dramatically expands the scope of political judgment to include most of the moral concerns critics such as Benhabib have raised objection to. Judgment by its very nature is *essentially* political: it only functions to the extent that it takes account of others. There can therefore, in principle, be no such thing as *moral* judgment. But this does not mean that political judgment does not serve most of the purposes of what is commonly called "moral judgment."

Yet, even given this more expansive conception of political judgment,

Arendt seems to have understood the role of thought and morality in politics to be more complex than her initial formulation would suggest. Arendt believes that without the depth and meaning that thought provides, political judgment will essentially remain "aesthetic": that is, it will remain superficial and only pay attention to the surface of things, while action will have no possibility for achieving its goal of immortalization, since ultimately only historical reflection on actions performed in a public realm can provide this. Sensitivity and cultivation are admirable, but they are ultimately not enough for true political judgment. Arendt cites as an example the "highly cultivated murderers" of the Third Reich, who read Hölderlin and listened to Bach and had impeccable family lives.[132] These individuals, she argues, were cultivated but also profoundly thoughtless, and as a result political judgment failed them. In other words, Arendt very much agrees with Machiavelli's claim in *The Prince* that political immortalization has certain built-in limitations that revolve around the judgment of immortality.[133] A truly virtuoso actor, though he can never be certain of how the story his actions initiate will turn out, has an intuitive sense of what the meaning of his actions may turn out to be, and this sense is only possible if the actor is also a thinker.

To Return Political Philosophy to the Citizens

I want now to argue that this theory of judgment indicates a unique and powerful conception of the relation between theory and practice, what we might call the non-sovereign theory of judgment associated with non-sovereign agency. Arendt has argued that the modern understanding of good judgment tends to revolve around the criteria of success and thus to define politics in terms of sovereignty. In order to challenge this sovereign understanding of political judgment, Arendt argued that her political appropriation of Kantian aesthetic judgment offered a rehabilitation of political opinion, or *doxa*, as she calls it after the Greek word. For Arendt, political thought is a matter of the opinion: any political assertion necessarily comes from our own perspective, and the only way it can have validity for others is if we can persuade them to see things similarly. In the realm of human affairs, in other words, there is no absolute validity; but this does not mean there is no validity. Political opinion has an intersubjective validity that, as we have seen, is grounded in distinctive features of the human faculty of common sense.

Arendt's argument for this came in her essay "Truth and Politics." "Truth and Politics" has often been among the key texts critics of her theory of judgment attack. The locus of these attacks is focused on her emphatic insistence that the validity of truth and politics are of different orders, and it is vital that they not be confused with each other.[134] Truth, she argues, compels our assent: we have no choice but to accept its claims. Political judgment, on the other hand, is a matter of opinion: I must be freely and genuinely persuaded of its claims on the basis of my common sense. On its face, this may seem difficult to grasp. As noted earlier, critics such as Ronald Beiner, perhaps her most articulate interlocutor, finds the idea unintelligible. He argues that in doing this, Arendt "slanders truth" when she labels it "coercive" and "tyrannical" by turns in the text of "Truth and Politics." Thus, Arendt ends up with a "defective phenomenology of political judgment," for any political opinion, he argues, must have truth at least as a regulative idea. "I engage in political debate with opposing points of views," he writes, "in order to challenge mistaken judgments and try to help the truth prevail. One fails to capture the authentic meaning of political judgment unless one understands sincerely intended judgment . . . as aimed at *true* judgment."[135]

Critics such as Beiner and Habermas misunderstand the nature of her claims about truth and political opinion, however. Judging citizens do not offer their *doxa* in order to simply add to the "wonderful diversity of opinions"; the stakes, rather, are far higher than that, for in Arendt's view, the more opinions one has access to, the more judgments one is exposed to, the better one's common sense will be. Moreover, in my reading of "Truth and Politics," Arendt was by no means "slandering" truth: her tone throughout the essay is in fact at least as defensive of truth as it is of politics, stating at the very beginning that what prompted her to write it was "the amazing amount of lies used in the 'controversy'" over *Eichmann in Jerusalem*.[136] In fact, what she seems above all interested in doing is explaining why any attempt to collapse the distinction between truth and political judgment or opinion is both dangerous and self-defeating.

She begins the essay by drawing a distinction between rational truth and factual truth. Rational truths base their validity on the structure of the human mind and result in such truth claims as are found in mathematics, science, and philosophy. Factual truths are occurrences in human history. To clarify what she means, she conveys the story of when Clemenceau was asked who was responsible for the outbreak of World War I. "This I do not know," he replied. "But I know for certain that they will not say that Belgium invaded Germany."[137] There is clearly a profound difference in the strength and reliability of the two different forms of truth, and Arendt is particularly concerned to examine just how vulnerable factual truths can be to manipulation once they have been politicized, since such truths always rely on the memory of human beings. But regardless of their relative vulnerabilities, Arendt insists that both rational and factual truths have a validity that is not political: they are established by specific individuals whose vocation is to arrive at these truths outside of the political realm and its inherent relativity. She calls these individuals "truth-tellers," as distinguished from the citizens who occupy the public realm. If we recall Arendt's account of the two-part structure of the human world, Arendt claims that it is made up of the human artifice, which is created through the activity of work and includes all our civilization's technology, science, art, history, and literature, and the web of human relations, which arises out of the human activity of action and exists as a kind of "overgrowth" on the human artifice. Truth-tellers are in that sense "workers" on the human artifice, in that they seek to establish certain objective structural elements of the common world. Truth-tellers, whether rational or factual, rely on objective procedures to arrive at their claims, whether it is through reason, logic, and experimentation in the case of rational truths, or through the careful examination of evidence established with eyewitness accounts, documents, records, and monuments. They both aspire to establish their claims on the basis of the compelling force of truth.[138]

In contrast to truth-tellers, Arendt argues, citizens exist within the web of human relations at different locations in the common world, thus having differing perspectives on these objective facts. It is the vocation of citizens, she asserts, to pass judgment—to offer what she calls their *doxa*—on these matters of fact. In "Truth and Politics," Arendt calls this "representative thought": "I form an opinion by considering a given issue from different viewpoints, by making present to my mind the standpoints of those who are absent." As we noted before, judgment or *doxa* is not about ingesting everyone's actual views within our own—we are not "counting noses," she says. Rather, with representative thought we are cultivating our judgment, developing an "enlarged mentality" that takes in the standpoints of as many other judges as possible. In doing so, I gain not the objectivity and self-evidence that truth-tellers are entitled to, but what she calls "impartiality," a position that is still my own, but that has been cultivated to be able to take in the perspectives of as many other judging citizens as possible.[139] Thus, for Arendt opinion, or *doxa*, does not simply refer any unreflective comment someone might drop in conversation about politics; an opinion is only truly *doxa* if it has been formulated out of a cultivated political *sensus communis*.

The upshot of all of this is that critics like Beiner and Habermas are wrong to claim that Arendtian political judgment fails to account for cognitive elements in political judgment. The validity of truth is presupposed in political judgment to the extent that it is always concerned with passing judgment on the meaning of preexisting truths established in the human artifice of the common world. In other words, before the validity of the political *sensus communis* can be appealed to, the objective validity of the truths on which we are to pass judgment must first be appealed to. The point critics seem to miss is that the crux of the matter turns on the question of validity. For Arendt, the nature of the validity of matters of factual and rational truth require that there should be, at least in principle, no debate about their conclusions: there should be only one right answer in matters of truth, and thus in this sense truth may perhaps justifiably, if benignly, be called tyrannical and compelling. However, in matters of political opinion, the nature of the validity being asserted means that it is quite possible for different judging subjects located in different positions in a common world to have very different opinions on political matters, yet each still be "right" in some sense.

When I say "this war is unjust" or "this policy wrongly restricts freedom" or "government surveillance has gone too far," there are of course objective facts that I draw on, but to claim mine are the only conclusions that have the force of political validity does indeed seem impossible and even tyrannical. While it is true that, as we debate about political affairs, I and my fellow judges will likely begin to approach consensus, there is no guarantee that this will be the case. In matters of political judgment, thinking in terms of right or wrong answers is not the appropriate way to consider the question; rather, it has to do with who has a more illuminating and perspicuous understanding of the matters we are examining. The real question, in other words, is to try to determine who is *more* right, who has a clearer, more cultivated *sensus communis*, who has the deeper, richer feeling for reality. Thus, when a citizen forms a *doxa*, they are in essence offering a political interpretation of the facts established by the truth-tellers, but this "political" aspect is the crucial element. It becomes a "political" interpretation when it has been fitted into the common world by the faculty of judgment, by having gained an impartial standpoint or enlarged mentality through representative thought. As a result, only judging citizens can truly be political theorists, because only judging citizens have access to a commonsense feeling for a public realm in a common world. There will therefore never be any single, correct political theory—no final, sovereign account of politics—because no political theorist can ever escape having to render their theories as *doxa*, and the one great mistake the tradition of political thought made was to imagine it could escape the fact that political opinion is always rendered as *doxa*.

Thus, when truth-tellers move beyond the sheer act of providing facts and seeks to frame facts appropriately—to explain their significance—they are no longer really acting in the capacity of historians, scientists, or reporters, and instead have now begun acting in their capacity as citizens, in that they are appealing to some kind of political common sense. Truth-tellers can also be judging citizens; but it is crucial to understand that when they do so, they are acting in different capacities, utilizing different faculties, and claiming different modes of validity. In an unpublished lecture from 1967 called "Intellectuals and Responsibility" Arendt said: "Intellectuals have greater responsibility because they know more . . . [but that] knowledge does not mean that they are able to arrive at better . . . judgments. . . . Their special responsibility lies in giving facts of the matter after which they resume their roles as judging citizens like everybody else. . . . Each one of us wears two hats. We . . . teach the truth as we see it . . . [but] in addition, we are also citizens, and take our responsibilities."[140] When truth-tellers make a truth claim, they are in a very real sense attempting to coerce the assent of those around them; however, when they draw conclusions about the political significance of those claims they must woo and persuade those around them to judge similarly to them. Truth-tellers cannot avoid having to take on both roles and to engage in both activities. When they try to collapse both activities into each other, according to Arendt, confusion and danger can only follow. As a result, one might say that political theorists, political scientists, and perhaps social scientists in general might be thought of as professional citizens, so to speak. Of course, like any other citizen, they are not paid to be citizens; nevertheless, one might argue that the services they perform for society are simply a more sophisticated version of the kind of judgment all citizens should ideally exercise. Intellectuals at their best, then, should serve as examples of judgment to their fellow citizens.

It seems difficult to exaggerate how important it must have been to Arendt that the difference between of these two modes of validity be maintained. Her work no doubt made her deeply aware that the modern tendency to collapse the distinction between the objectivity of the truth-tellers and the impartiality of political judgment is what lay behind the ideological and totalitarian political thinking that had become so virulent in the first half of the twentieth century.[141] At first glance, it may seem counterintuitive to suggest that appealing to the higher standard of certainty implied in the ideal of objectivity could be dangerous; however, history shows that this has very much been the case. Twentieth-century political history shows that when political opinions—the reflections and *doxa* of specific individuals about a common world—were attributed the kind of validity that only truth can guarantee, the result was a variety of ideologies. Marxism, fascism, Leninism, anti-Semitism, liberalism, conservatism, socialism, and so on, all began simply as political opinions, but at various points claimed to be truths. When this happens, it becomes impossible to rationally distinguish between what is fact and what is opinion, since they both aspire to the same form of validity. As a variety of ideologies with radically different worldviews all claimed to hold a monopoly on objectivity, facts increasingly came to be treated as mere matters of opinion, mere inconveniences. Some ideologies came to believe that they could pick and choose their own sets of facts, could even manufacture facts if necessary or, in the case of totalitarian regimes, simply rewrite history altogether, and be justified in doing so because it was the ideology that represented reality, not the facts.[142] Even today, we see many of these same political pathologies in contemporary political discourse. Many political movements regularly assert their belief that they are entitled to report their own sets of facts and justify it as presenting an alternate point of view, such as in the case of those who deny man-made global warming or support teaching intelligent design theories in public schools. This kind of politicization of scientific evidence is why Arendt was so emphatic in "Truth and Politics" about maintaining the distinction between truth and opinion. While the establishment of truth is open to the same kind of human error all human activities are open to, it is dangerous and foolhardy to ever politicize the process of truth telling. For Arendt, the relativity inherent in politics requires the existence of an objective common world to give it stability, and to the extent that truth telling is one crucial activity we employ to add to this stable human artifice, any attempt to politicize that process can only be destructive of our common world.

A New Foundation for Modern Politics?

In conclusion, we can now glimpse what Arendt was up to in her broader positive project. It seems that Arendt believed only an authentic practice of political philosophy could bring about a new foundation for Western politics. As we've seen, Rome seemed to represent a very attractive political ideal for Arendt; unfortunately, we cannot go back to Rome or any other bygone era. Modernity had long since fatally undermined the Roman trinity of tradition, religion, and authority that had underwritten Western politics for so long. That trinity could not simply be reconstituted, because it had arisen in a very specific set of political circumstances that could never be consciously reenacted, as the modern revolutionaries in her view had tried to do. Arendt always insisted that political and historical events were concrete occurrences that were unique and unrepeatable. A renewed Western political realm could not be recreated through "theory" in some sort of sovereign act of fabrication, as left- and right-wing revolutionaries had tried to do. She was convinced that in our time there can no longer be a separation between those who think and those who act. For the first time in Western history, the modern era demands that citizens be not only judging and acting citizens but also thinking citizens. In essence, Arendt was claiming that we must go back to the first exemplars of impartiality, to the ancient historians. Greek politics had sought to ignore thought, which they understood as the life of the mind of the philosophers; the Romans did not need to think because they had a tradition that made thinking unnecessary; finally, the modern revolutionaries, who attempted to complete the same task that has been left to us—the refounding of Western politics—had failed because they adopted the tradition of political thought's mistaken notion of thinking as fabrication. Instead, individual citizens have to think, to judge, and to act politically for themselves, without the direction of a sovereign theorist.

This seems to be why Arendt was so urgently concerned with understanding the nature of true political philosophy. In the prologue to *The Human Condition*, Arendt denied that it was her obligation in the book to tell her readers how to respond to the modern predicament. "To these preoccupations and perplexities," she writes, "this book does not offer an answer. Such answers are given every day, and they are matters of practical politics, subject to the agreement of many; they can never lie in theoretical considerations or the opinion of one person, as though we dealt here with problems for which only one solution is possible."[143] This was not a literary flourish; it expressed the deepest elements of her political thought, a thought that centered around how to imagine an authentic political philosophy that only true citizens could practice together. In the modern world, political judgment means that each citizen is both a political theorist and a political actor, and no one can do this thinking and acting for the citizen. What we can do is appeal to a political common sense, and as we do so, our judgments will begin to condition and cultivate each other and eventually perhaps to approach consensus. Authentic political philosophy, in other words, is essentially participatory: its results are wholly contingent upon the judges involved, and though they are all reflecting on an objective world that they all have in common, there can be no certain outcome to the deliberations of these judges, for they are all plural beings located at different places in the world. But the essential element is that those who participate *must* be true citizens in the Arendtian sense: those who have cultivated "a taste for public freedom," who have a commitment to a common world, and who are willing to take responsibility for that world by judging and acting politically. In that sense, Arendtian judgment is highly republican. As she notes at the end of *On Revolution*, this participation will in principle be open to all, but the reality is that not everyone will have the taste for public freedom, and that is certainly everyone's right.[144] But it is incumbent on us to encourage and empower as many as possible to participate and to deliberate: the more judging citizens are involved, rendering their *doxa*, the better their deliberations and the more enlarged their political *sensus communis* will be, and thus the better all of our political judgments will be.

Conclusion
Only the Citizen's Judgment

Concluding Thoughts

We have seen Arendt make a number of bold claims in this study. A full assessment and reflection on the implications of these ideas lies beyond the scope of this book, and this study should instead be viewed as a place to begin exploring their significance. I do, however, want to offer some critical comments on the value of these ideas, not just for today, but perhaps even more significantly for the near future. As descendants of a venerable tradition, much political reflection tends to operate in something of a retrospective mode: we look back to the ideas of our tradition to gain insight into our political world. Nothing in this study is intended to cast doubt on the value, even imperative, of doing this. Part of what made Hannah Arendt unique was her determination to seriously explore the future of political theory. I believe that the very near future will likely pose fundamentally different political challenges from the social world we currently inhabit, challenges I believe Arendt's political thought is uniquely positioned to help us meet. In this concluding chapter, I want to briefly explore this future and Arendt's potential value to it. First, however, some brief critical comments on the ideas discussed in this study are in order.

To begin with, I believe there are some problems, or perhaps, rather, limitations, in her genealogy of modernity. I argued before that her position is more subtle and illuminating than is often thought. She is clearly correct in her claim that modern science's Archimedean perspective has become by far the most prestigious and overwhelmingly predominant cultural perspective of the modern world, deeply conditioning human agency and politics. However, I believe Arendt gave modern scientism too much causal significance in her genealogy of modernity. It does not necessarily follow that because modern individuals have adopted the scientific outlook as their default perspective on the world, modern science must therefore have instigated that world, and Arendt's theory of modernity seems to accept this fallacy. A more complete explanation for the rise of the modern world would probably have to find a kind of reflexivity between the scientific outlook and the political economic forces that allowed the scientific perspective to even become politically viable. Obviously, there were a number of technological advances and modes of productive organization without which the industrial revolution could never have occurred, and which Arendt only vaguely acknowledges. Indeed, the single most important factor in the rise of modern capitalism, and thus modern society, was likely the industrial turn to widespread use of hydrocarbon fuels, whose extraordinary efficiency and convenience arguably made the emergence of commercial society a foregone conclusion.[1] All this does not mean that Arendt's descriptions of modern society were wrong, but it does probably mean that there are some significant gaps in her genealogical argument.

Another area of concern has to do Arendt's overly bleak assessment of modern society, an analysis that at times boarders on mean-spiritedness. In her less provocative moments, Arendt was certainly willing to recognize that modern private life can be satisfying. There are a comparatively enormous variety and accessibility of pleasures both high and low in the modern world, none of which, if taken in moderation, can be rejected without refusing to partake in the whole human experience. To claim that modern life is necessarily a bad life defies credulity, especially compared to many other times and places in human history. The fact that Arendt at times suggested otherwise no doubt was largely for polemical purposes. But it is also true that, looked at from the perspective of her larger concerns with humanity's greatest threats, freest capacities, and most singular experiences, the aspirations of modern life no doubt seemed unbearably mundane and bourgeois by comparison. There is without question a certain sedentariness and seductiveness to bourgeois existence, one that may pose a very real threat to human agency simply because it arguably seeks to make true action unnecessary.

Another worry is one that we have seen raised from the beginning of this book, perhaps best expressed by Christian Bay, who chided Arendt for her "lack of seriousness about modern problems." This critique may in many ways be accurate: Arendt's non-sovereign political ideals seem very much to exist at a distance from the political approaches of the modern world. Citizens in modern mass commercial societies have little real incentive to engage in what Arendt called "public freedom," to seek to exercise their freedom in a public realm where their actions can change the world, while true political judgment is rarely called for in citizens, except in very limited circumstances such as choosing a party affiliation or candidate. Modern politics has increasingly emphasized markets and institutions to organize its citizens, doing its best to remove responsibility for politics from inconstant human action and intention. In this context, Arendt's lionization of political participation and citizen judgment often seems hopelessly naive or utopian. While this is in many ways a fair critique, contemporary political theory has often been inspired by Arendt and others like her, arguing that the realization of global and communal social justice may require more participatory political engagement, democratic deliberation, and thoughtful political judgment from the broader citizenry. Indeed, at least on a conceptual level, I believe Arendt's account of political judgment has a number potential theoretical contributions to deliberative and democratic political thought, arguably providing an account of the ontological conditions of the a priori conceptual structures deliberative democrats have historically based their political theory on. It seems that any truly deliberative political practice would have to existentially presuppose a number of the structures of judgment Arendt outlined, including the concept of a common world, the intersubjective (rather than universal) validity of political opinion, an inherent sense of public-spiritedness, along with her theory of judgment's openness, cosmopolitanism, and intercultural validity. Yet, as inspiring as deliberative pursuits of social justice are, it is hard to imagine they will become a serious force in modern politics, and especially so in Arendt's case, thanks to the modern structures and forces that work against real public engagement among modern citizens. Modern citizens generally seek to express their freedom in the private sphere, and, as a result, Arendt's politically participatory conception of agency often seems downright odd when discussed in the modern context. So long as modern politics successfully channels its citizens' activities though impersonal markets, institutions, and legal structures, the criticism that Arendt's ideals are utopian and possibly irrelevant will always have salience. But as I will argue shortly, this may very soon cease to be the case.

Finally, if there is any truly problematic aspect of Arendt's work, it is her style of communicating her ideas. I believe Arendt had her reasons for conveying her ideas in the idiosyncratic manner she did; still, one wonders if the negatives of her way of thinking, researching, and communicating ultimately outweighed the positives. There are a number of dimensions to her thought that she never made explicit enough, and it begs the question of how valuable a thinker can be if her texts ultimately do not make some of the fundamental meaning of her ideas readily available to readers. In my opinion, there are both pragmatic and ethical problems involving her style. Pragmatically, it is certainly true that the practical value of her ideas are diminished by her abstruseness. Yet, at a more essential level, her style raises even more disturbing ethical questions. It is hard not to perceive a certain egocentric quality in Arendt's thought, almost as though the thinking activity itself was the important part for her, while the extent to which her ideas were fully understood too often seemed of secondary importance. While there is something to be said for this contemplative hierarchy of intellectual activities, and it is certainly not unprecedented in the history of philosophy, it also seems rather self-involved and shortsighted—at least, in the context of political theory. The result of this kind of aloofness is that the community of scholars and citizens who care about these matters are not given the full benefit of a unique and challenging perspective, and the ideas themselves are never given adequate refinement and critique. It appeared to be simply a personal failing on Arendt's part and, indeed, one that has diminished her legacy.

Nevertheless, the reader may still think that this book has left too many of Arendt's ideas unchallenged. In some ways, this is a fair criticism; however, there were reasons for this that had to do with some unusual complications involved in this study. One complication had to do with what I have argued is this book's significant departures from previous work on Arendt. Undertaking what might be called a "revisionist" interpretation by its very nature means that one must spend quite a bit of time explaining how this new perspective challenges previous interpretations in essential ways. As a result, it is probably fair to claim that I have spent more time attacking Arendt's critics and defending her ideas than I have critically assessing Arendt myself. However, a second aspect of this project, involving her attack on the tradition of political thought, has made criticizing Arendt even more difficult. Since many of the common political categories and assumptions that one would appeal to in criticizing her are rooted in the tradition's conceptual framework, it becomes very difficult to criticize Arendt without implicitly invoking categories she has already claimed are politically inauthentic. As a result, providing a more extensive critique of Arendt in this study would have involved adopting one of two approaches: either to insist on the tradition's perspective against Arendt's views, or to attempt to achieve some third perspective–a prospect that, to say the least, is daunting and well beyond the scope of this study. The fact is that many of the categories of the tradition are so distant from

Arendt's that they simply cannot easily be reconciled with her perspective, and attempting to ignore this exclusivity of the two perspectives will inevitably result in a deep and fundamental tension, if not self-contradiction. Though it is probably evident to any reader that I am partial to Arendt's perspective, my goal here has not necessarily been to assert the superiority of one perspective over the other, but instead has been to try to maintain the appropriate distance between the two viewpoints.

To illustrate this, I want to consider how these two perspectives approach the question of the relationship between justice and freedom. The vast difference in how these viewpoints understand this relationship is not just an isolated conceptual contradiction; rather, it indicates a fundamental incompatibility. Of course, it is difficult, if not impossible, to generalize how the entire tradition of political thought has understood the relationship between justice and freedom. Indeed, it is arguably true that the question was only taken seriously by modern political philosophers when freedom became a much more prominent political ideal. Nevertheless, it seems unarguable that justice has ultimately always had, as Rawls would say, "lexical priority" within the tradition's conceptual framework: that is, justice has always been understood to have priority, since freedom, as the tradition understood it, requires just conditions for its exercise. This, of course, does not mean that there are not potential tensions between the full realization of justice and freedom in the tradition's outlook: modern political thought, after all, might reasonably be characterized as a grand reflection on the tension between individualism and political and social equality. Thus, though certainly concerns for freedom might attenuate the pursuit of justice, in the end, from the tradition's perspective, justice must have political priority, for without at least some baseline conditions of civil and social justice freedom cannot even occur.

By contrast, Arendt's view of the relationship between justice and freedom is far more ambiguous, involving an *essential* tension at its very core. Indeed, in terms of Arendt's account of free human action, it appears that where conditions of social and political justice are more fully realized, less scope and significance are available to true human agency. This, in my view, is a fundamental problem with previous theories of non-sovereign agency, which I believe still work within the tradition's assumption of the priority and primordiality of justice before freedom.[2] Patchen Markell, for example, writes, "My guiding rubric—'politics of acknowledgment'—must not be misunderstood. Such a politics consists in the first instance in a distinctive, yet fairly general, account of the meaning of justice in relations of identity and difference, one that is rooted in the ontological picture, and the diagnoses of *in*justice."[3] The problem with this objective is that any attempt to make non-sovereign agency a goal of social justice must inevitably result in action's becoming domesticated and to some extent impotent. For Arendt, agency is not a *result* of justice; rather, it is the extraordinary *origin* of justice and all other human worldly states of affairs. In fact, justice by almost any imaginable conceptualization must inevitably seek to mitigate or even negate many of the most fundamental characteristics of Arendtian action: its potency and unpredictable, uncontrolled nature; its capacity to begin new worldly states of affairs; its *sui generis* status and ability to disclose the unique identity of the actor. The fact is that the more obstacles justice removes from agency's path, the less significant, potent, and self-disclosive the action will be. In essence, it was Arendt's view that the consequence of the modern aspiration to achieve human freedom through the realization of conditions of social justice has been to make agency *boring.*

Of course, while Arendt generally seemed to detest this state of affairs, it is not as though modernity had any choice in the matter, and she appeared to recognize this fact also. In an increasingly complex and interdependent socioeconomic world, where for the first time in history literally millions of citizens now demanded their equal share of political and social agency, the idea that everyone could have access to the kind of potency that action at its highest level possesses would have meant counseling a politics of worldwide chaos. And so we might say that modernity has done the best it could—indeed, that in many ways it is an impressive achievement. Arendt clearly disdained the idea that the rare, *sui generis*, self-revelatory, and highly potent activity she understood as action—an activity that in any realistic sense occurs but a few times in a human lifetime—could be identified with the banal and mundane activities of bourgeois private life and careerism. This does not mean there is anything necessarily sinister or even morally problematic with modern democracy and bourgeois life, other than perhaps the mistaken notion its citizens have about the significance of their activities. But from Arendt's perspective, it simply remains imperative that we call this state of affairs what it is: a peaceful, predictable, conformist, although highly pleasant way of life.

In view of this apparently unavoidable bourgeois character of modern society, one question we are left with is the basic worth of Arendt's critique. In other words, if our current social and political arrangements are so imperative, why bother attacking them with such radical and fundamental depth?

Why not instead focus our criticism on practical and feasible policy outcomes that might contribute to greater social justice? This is one of the most common criticisms I have heard from Arendt's readers over the years, and I must admit that, frankly, it never fails to strike me as an extraordinarily uncritical attitude. Beyond the rather degrading implication that intellectual life can be reduced to a utilitarian activity, I believe there are a number of valuable aspects to the kind of radically "impractical" critique Arendt can be thought to have offered. For one, it may point toward private experiences that challenge the status quo, since not all critical resistance must realize itself in social and political action in order to have social value. To take two examples, artistic expression and countercultural experimentation have been common ways modern citizens have critically resisted the modern world, and it seems likely Arendt may have lessons to teach even in these contexts. Second, even from a revolutionary standpoint, the line of critical theory proceeding through Hegel, Marx, and the Frankfurt School has certainly not always demanded that there be clear policy implications and obvious political action resulting from critical reflection on modern politics and society.[4] While Arendt herself did not seem especially friendly to critical social thought, her critique might still arguably represent quite a powerful negation of modern society. However, third and lastly, in the concluding pages of this book I argue that in the not-too-distant future Arendt's ideas may prove to be far more practically relevant than many think.

The Coming Need for Renewed Citizen Agency and Judgment

In this final section, I want to think beyond where Arendt ended her reflections on the renewal of politics and judgment by placing her work in dialogue with another of my research interests: modern sustainability theory. Through much of the twentieth century, critics of modernity like Arendt focused their attacks on concerns over cultural alienation or social justice. However, near the end of Arendt's life a more material set of concerns were increasingly raised about the potential unsustainability of modern commercial society in books such as Rachel Carson's *Silent Spring*, the Club of Rome's *The Limits to Growth*, and E. F. Schumacher's *Small Is Beautiful*.[5] There is no significant evidence suggesting Arendt ever seriously considered this question. In the years since, however, this question has become among the most pressing concerns of contemporary politics, one that I believe should lead us to reassess the practical value of Arendt's ideas. The economic and ecological unsustainability of contemporary commercial society may very well indicate that modern faith in the political effectiveness of markets and liberal institutions will soon prove outmoded. Our world in the near future will pose a variety of political and practical problems whose urgency will only increase the longer human beings fail to take responsibility for them. I believe these problems will demand direct political action and good political judgment not just from leaders and power brokers but from a robust, diverse, committed, and cosmopolitan citizenry. As a result, theorizing a new politics along Arendtian lines is likely to become much more directly relevant to political theory.

The notion that Arendt's political ideals are irrelevant to modern politics is a conclusion largely drawn from the circumstances of modern society and political economy. Given the huge populations involved, modern political regimes have increasingly come to rely on market and institutional structures to organize citizens. This is not to suggest that citizens in modern democracies have no political virtues and are not encouraged to develop such virtues in a variety of ways by their states; but as much as possible, modern states have done their best to focus citizens' agency primarily in private activities through participation in markets and institutions. However, two hundred years ago Arendt's political ideals would have seemed far less irrelevant. As has been noted for some time now, the liberal tradition was not the only political tradition in the early modern era, but instead coexisted with a republican tradition that believed that a healthy regime required a civically engaged and responsible citizenry.[6] This was often the justification used for the widespread restrictions on citizenship in early modern regimes, which included, among others, property ownership, education, religion, gender, and racial restrictions. However, during the nineteenth century, citizenship ceased to be understood as an exclusive status presuming significant public engagement and obligations, and instead increasingly became a basic right to political inclusion in the body politic. The liberal tradition's emphasis on institutionalism, commercial activity, and privacy came to be the dominant political outlook of modern politics, while the republican emphasis on civic engagement largely disappeared as an explicit ideology. This victory of liberalism did have a certain normative logic, in that all individuals living in a political society should be entitled to a variety of basic rights and liberties; yet, it is striking how quickly and decisively the republican notion of citizenship became displaced in modern society. Why did political regimes become convinced they could rely on markets and institutions to organize their populations and to seek to downplay their citizens' sense of civic responsibility?

This is, of course, a complex question and there were a number of factors involved, but the near coincidence of the full realization of the industrial revolution suggests it is obviously among the primary causes. Indeed, the history of the past 150 or so years makes clear that the legitimacy with which liberal democratic institutions and market society are viewed has a strong relationship to periods of economic growth and decline. During periods of recession or depression, modern politics often gave way to a variety of political pathologies, such as political fanaticism, ideological thinking, class- or identity-based factionalism, high crime rates, and general social unrest. The near-religious faith and commitment citizens and political elites have to the beneficence and absolute necessity of continually advancing economic growth make it the one untouchable assumption of modern politics and public policy. And this is with good reason: a liberal politics without at least the plausible possibility of social and economic advancement for the majority of its citizens would have a very difficult time justifying its institutional and market-based politics. While it arguably cannot account for all of the political stability of the post–World War II period of the twentieth century, there is little doubt that the relatively broad improvement in the economic security and expectation of individual advancement among Western populations, coupled with the (until recently) relative stability of the business cycle, lies at the foundation of the success of contemporary liberal politics.

If the story I have just told is true, the potential unsustainability of the modern capitalist political economy would necessarily pose a major threat to this liberal political dominance, for it would seem to effectively undermine its modus operandi. I want now to explain why I believe this concern is no longer a mere possibility; it is effectively an accomplished fact, whose consequences will only become more dire the longer modern society fails to respond by reorganizing its basic cultural, economic, and political arrangements. Current research offers convincing reasons to believe that economic growth in the near future will, at best, remain at very low levels, if not disappear completely, with the result that it will no longer be able to serve as the political economic foundation of liberal society. We very likely may soon have to live in what the ecological economist Herman E. Daly calls a "steady-state economy." In such a context, I believe Arendt's ideas about political judgment and agency will have far more directly practical and political relevance.

Limits-to-growth arguments in political economy inevitably tend to be unpopular, and thus infrequent; but recently two high-quality sources arguing for substantial limits to future economic growth have appeared: Thomas Piketty's *Capital in the Twenty-First Century* (2014) and Richard Heinberg's *The End of Growth* (2011).[7] Each book presents distinct but complimentary arguments that the modern assumption of perpetually enhanced economic growth will effectively end within this century. Piketty's argument is based in economic history, while Heinberg's is based on an analysis of peak resource production. There is little overlap in either the evidence or the arguments of the two books, and when taken together it is difficult to escape the conclusion that modern commerce, if it does exist in the future, will likely be far less robust, socially prominent, and politically predominant. Of course, it is likely that there will still be much use of markets, just as there always has been, but they would likely be much more "embedded" within society, as Karl Polanyi once put it, rather than understanding themselves as providing the model for society's basic structure.[8]

In *Capital in the Twenty-First Century*, Thomas Piketty begins his argument by noting that many of the economic models that support America's generally rosy outlook on economic growth come from American economics' general lack of engagement with economic history. The widespread assumption in economically advanced countries that economic growth should average around 3–4 percent a year is based on several historically anomalous time periods that have occurred since the industrial revolution. In fact, a variety of unique circumstances contributed to the high levels of growth that the modern world has seen, particularly in the twentieth century. To begin with, Piketty points out that simple population growth greatly contributes to economic growth, estimating that from 1700 to 2012 about half of modern economic growth was due to population growth. This demographic contribution to modern economic growth came as a result of the rapid modern expansion of population sizes due to advances in medical knowledge, better sanitary conditions, improved nutrition, and general well-being. A second contributing factor was the advances in technology and efficiency along with the general economic development that characterized the period since the industrial revolution.[9] Finally, the last contributing factor was the shocks to capital experienced during the twentieth century, such as the various economic crises and the two world wars.[10] These had the effect of destroying the capital that resulted from earlier periods of growth and encouraged rapid recovery development.

According to Piketty, these factors suggest that growth will be substantially attenuated during the twenty-first century. Current research suggests that global population growth will begin to stabilize in the coming century, falling to 0.4 percent in 2030, and settling around 0.1 percent in 2070—down from the spectacular peak of nearly 2 percent from 1950 to 1990.[11] This decline in global population growth is likely to affect the economies of currently developed countries as much as it affects the developing countries that are still seeing relatively high rates of demographic growth, since the globalized world economy has allowed the developed countries to capitalize on the higher rates of growth in developing countries. Moreover, past growth rates, as impressive as they seemed, at their highest levels averaged about 1.6 percent between 1913 and 2012, but previously were much lower: 0.9 percent during 1820 to 1913, and 0.1 percent during 1700 to 1820. But keep in mind that a large portion of the twentieth century's 1.6 percent growth was due to huge population increases, and when this demographic related growth is factored out, global growth during this period drops to around 0.8 percent. The fact of the matter is that the only time there is noticeably higher growth on the order of 3–4 percent is when countries are involved in a developmental "catch up" process, such as has been seen recently in China. "The key point," Piketty writes, "is that there is no historical example of a country at the world technological frontier whose growth in per capita output exceeded 1.5 percent over a lengthy period of time." Thus, Piketty argues that the global economic system is in the process of transitioning back to a lower growth regime. He is apprehensive about predicting exactly what the future growth rate will be. For the sake of his broader argument, Piketty adopts a median scenario of around 1.2 percent: slightly down from a more optimistic reading of these facts, which could rise as high as 1.5 percent, but substantially higher than Robert Gordon's prediction of 0.5 percent, which Piketty considers "a little too dark."[12] But as Piketty explains in the rest of the book, even a 1.2 percent growth rate could lead to a variety of widespread political and economic problems, which he believes neither the market nor current paradigms of public policy will be able to adequately address, and that some more radical approaches will be in order.

Sobering as Piketty's economic forecast may seem, there are compelling reasons to believe that his projections are substantially too optimistic. Modern economics' faith that capitalism will be able to continue in anything resembling its current form is heavily reliant on a belief that effective substitution of energy sources and durable gains in efficiency and productivity through technological development are both perpetual and ongoing processes inherent to capitalism. Piketty at points deals with these two concepts, recognizing that they are potential vulnerabilities to even the limited growth he is projecting. He notes that his projections are predicated on the assumption that effective substitutions for hydrocarbons will be developed. As for the notion of durable gains in efficiency, while he recognizes the viability of Robert Gordon's argument for the diminishing economically relevant returns on technological development, he tends to downplay this concern without offering any real explanation why.[13] In both cases, it is likely that these assumptions are much more problematic than Piketty thinks.

In terms of the supposed long-term productivity gains we might derive from technological developments, there is good reason to believe that the law of diminishing returns has characterized these gains and will continue do so.[14] As Piketty notes, Gordon's basis for claiming that growth will fall to .05 percent between 2050 and 2100 comes from his analysis of previous waves of technological change. Gordon claims that earlier forms of technology since the industrial revolution, such as the steam engine or the development of electric infrastructure, produced much more economic growth than ensuing developments, such as the more recent information technology revolution, because these earlier technologies had a more disruptive effect on society leading in turn to more economic activity. Gordon argues that future technological developments are likely to be even less growth inducing.[15] Moreover, one does not need to rely solely on historical evidence; there are persuasive theoretical reasons to recognize that diminishing returns will increasingly characterize further technological development. Mats Larsson points out that since there are ultimately a limited number of economically relevant human activities—transportation, communication, manufacturing, trading, accounting, and so on—it is likely that we are very close to the limits of any possible economically relevant efficiency gains these activities could achieve.[16] Thus, while it is certainly possible that we may achieve substantially more computing power, for instance, it is not clear that this improvement will produce substantial economic growth, since in the end most economically relevant activities can only be sped up so much before further advances become more or less redundant. Gordon, for his part, is in agreement with this analysis, arguing that there will likely be a decoupling effect in the near future, where we may see robust technological development in the coming century that produces relatively little economic impact.

However, as Richard Heinberg argues in *The End of Growth*, the greatest drag on future economic growth may very well be modern capitalism's inability to find an energy resource of comparable efficiency to what hydrocarbons have meant for its long-term growth. Heinberg frames the book's argument by noting that economies function as systems: they operate according to certain endogenous rules, are characterized by a variety of inputs and outputs, and tend to be driven either by virtuous or vicious self-reinforcing cycles.[17] If one thinks about successful systems in nature, such systems need to have robust reproductive capacities in order to maintain positive self-reinforcing cycles of population growth, which allow the system to absorb periodic shocks and negatively impacting events without falling into a negative cycle. Heinberg argues that modern capitalism developed according to similar principles. In order to create the self-reinforcing cycles of development it has seen for the past two centuries, it needed a power source that could supercharge the cycle of development, allowing it to maintain the robust profit margins that were reinvested as capital in the system for future growth (that is, a virtuous self-reinforcing cycle), but also to absorb the negative shocks it experienced in its development without allowing these shocks to spiral into vicious cycles. Heinberg points out that hydrocarbon fuels were the ideal energy source to power the cycle of modern capitalism.[18] They could be extracted from the earth's crust cheaply, were portable, required little treatment in order to store, and delivered much more energy per unit than earlier power sources. The ratio of energy returned to energy invested (EROI) of oil was something on the order of 100:1, an incredible level of efficiency that was virtually guaranteed to create a supercharged self-reinforcing cycle of economic development.

Unfortunately, there is no existing renewable energy source that can even begin to approach the EROI levels that hydrocarbon fuels once had, whose own efficiency has now begun to substantially decrease as the low-hanging fruit of the earth's fossil fuel resources have essentially been used up. Of course, it is possible that renewables could someday become as efficient as hydrocarbons once were through further technological innovations, but this is certainly not guaranteed and it does not reflect existing technology. The faith many have that technological development will inevitably lead to such efficiency is in fact just that: faith. It relies on projections based on as-yet-undiscovered innovations and implementation solutions, many of which may be very difficult to achieve given certain physical laws.[19] There is evidence that renewables, at least in their current niche state, have or will soon have comparable EROI levels to current hydrocarbon fuels, but this is not because renewables have become extraordinarily more efficient.[20] Instead, it is because hydrocarbon production has become increasingly less efficient as easily reaped stocks have become depleted. As Heinberg notes, "We are trying to do something inherently very difficult—replace one fuel, which nature collected and concentrated, with another fuel which requires substantial effort on our part to achieve the same result."[21] Moreover, the efficiency data of current renewables is drawn from their position as a niche resource: they will likely become less efficient and more complicated when they are expected to provide energy for the current global economy, let alone respond to a future with far higher energy demands due to further development. Furthermore, there are likely to be even deeper systemic problems raised by the shift to renewables, which will make the economic growth Piketty envisions even less likely. Because energy production requires high investments of initial capital, extensive infrastructure, and high costs in bringing it to the market, there tends to be a significant time delay between initial capital investments and sale of the finished product, which means that effective energy production requires relatively stable prices over extended periods of time. As a result, there is inevitably an economically efficient price range that energy investment requires in order to attract further investment. When prices fall outside this range, it tends to lead to market instabilities and negative effects on growth. Thus, we have seen rather dramatic swings in energy prices in the past few years, and this is no doubt largely due to the increasingly lower EROI of hydrocarbon fuels. As this "Goldilocks zone" for energy prices shrinks due to lower levels EROI efficiency, Heinberg predicts that the virtuous self-reinforcing cycles that capitalist development was based on could very well turn into vicious cycles with the potential to undermine capitalism itself.[22]

This last possibility is obviously an apocalyptic scenario, and, as I am not an economist, I am hesitant to draw the kind of dramatic conclusion Heinberg does, which essentially amounts to an assertion that commercial society is soon to be effectively undermined.[23] However, as I noted earlier, Piketty and Heinberg are presenting distinctly different arguments for lower future growth, which rely on distinct kinds of evidence with very little overlap. Moreover, this "Goldilocks zone" problem is not just limited to energy production but affects any kind of large-scale resource production, many of which have no obviously efficient substitutes, such as, for instance, fresh water. I have also not even considered the massive problems associated with overconsumption, waste, pollution, deforestation, threats to global biological services and biodiversity, overpopulation, and agribusiness, which are harming our environment in a variety of unsustainable ways that go beyond hydrocarbon-produced pollution, and which when addressed will also negatively impact economic growth. It thus seems that we have to take it as a deadly serious and perhaps even likely scenario that the world we are soon to inhabit will be one characterized by very low levels of economic growth—probably quite a bit lower than even Piketty's moderate pessimism is predicting.

The political challenges of living in such a low-growth regime are likely to be profound. During the twentieth century, the worst cases of fanaticism, tyranny, and political self-destruction occurred during periods of economic weakness, where growth could not be guaranteed as the saving grace of liberal politics. It is often thought that citizens in contemporary Western democracies are now too savvy and democratically cultivated to fall into the political mass fanaticism of past generations, but this is probably wishful thinking. There are ample amounts of political fanaticism in contemporary liberal politics—some of it in high political offices—and we have every reason to believe that it is not more widespread because most citizens are in a position to be distracted from politics by private concerns. But if growth ceases to be able to underwrite the political stability of the modern world, we will essentially be in uncharted waters. Simply put, it is unclear exactly what incentive citizens will have to support their political institutions and to behave in socially productive ways—other than perhaps sheer physical security—after the promise of perpetual economic advancement has ceased to be a realistic political device. The relationship between modern citizens and their political regimes would therefore likely have to be profoundly reconceived. But on what basis could this be done?

Of course, there is always the possibility that some unforeseen solution—whether it is a technological discovery or something else completely—will emerge to render these concerns moot, but as such a solution does not yet exist, it seems foolhardy not to consider how we could respond in the absence of such a panacea. It would seem that there are two potential political directions we might take, both of which Arendt spent a great deal of time conceptualizing. One would be the "sovereign" approach, which would push for greater state power, centralization, command and control, regulation, and surveillance. This would be the approach most likely necessary in order to maintain something even in the neighborhood of modern levels of production, materialism, and commercial society, which of necessity demands high levels of interdependence, specialization, regulation, and efficient resource and product distribution. However, the second path we might take would be the "non-sovereign" approach. It would be—not just in practice but even in its basic existential orientation—a profound shift in how we organize our world and what we aspire to both as individuals and as communities. It would no longer be one that idealizes extraordinary wealth, plastic and physically unhealthy forms of beauty and sexuality, and often pointless careerism; engages in holocaust-like treatment of animals; perhaps irrevocably harms our ecosystem by damaging our climate, destroying biodiversity and biological services, and poisoning our food chain with hydrocarbon fuels and massive plastic waste deposits; and seeks to make us content with relationships and communities characterized by nihilism, alienation, materialism, and superficiality. Instead, this would be a political world that relied heavily on the political judgment and agency of individual citizens, whose political, economic, and social organization would be far more decentralized, localized, republican, and federalized—ideally to a global level. This non-sovereign approach is one that Hannah Arendt long advocated for.

Arendt believed that if humanity was ever to rediscover the treasure of public freedom, it would have to do so through just such a robustly participatory, federated, and cosmopolitan non-sovereign political organization.[24] Her model for this was early America, which, despite its flaws, she believed had enacted the only successful revolution. She had in mind the civically active America that Tocqueville had described, rooted in the principle of federalism, which she believed was the most ingenious idea in all of American political history.[25] This was an idea that she believed allowed for a vast expansion of the public realm, while at the same time retained the possibility for people at the most local levels to act politically and obtain at least a small share of "public happiness."[26] If the idea of sovereignty could be overcome, this expansion of the public realm through the principle of federalism might eventually even be extended to a global level and thus facilitate a non-sovereign association of states like that of Rome. "If politics is defined in its usual sense," she wrote, "as a relationship between rulers and the ruled, the hope [of a global government] is, of course, purely utopian. . . . If, however, we understand politics to mean a global dominion in which people appear primarily as active agents who lend human affairs a permanence they otherwise do not have, then this hope is not the least bit utopian."[27] Indeed, global non-sovereign politics is a clear consequence of Arendt's Kantian account of a political *sensus communis*, as an a priori structure that extends to *any* judging subject—a point that is not lost on her in the Kant lectures. She writes: "One judges always as a member of a community, guided by one's community sense, one's *sensus communis*. But in the last analysis, one is a member of a world community by the sheer fact of being human; this is one's 'cosmopolitan existence.'"[28] Arendt's "right to have rights," then, rather than being an argument for parochialism and communitarianism, could conceivably extend to the whole world.

This advocacy, outlined primarily at the end of *On Revolution*, for a localized, federalized, and republican politics has often been perceived as a curious utopian oddity by most of her readers. Yet, many theorists who have confronted the question of modern sustainability have increasingly come to the conclusion that only a similar kind of non-sovereign reorganization of humanity's political economy and activities could achieve true sustainability.[29] Only such a non-sovereign reorganization of modern political economy, they argue, could wrest control of global capitalism and place our economic arrangements under human intention, by making individual people in concrete worldly locales directly responsible for their own local means of production.[30] Instead of attempting to maintain at a global level the unsustainable "throughput" consumer economy on which modern growth is based, this non-sovereign world would seek to realize what Herman Daly envisioned as a "steady-state economy," which focused far less on producing consumer goods and more on essential human needs and well-being.[31] This of course does not mean regressing back to some kind of preindustrial subsistence-based way of life; but it would mean profoundly altering our materialistic way of life toward something that is sustainable in the here and now, with existing technological solutions, and not in some hoped-for Promethean scenario. This arrangement would no doubt be less efficient and require a dramatic change in our social values, lifestyles, and fundamental aspirations. But it would also almost certainly be more realistic than the belief that the lifestyle of the American middle class—in a country that constitutes 5 percent of the world's population but consumes a far outsized proportion of its resources—could possibly be sustained indefinitely at a national level, let alone extended to the world as a whole. Indeed, for much of the earth's population, this would likely result in a marked improvement in their material conditions, since if it were realized it would mean ending corrupt local rulership and parasitic Western stealth imperialism. Such a world would certainly place far greater burdens on citizens, requiring a much more robust and potent conception of political action, and demand a broader, more thoughtful, public-spirited, and cosmopolitan form of political judgment. But while many sustainability theorists see this potential post-growth world as something of a consolation prize for having given up modern Prometheanism, we have seen Arendt argue that political arrangements similar to this new world could in fact hold the potential of a new realization of human freedom.

* * *

The foregoing may seem like a dour note to end this book on, but perhaps it is only in contrast with modernity's near endless capacity for Promethean progressive imagination. Anyone who has lived in the grown-up human world for any extended period of time knows that while these modernist fantasies are pleasant thoughts, they are also an infinity removed from the messy, occasionally absurd activities and relationships where we actually find meaning in life. Real human life takes place in relationships that are complicated and mysterious and tragic and pleasurable—and an indefinite number of other adjectives I do not have time to list. While these relations are the context of human action, most of our lives and our relationships are not moments of human action: mostly, we don't change the world, and to the extent we change anyone's life, we expect it will be only a little, if hopefully for the better. Mostly, we hope that when we are remembered, it will be because we made the lives of those around us just a little better for having known us. But every once in a while, our action with others comes to have a greater meaning; now and then we do act, and we hope the world is a better place because of it. In this frustrating and splendid web of human relationships we live our lives and find their meaning, and no Promethean modernist future is likely to ever change this "non-sovereign" character of our human agency. At least, we should sincerely hope it does not, since whatever that world would be, it would not be recognizably human. The future of human civilization may very well depend on our recognizing this fact by returning genuine political agency back to the flawed, limited people who act in a complicated, confusing web of human relationships and a world of human artifice that increasingly demands that they begin respecting its natural and political limits.

My hope is that this book has offered a starting point for further exploration of the capacities on which humanity will have to rely if it is to confront the challenges of the modern world going forward. Hannah Arendt devoted her life's work to theorizing these capacities, perhaps in the hope that her explorations might offer a new political direction if humanity ever chose to pursue one. At the very least, then, Arendt has not left us with a mere utopian fantasy; she has provided a profound set of articulations of the nature of human agency and political judgment in confronting the challenges posed by the modern world. She has offered powerful arguments defending our right to demand that responsibility and freedom can be returned to actual human beings. If nothing else, Hannah Arendt has shown us that the possibility for changing the world and making it something truly human has not yet departed from among the fundamental human capacities; perhaps it only awaits our willingness to take responsibility for our world again.

Notes

Preface

1. Cf. Nicholas Lobkowicz, *Theory and Practice: History of a Concept from Aristotle to Marx* (Notre Dame, IN: University of Notre Dame Press, 1967); Sheldon S. Wolin, *Politics and Vision: Continuity and Innovation in Western Political Thought*, expanded ed. (Princeton, NJ: Princeton University Press, 2004), 3–4, 17–22; Richard J. Bernstein, *Praxis and Action: Contemporary Philosophies of Human Activity* (Philadelphia: University of Pennsylvania Press, 1971), ix–xii.

Introduction

1. Dana Villa, "Hannah Arendt, 1906–1975," *Review of Politics* 71:1 (Winter 2009), 28.

2. Elisabeth Young-Bruehl quotes comments like "it is a masterpiece" and "she is comparable to Marx." Young-Bruehl, *Hannah Arendt: For Love of the World*, 2nd ed. (New Haven, CT: Yale University Press, 2004), xxxvii.

3. Ibid., xxxviii.

4. Arendt, "On Hannah Arendt," in *Hannah Arendt: The Recovery of the Public World*, ed. Melvin A. Hill (New York: St. Martin's, 1979), 307.

5. Young-Bruehl, *Hannah Arendt: For Love of the World*, 381.

6. Irving Howe, "Banality and Brilliance: Irving Howe on Hannah Arendt," *Dissent*, June 5, 2013, accessed at http://www.dissentmagazine.org/online_articles/banality-and-brilliance-irving-howe-on-hannah-arendt.

7. Young-Bruehl, *Hannah Arendt: For Love of the World*, 404ff.; Richard Bernstein, "Rethinking the Social and the Political," in *Philosophical Profiles: Essays in a Pragmatic Mode* (Philadelphia: University of Pennsylvania Press, 1986), 246; Villa, "Hannah Arendt, 1906–1975," 30. Young-Bruehl notes that *On Revolution* was virtually required reading in the early days of the free speech movement at Berkeley.

8. McCarthy, "Editor's Postface," in Arendt, *The Life of the Mind*, ed. Mary McCarthy (New York: Harcourt, 1978), 243ff.

9. Arendt, "Preface: The Gap Between Past and Future," 14–15. Full source information for Arendt citations can be found in the bibliography.

10. Arendt, "On Hannah Arendt," 338.

11. Ibid., 307–310.

12. Hannah Arendt and Karl Jaspers, *Correspondence, 1926–1969*, ed. Lotte Kohler

and Hans Saner, trans. Robert Kimber and Rita Kimber (New York: Harcourt Brace Jovanovich, 1992), 327.

13. Ibid., 289.

14. Hannah Arendt and Martin Heidegger, *Letters, 1925–1975*, ed. Ursula Ludz, trans. Andrew Shields (New York: Harcourt, 2004), 121 n. 8.

15. Arendt, "Philosophy and Politics: The Problem of Action and Thought After the French Revolution," unpublished lecture and manuscript (1954). Subsequent citations to this and other works in the Library of Congress (LOC) collection will be cited by LOC page numbers.

16. Arendt, "Philosophy and Politics," *Social Research* 71:3 (Fall 2004), 427–454.

17. Arendt, "Introduction *into* Politics," in *The Promise of Politics*.

18. Kohn, introduction to Arendt, *The Promise of Politics*, xvii.

19. Ibid., xvii.

20. Arendt, "Introduction into Politics," lecture course at University of Chicago (1963). This is a completely different instance of writing from the earlier manuscript.

21. Arendt, "Philosophy and Politics: What Is Political Philosophy?" lecture course at New School for Social Research (1969).

22. Ronald Beiner, "Interpretive Essay," in Arendt, *Lectures on Kant's Political Philosophy*, ed. Ronald Beiner (Chicago: University of Chicago Press, 1982); Beiner, "Rereading Hannah Arendt's Kant Lectures," in *Judgment, Imagination, and Politics: Themes from Kant and Arendt*, ed. Ronald Beiner and Jennifer Nedelsky (Lanham, MD: Rowman & Littlefield, 2001); Richard Bernstein, "Judging—the Actor and the Spectator," in *Philosophical Profiles*; Peg Birmingham, "Hannah Arendt: The Spectator's Vision," in *The Judge and the Spectator: Hannah Arendt's Political Philosophy*, ed. Joke J. Hermsen and Dana R. Villa (Leuven, Belgium: Peeters, 1999); John Glenn Gray, "The Abyss of Freedom—and Hannah Arendt," in *Hannah Arendt: The Recovery of the Public World*, ed. Melvyn A. Hill (New York: St. Martin's Press, 1979); Dana Villa, "Thinking and Judging," in Hermsen and Villa, *The Judge and the Spectator*.

23. Arendt seems to suggest this in *The Life of the Mind* at the end of the "Thinking" volume (215–216), and two of her closest friends, John Glenn Gray and Mary McCarthy, attest that this was her intention also. See Gray, "The Abyss of Freedom," 225–226; and McCarthy, "Editor's Postface," 242.

24. Both Arendt and McCarthy state that "Judging" was intended to be a concluding section of the "Willing" volume. See Arendt, *The Life of the Mind*, "Thinking," 213, and "Willing," 242.

25. Arendt, *The Human Condition*, 16–17, 324–325.

26. Ibid., 16.

27. Ibid., 17.

28. Arendt, *The Life of the Mind*, "Thinking," 6–7.

29. Hannah Arendt and Mary McCarthy, *Between Friends: The Correspondence of Hannah Arendt and Mary McCarthy, 1949–1975*, ed. Carol Brightman (New York: Harcourt Brace, 1969), 213.

30. Arendt, "On Hannah Arendt," 305–306.

31. See Beiner, "Interpretive Essay"; Beiner, "Rereading Hannah Arendt's Kant

Lectures"; Bernstein, "Judging—the Actor and the Spectator"; Birmingham, "Hannah Arendt"; Gray, "The Abyss of Freedom"; and Villa, "Thinking and Judging"; see also Seyla Benhabib, "Judgment and the Moral Foundations of Politics in Hannah Arendt's Thought," in Beiner and Nedelsky, *Judgment, Imagination, and Politics*; Annelies Degryse, "*Sensus communis* as a Foundation for Men as Political Beings: Arendt's Reading of Kant's Critique of Judgment," *Philosophy and Social Criticism* 37:3 (2011), 345–358; Maurizio Passerin d'Entrèves, "'To Think Representatively': Arendt on Judgment and the Imagination," *Philosophical Papers* 35:3 (2006), 367–385; Robert J. Dostal, "Judging Human Action: Arendt's Appropriation of Kant," in Beiner and Nedelsky, *Judgment, Imagination, and Politics*; Alessandro Ferrara, *The Force of Example: Explorations in the Paradigm of Judgment* (New York: Columbia University Press, 2008), chap. 2, "Making Sense of the Exemplary"; Bryan Garsten, "The Elusiveness of Arendtian Judgment," in *Politics in Dark Times: Encounters with Hannah Arendt*, ed. Seyla Benhabib (New York: Cambridge University Press, 2010); Jürgen Habermas, "Hannah Arendt's Communications Concept of Power," *Social Research* 44:1 (Spring 1977), 22–23; George Kateb, "The Judgment of Hannah Arendt," in Beiner and Nedelsky, *Judgment, Imagination, and Politics*; David L. Marshall, "The Origin and Character of Hannah Arendt's Theory of Judgment," *Political Theory* 38:3 (2010), 367–393; Kirstie M. McClure, "The Odor of Judgment: Exemplarity, Propriety, and Politics in the Company of Hannah Arendt," in *Hannah Arendt and the Meaning of Politics,* ed. Craig Calhoun and John McGowan (Minneapolis: University of Minnesota Press, 1997); Andrew Norris, "Arendt, Kant, and the Politics of Common Sense," *Polity* 29:2 (Winter 1996), 165–191; Paul Ricoeur, "Aesthetic Judgment and Political Judgment According to Hannah Arendt," in *The Just*, trans. David Pellauer (Chicago: University of Chicago Press, 2000); Peter J. Steinberger, "Hannah Arendt on Judgment," *American Journal of Political Science* 34:3 (August 1990), 803–821; Tracy B. Strong, "Without a Banister: Hannah Arendt and Roads Not Taken," in *Politics Without Vision: Thinking Without a Banister in the Twentieth Century* (Chicago: University of Chicago Press, 2012), 325–369; Leslie Paul Thiele, "Judging Hannah Arendt: A Reply to Zerilli," *Political Theory* 33:5 (October 2005), 706–714; Albrecht Wellmer, "Hannah Arendt on Judgment: Unwritten Doctrine of Reason," in Beiner and Nedelsky, *Judgment, Imagination, and Politics*; Sanem Yazicioglu, "Arendt's Hermeneutic Interpretation of Kantian Reflective Judgment," *Philosophy Today* 54:4 (December 2010), 321–332; Linda Zerilli, "'We Feel Our Freedom': Imagination and Judgment in the Thought of Hannah Arendt," *Political Theory* 33:2 (April 2005), 158–188; Zerilli, "Response to Thiele," *Political Theory* 33:5 (October 2005), 715–720.

32. Bernstein, "Judging—the Actor and the Spectator," 237; Beiner, "Interpretative Essay," 134–135.

33. Arendt, "On Hannah Arendt," 305.

34. Arendt, "Philosophy and Politics: What Is Political Philosophy?" (1969), LOC 024461.

35. Arendt, "Concern with Politics in Recent European Philosophical Thought," 432–433.

36. Arendt, "What Is Freedom?" 142ff., esp. 161–163; Arendt, *The Human Condition*, 234ff.; Arendt, *The Life of the Mind*, "Willing," 195ff.

37. Arendt, *On Revolution*, 20ff.

38. Arendt, "Introduction *into* Politics," in *The Promise of Politics*, 117.

39. Arendt, "Philosophy and Politics: What Is Political Philosophy?" (1969), LOC 024461.

40. Gadamer, for instance, in *Truth and Method*, understands his own theory of judgment as a reaction to Kant's third *Critique*. For more directly non-Arendtian "reappropriations" of Kant's third *Critique*, see, for example, Rudolf A. Makkreel, *Imagination and Interpretation in Kant: The Hermeneutical Import of the "Critique of Judgment"* (Chicago: University of Chicago Press, 1990); Makkreel, "Reflective Judgment, Orientation, and the Priorities of Justice," *Philosophy and Social Criticism* 27:3 (2001), 105–110; Makkreel, "The Role of Judgment and Orientation in Hermeneutics," *Philosophy and Social Criticism* 34:1–2 (2008), 29–50; Alessandro Ferrara, *Justice and Judgment: The Rise and the Prospect of the Judgment Model in Contemporary Political Philosophy* (Thousand Oaks, CA: Sage, 1999); Ferrara, *The Force of Example*; Maria Pia Lara, *Narrating Evil: A Post-Metaphysical Theory of Reflective Judgment* (New York: Columbia University Press, 2007).

41. Max Deutscher, *Judgment After Arendt* (Burlington, VT: Ashgate, 2007).

42. Garsten, "The Elusiveness of Arendtian Judgment," 318.

43. Margaret Canovan, *Hannah Arendt: A Reinterpretation of Her Political Thought* (New York: Cambridge University Press, 1992), 269–272.

44. Seyla Benhabib, *The Reluctant Modernism of Hannah Arendt*, new ed. (New York: Rowman & Littlefield, 2000), 172ff.; Dana Villa, *Arendt and Heidegger: The Fate of the Political* (Princeton, NJ: Princeton University Press, 1996), 102–107.

45. Michael McCarthy, *The Political Humanism of Hannah Arendt* (New York: Lexington Books, 2012), 288.

46. Occasionally interpreters have mentioned the possibility that Arendt's work as a whole could be understood this way, but the idea has never been pursued in any substantial form. See, for instance, Elisabeth Young-Bruehl, "Reflections on Hannah Arendt's *The Life of the Mind*," in *Hannah Arendt: Critical Essays*, ed. Lewis P. Hinchman and Sandra K. Hinchman (New York: SUNY Press, 1994); and Canovan, *Hannah Arendt: A Reinterpretation of Her Political Thought*, 255ff.

Chapter 1

1. Bernstein, "Rethinking the Social and the Political"; Mary Dietz, "'The Slow Boring of Hard Boards': Methodical Thinking and the Work of Politics," *American Political Science Review* 88:4 (December 1994), 873–886; J. Peter Euben, "Hannah Arendt at Colonus," in *Platonic Noise* (Princeton, NJ: Princeton University Press, 2003); Habermas, "Hannah Arendt's Communications Concept of Power"; Bonnie Honig, "The Politics of Agonism: A Critical Response to 'Beyond Good and Evil: Arendt, Nietzsche, and the Aestheticization of Political Action' by Dana R. Villa," *Political Theory* 21:3 (August 1993), 528–533; Hanna Fenichel Pitkin, "Justice: On Relating Private and Public," *Political Theory* 9:3 (August 1981), 327–352; Sheldon S. Wolin, "Hannah Arendt: Democracy and the Political," *Salmagundi* 60 (Spring–Summer 1983), 3–19.

2. Mary McCarthy, quoted in Arendt, "On Hannah Arendt," 315.

3. Bernstein, "Judging—the Actor and the Spectator," 237ff.; Beiner, "Interpretative Essay," 134–135.

4. Beiner, "Interpretative Essay," 92.

5. Arendt, "Karl Marx and the Tradition of Western Political Thought," 282.

6. Arendt, "Preface: The Gap Between Past and Future," 5.

7. Ibid., 6.

8. Arendt, "What Is Authority?" 141.

9. Arendt, "On Hannah Arendt," 336.

10. Arendt, "A Reply to Eric Voegelin," 401ff.

11. Ibid., 403.

12. Ibid., 403–404.

13. Arendt's approach has recently found defenders among empirically oriented social scientists, and particularly among sociologists. See, for instance, Peter Baehr, *Hannah Arendt, Totalitarianism, and the Social Sciences* (Stanford, CA: Stanford University Press, 2010); and Robert Fine, *Political Investigations: Hegel, Marx, Arendt* (New York: Routledge, 2001). Baehr, in particular, provides a considered defense of Arendt's theory and approach to analyzing totalitarian phenomena.

14. Arendt, "Walter Benjamin, 1892–1940," 195ff., 201.

15. Ibid., 201.

16. Arendt seems to have begun characterizing her approach by this name in a letter to Kurt Blumenfeld in 1960 (see Young-Bruehl, *Hannah Arendt: For Love of the World*, 95 n. 22). Arendt fleshed out more specifically what she had in mind in using this term in her characterization of Walter Benjamin's approach (and Heidegger's, for that matter) in her essay "Walter Benjamin," (200–201), which had originally been the introduction to a collection of Benjamin's essays that she edited, called *Illuminations* (1968). She also mentions the approach in *The Human Condition*, 94ff.

17. Arendt, "Walter Benjamin," 205–206.

18. Arendt, "Understanding and Politics," 311.

19. Arendt, "Preface: The Gap Between Past and Future," 14.

20. Arendt, "What Is Authority?" 101ff.

21. Arendt, "Preface: The Gap Between Past and Future," 14.

22. Arendt, *The Human Condition*, 205.

23. Ibid., 259.

24. Ibid., 205.

25. Arendt, "What Is Freedom?" 168–169.

26. Ibid., 168–169.

27. My account of Heidegger draws on the following works: Walter A. Brogan, *Heidegger and Aristotle: The Twofoldness of Being* (Albany: State University of New York Press, 2005); John Caputo, *Radical Hermeneutics: Repetition, Deconstruction, and the Hermeneutic Project* (Bloomington: Indiana University Press, 1987); Robert J. Dostal, "Time and Phenomenology in Husserl and Heidegger," in *The Cambridge Companion to Heidegger*, 2nd ed., ed. Charles B. Guignon (New York: Cambridge University Press, 2006); Hubert L. Dreyfus, "Heidegger on the Connection Between Nihilism, Art, Technology, and Politics," in Guignon, *Cambridge Companion to Heidegger* ; Michael Allen Gillespie, "Martin Heidegger's Aristotelian National Socialism," *Political Theory* 28:2 (April 2000), 140–166; Gillespie, "Radical Philosophy to Political Theology," in *The Oxford Handbook*

of Theology and Modern European Thought, ed. Nicholas Adams, George Pattison, and Graham Ward (Oxford: Oxford University Press, 2013); Theodore Kisiel, *The Genesis of Heidegger's "Being and Time"* (Berkeley: University of California Press, 1993); Richard Polt, *Heidegger: An Introduction* (Ithaca, NY: Cornell University Press, 1999); Tracy B. Strong, "Martin Heidegger and the Space of the Political," in *Politics Without Vision: Thinking Without a Bannister in the Twentieth Century* (Chicago: University of Chicago Press, 2012); Charles Taylor, "Engaged Agency and Background," in Guignon, *Cambridge Companion to Heidegger*; Mark A Wrathall, "Truth and the Essence of Truth in Heidegger's Thought," in Guignon, *Cambridge Companion to Heidegger*.

28. Benhabib, *The Reluctant Modernism of Hannah Arendt*; Lewis P. Hinchman and Sandra K. Hinchman, "In Heidegger's Shadow: Hannah Arendt's Phenomenological Humanism," *Review of Politics* 46:2 (April 1984), 183–211; Jacques Taminiaux, *The Thracian Maid and the Professional Thinker: Arendt and Heidegger*, trans. and ed. Michael Gendre (Albany: State University of New York Press, 1997); Dana Villa, *Arendt and Heidegger*; Villa, "The Anxiety of Influence: On Arendt's Relationship to Heidegger," in *Politics, Philosophy, Terror: Essays on the Thought of Hannah Arendt* (Princeton, NJ: Princeton University Press, 1999); Villa, "Arendt, Heidegger, and the Tradition," *Social Research* 74:4 (Winter 2007).

29. Accessed at http://www.bard.edu/arendtcollection/marginalia.htm#h.

30. Young-Bruehl, *Hannah Arendt: For Love of the World*. Mainly discussed in chapter 2 (pp. 42–76).

31. Ibid., 75.

32. Arendt and Heidegger, *Letters*, 120.

33. Arendt, "Martin Heidegger at Eighty," 1.

34. Martin Heidegger, *Being and Time*, trans. John Macquarrie and Edward Robinson (New York: Harper and Row, 1962), 51–53, 58ff. (all citations are to this edition of *Being and Time* unless otherwise specified). This approach, obviously, originated with Kant and Hegel, though Heidegger is typically seen as the pioneer of the resurgence it has had in the twentieth century. For a helpful introduction to this approach, see Charles Taylor, "Engaged Agency and Background"; and Taylor, "The Validity of Transcendental Arguments," in *Philosophical Arguments* (Cambridge, MA: Harvard University Press, 1995).

35. This has been a fairly popular form of philosophical argumentation during the last century or so. Daniel Dennett has recently called this kind of argument "intuition pumps." See Daniel C. Dennett, *Elbow Room: The Varieties of Free Will Worth Wanting* (Cambridge, MA: MIT Press, 1984), 12. The later Wittgenstein, for instance, was well known for the use of thought experiments in order to establish his claims about the nature of language, while other philosophers, such as Charles Taylor, John Searle, and Thomas Nagel have made famous arguments based on the use of these kinds of thought experiments.

36. Heidegger, *Being and Time*, 19.

37. Ibid., 21–24.

38. This draws on Charles Taylor's characterization in "Engaged Agency and Background," 210ff.

39. Arendt, "A Reply to Eric Voegelin," 407–408.

40. Ibid., 408.

41. Arendt, *The Human Condition*, 10.

42. Ibid., 10–11.

43. Ibid., 9.

44. Heidegger, *Being and Time*, 78ff.

45. Accessed at http://www.bard.edu/library/arendt/pdfs/Heidegger-SeinundZeit.pdf.

46. Arendt, *The Human Condition*, 7.

47. Arendt, "Concern with Politics in Recent European Philosophical Thought," 443.

48. Heidegger, *Being and Time*, 78ff., 91ff.

49. Martin Heidegger, "The Origin of the Work of Art (Early Draft)," in *The Heidegger Reader*, ed. Günter Figal, trans. Jerome Veith (Bloomington: Indiana University Press, 2009), 35, 135. Thanks go to Richard Polt's *Heidegger: An Introduction* for pointing me to this turn of phrase.

50. The most well-known place Heidegger criticized value thinking was in the "Letter on Humanism," in *Basic Writings*, rev. and expanded ed., ed David Farrell Krell (New York: HarperCollins, 1993), 251ff., which Arendt was known to have called Heidegger's *Prachtstück*, or "his most splendid effort" (216).

51. Heidegger, *Being and Time*, 173ff.

52. Ibid., 79ff.

53. Ibid., 79ff., 169ff.

54. Ibid., 80.

55. Ibid., 19.

56. Ibid., 24–28, 35–37.

57. Ibid., 377.

58. Heidegger, "Letter on Humanism," 230.

59. Heidegger, *Being and Time*, 377.

60. Ibid., 424ff. The German word is *Geschichtlichkeit*. I use the translation of Macquarrie and Robinson, who translate the word as "historicality." However, the common practice when discussing this idea of Heidegger's has been to use Stambaugh's "historicity," and so I will also follow this practice. Cf. Martin Heidegger, *Being and Time*, trans. Joan Stambaugh, rev. Dennis J. Schmidt (Albany: State University of New York Press, [1953] 2010).

61. Heidegger, *Being and Time*, 425.

62. Ibid., 150, 365, 427.

63. Ibid., 444ff.

64. Ibid., 365, 427.

65. Ibid., 434–437.

66. Ibid., 310–324; see also Martin Heidegger, "What Is Metaphysics?" in *Basic Writings*, 90ff.

67. Heidegger, *Being and Time*, 284–311.

68. Ibid., 376ff., 387ff.

69. Ibid., 313.

70. Ibid., 342ff.

71. Ibid., 343; Martin Heidegger, "On the Essence of Truth," trans. John Sallis, in *Basic Writings*, 111ff.

72. Heidegger, "On the Essence of Truth," 130ff.

73. The development of Heidegger's engagement with Aristotle's *Ethics* through the 1920s has been well documented. For a concise treatment, see Gillespie, "Martin Heidegger's Aristotelian National Socialism." For book-length treatments of the Aristotelian background, see Brogan, *Heidegger and Aristotle*; and for how it eventually became *Being and Time*, see Kisiel, *The Genesis of Heidegger's "Being and Time."* Arendt's Aristotelianism clearly comes through her adoption of many of Heidegger's existentialist ontological commitments. Moreover, her conceptions of action as *praxis*, while it draws on pre-Aristotelian sources, would not have been possible if she had not first been responding to Aristotle. The breadth of how extensively Arendt drew on Aristotle's various practical philosophical texts can be demonstrated by consulting her *Denktagebuch*, or thought journal, which was published in Germany in 2002. It shows that in the early to mid-1950s she took notes on the *Politics*, the *Rhetoric*, and the *Poetics*, and several of Aristotle's *Ethics*.

74. Gillespie, "Martin Heidegger's Aristotelian National Socialism," 151ff.

75. This is dealt with through Heidegger's argument that theoretical thinking derives from technical know-how (an argument Arendt sought to develop more concretely in *The Human Condition*), which he fleshes out through phenomenological argumentation and an extensive critique of Descartes, covered roughly in *Being and Time*, 67–138 , with a more concise formulation at 408–415.

76. Gillespie, "Martin Heidegger's Aristotelian National Socialism," 150–151.

77. Arendt, *The Life of the Mind*, "Willing,"184–185.

78. Heidegger, "Letter on Humanism," 217.

79. See Benhabib, *The Reluctant Modernism of Hannah Arendt*; Canovan, *Hannah Arendt*; McCarthy, *The Political Humanism of Hannah Arendt*; Hanna Fenichel Pitkin, *The Attack of the Blob: Hannah Arendt's Concept of the Social* (Chicago: University of Chicago Press, 1998); Dana Villa, "Introduction: The Development of Arendt's Political Thought," in *The Cambridge Companion to Hannah Arendt*, ed. Dana Villa (New York: Cambridge University Press, 2000).

80. Arendt, *The Origins of Totalitarianism,* 3rd ed., 389ff., 461ff., 469ff.

81. Arendt, "Concern with Politics in Recent European Philosophical Thought," 443.

82. Ibid., 432–433, 443–445; Arendt, "What Is Existential Philosophy?" 186.

83. Arendt, "Concern with Politics," 432.

84. Ibid., 433.

85. Arendt, "What Is Existential Philosophy?" 176–180.

86. Arendt, "The Concept of History," 42–44, 61; Arendt, *The Human Condition*, 10–11, 175–188.

87. Arendt, *The Human Condition*, 7–9, 176–178.

88. Ibid., 177–178.

89. Ibid., 184.

90. Arendt, "What Is Freedom?" 168–169.

91. Arendt, "Philosophy and Politics: What Is Political Philosophy?" lecture course (1969), LOC 024429–30, 47; though this is by far her most substantial engagement, Arendt mentions *athanatizein* in a number of other places, including "The Concept of History," 46; *The Human Condition*, 17ff.; *The Life of the Mind*, "Thinking," 129ff.; "Introduction into

Politics," lecture course (1963), LOC 023807; "Philosophy and Politics: The Problem of Action and Thought After the French Revolution," (1954), LOC 023360ff.

92. Arendt, "Philosophy and Politics: What Is Political Philosophy?" (1969), LOC 024429.

93. Ibid., 024447.

94. Ibid.; Arendt, "The Concept of History," 46–47.

95. Arendt, "Philosophy and Politics: What Is Political Philosophy?" (1969), LOC 024446–47.

96. Ibid., 024444.

97. "Arendt, "Introduction *into* Politics," in *The Promise of Politics*, 131; Arendt, "What Is Freedom?" 145, 149, 159; Arendt, *The Life of the Mind*, "Willing," 198–200.

98. Arendt, "Philosophy and Politics: What Is Political Philosophy?" (1969), LOC 024443–45.

99. Arendt, *The Human Condition*, 14–21; Arendt, "Philosophy and Politics: What Is Political Philosophy?" (1969), LOC 024430–39.

100. Arendt, *The Human Condition*, 184; Arendt, "What Is Freedom?" 153.

101. Arendt, *The Human Condition*, 220ff.; Arendt, "The Concept of History," 46–47; Arendt, "Philosophy and Politics: What Is Political Philosophy?" (1969), LOC 024420ff.

102. Arendt, "The Concept of History," 46–47.

103. Arendt, *Lectures on Kant's Political Philosophy*, 22–23; Arendt, "Concern with Politics in Recent European Philosophical Thought," 429.

104. Arendt, "The Concept of History," 47.

105. Ibid., 16ff.

106. Arendt tacitly acknowledges this in "Philosophy and Politics: What Is Political Philosophy?" (1969), LOC 024421.

107. Ibid.

108. Arendt, "The Concept of History," 42.

109. Charles Taylor, who, drawing on the work of Merleau-Ponty, also employs this approach, has more recently called it "philosophical anthropology." See his introduction to *Philosophical Papers*, vols. 1 and 2 (Cambridge: Cambridge University Press, 1985). Elsewhere Stephen K. White has referred to this approach as "weak ontology." See White, *Sustaining Affirmation: The Strengths of Weak Ontology in Political Theory* (Princeton, NJ: Princeton University Press, 2000).

110. Arendt, *The Human Condition*, 5.

111. Ibid., 7–9.

112. Ibid., 7.

113. Ibid., 96ff.

114. Ibid., 105.

115. Arendt, "The Concept of History," 58; Arendt, *The Human Condition*, 7.

116. Arendt, *The Human Condition*, 143–144.

117. Ibid., 7.

118. Ibid., 236.

119. Ibid., 9, 177–178.

120. Ibid., 205–207; Arendt, *The Promise of Politics*, 46; Arendt, "What Is Freedom?" 150ff.; Arendt, "Philosophy and Politics: The Problem of Action and Thought After the French Revolution" (1954), LOC 023367.

121. Arendt, *The Human Condition*, 205; Arendt, *The Promise of Politics*, 46; Arendt, "The Concept of History," 42–48.

122. Arendt, *The Human Condition*, 181–186.

123. Ibid., 182–183.

124. Ibid., 189–192.

125. Ibid., 130–132.

126. Ibid., 182–183.

127. Ibid., 200.

128. Ibid., 178–179.

129. Arendt, "What Is Authority?" 107–115; Arendt, "Karl Marx and the Tradition of Western Political Thought," 290–298; Arendt, *The Human Condition*, 225–230.

130. Arendt, "What Is Authority?" 107ff.; Arendt, "Karl Marx and the Tradition of Western Political Thought," 290–298; Arendt, *The Human Condition*, 20, 178–180, 291ff.; Arendt, "Philosophy and Politics: The Problem of Action and Thought After the French Revolution," LOC 023361–73 (see 64, for instance); Arendt, "Introduction into Politics," lecture course (1963), LOC 023846; Arendt, "The Concept of History," 46–47.

131. Arendt, *The Human Condition*, 291; Arendt, "Philosophy and Politics" (2004), 437–441; Arendt, *The Life of the Mind*, "Thinking," 98–101, 179–181ff.; Arendt, "The Concept of History," 46–47.

132. Arendt, "Philosophy and Politics: The Problem of Action and Thought After the French Revolution" (1954), LOC 023361. In the last sentence, Arendt crossed out the part in brackets and scribbled in the following incomplete phrase: "was so [illegible word] [illegible word] with . . ." It seems obvious that she only intended to smooth out the language of the sentence, and not to alter the basic idea, so I have reinserted the crossed out phrase in lieu of it.

133. Arendt, "What Is Freedom?" 142ff., esp. 161–163; Arendt, *The Human Condition*, 234ff.; Arendt, *The Life of the Mind*, "Willing," 195ff.

134. Arendt, *The Human Condition*, 220–235; Arendt, "What Is Authority?" 139ff.; Arendt, "What Is Freedom?" 161ff.

135. Joan Cocks, *On Sovereignty and Other Political Delusions* (New York: Bloomsbury Academic, 2014), 87ff.; Sharon Krause, "Beyond Non-Domination: Agency, Inequality and the Meaning of Freedom," *Philosophy and Social Criticism* 39:2 (January 2013), 187–208; Patchen Markell, *Bound by Recognition* (Princeton, NJ: Princeton University Press, 2003), 5; Dana Villa, "Beyond Good and Evil: Arendt, Nietzsche, and the Aestheticization of Political Action," *Political Theory* 20:2 (May 1992), 275, 277–278; Linda Zerilli, *Feminism and the Abyss of Freedom* (Chicago: University of Chicago Press, 2005), 116–119.

136. Arendt, "What Is Freedom?" 161–169.

137. Arendt, "The Concept of History," 60.

138. Arendt, *The Human Condition*, 220–235.

139. Charles Taylor, "How Is Mechanism Conceivable?" in *Philosophical Papers*, vol. 1 (Cambridge: Cambridge University Press, 1985).

140. Martin Heidegger, "The Question Concerning Technology," in *Basic Writings*, 313–320; cf. Heidegger, *Plato's Sophist*, trans. Richard Rojcewicz and André Schuwer (Bloomington: Indiana University Press, 1992); on this point, see Richard Rojcewicz, *The Gods and Technology: A Reading of Heidegger* (Albany: State University of New York Press, 2006), 15–44.

141. Immanuel Kant, *Critique of Pure Reason*, trans. Werner S. Pluhar (Indianapolis, IN: Hackett, 1996), A80/B106ff.

142. Ibid., A169/B211ff.; A211/B257ff.

143. Ibid., A169/B211.

144. Arendt, *The Human Condition*, 175ff., 190; Arendt, "Introduction *into* Politics," in *The Promise of Politics*, 95, 190.

145. Arendt, *The Life of the Mind*, "Willing," 32–33, 59–63.

146. Arendt, *The Human Condition*, 222ff.; Arendt, "The Great Tradition II: Ruling and Being Ruled," 947; Arendt, "What Is Freedom?" 164; Arendt, "Philosophy and Politics: What Is Political Philosophy?" (1969), LOC 024431.

147. Arendt, *The Human Condition*, 181–192.

148. Studies have borne out the effectiveness of the recovery movement. For example, see Henry A. Montgomery, William R. Miller, and J. Scott Tonigan, "Does Alcoholics Anonymous Involvement Predict Treatment Outcome?" *Journal of Substance Abuse Treatment* 12:4 (July–August 1995).

149. For instance, see Arendt, *Responsibility and Judgment*, 112; Arendt, "The Concept of History," 62; Arendt, "Lying and Politics," 11–12; Arendt, "Truth and Politics," 243–244.

150. Arendt, *The Life of the Mind*, "Willing," 216–217; Arendt, *The Human Condition*, 220–247.

151. Arendt, "Some Questions Concerning Moral Philosophy," 112; Arendt, "The Concept of History," 62; Arendt, "Lying and Politics," 11–12; Arendt, "Truth and Politics," 243–244.

152. Arendt, *The Life of the Mind*, "Willing," 216–217; Arendt, *The Human Condition*, 220–247.

153. Arendt, "Introduction *into* Politics," in *The Promise of Politics*, 99.

154. Arendt, *The Life of the Mind*, "Thinking," 216.

155. Arendt, "Introduction *into* Politics," in *The Promise of Politics*, 125.

156. Arendt, *The Human Condition*, 7.

157. Ibid., 184.

158. Ibid., 205; Arendt, "The Concept of History," 42–48; Arendt, *The Promise of Politics*, 46.

159. Arendt, *The Human Condition*, 50–53.

160. Ibid., 53.

161. Ibid., 35ff.

162. Ibid., 253, emphasis added.

163. Arendt, "On Humanity in Dark Times," 19, emphasis added; see also 4, 10–13; Arendt, "Introduction *into* Politics," in *The Promise of Politics*, 106–107.

164. Arendt, "Some Questions Concerning Moral Philosophy," 112.

165. Arendt, *The Human Condition*, 49; cf. 42.

166. Ibid., 198ff.

167. Arendt, "Introduction *into* Politics," in *The Promise of Politics*, 106.

168. Arendt, *The Human Condition*, 57; Arendt, *The Promise of Politics*, 41–42.

169. Arendt, *The Human Condition*, 198–199.

170. Ibid., 198.

171. Ibid., 51–52.

172. Ibid., 198; see also 182–183. Cf. Arendt, "On Humanity in Dark Times," 4ff.

173. Arendt, *The Human Condition*, 182–184, 199ff.

174. Arendt, "The Concept of History," 58; Arendt, *The Origins of Totalitarianism*, 3rd ed., 191–197, 300–302.

175. Some of the most reflective discussions of this question are found in deliberative democratic theory. See Jürgen Habermas, "Three Normative Models of Democracy," in *Inclusion of the Other: Studies in Political Theory*, ed. Ciaran Cronin and Pablo De Greiff (Cambridge, MA: MIT Press, 1998); Seyla Benhabib, "Feminist Theory and Hannah Arendt's Concept of Public Space," *History of the Human Sciences* 6:97 (1993), 97–114; Seyla Benhabib, "Toward a Deliberative Model of Democratic Legitimacy," *Democracy and Difference*, ed. Seyla Benhabib (Princeton, NJ: Princeton University Press, 1996).

176. Arendt, "On Hannah Arendt," 316.

177. Arendt, *The Human Condition*, 167–174; Arendt, "The Nation," 207; Arendt, *The Origins of Totalitarianism*, 3rd ed., 300–302; Arendt, "The Concept of History," 89–90.

178. Arendt, "Introduction *into* Politics," in *The Promise of Politics*, 139–140.

179. Ibid., 136–138.

180. Arendt, *The Human Condition*, 159–160.

181. Ibid., 33–35, 38–41.

182. Ibid., 38–43; Arendt writes: "The larger the population in any body politic, the more likely it will be the social rather than the political that constitutes the public realm" (43). See Arendt, "On Humanity in Dark Times," 4, for a discussion of the how the modern public realm has lost its power to illuminate, that is, to disclose the "who" of the actors.

183. Arendt, "Introduction into Politics," lecture course (1963), LOC 023846.

184. Arendt, "What Is Freedom?" 153.

185. Plato, *Republic*, trans. G. M. A. Grube, rev. C. D. C. Reeve (Indianapolis, IN: Hackett, 1992), 357b–358a.

186. Patchen Markell, "Arendt's Work: On the Architecture of *The Human Condition*," *College Literature* 38:1 (Winter 2011), 15–44.

187. Arendt, "The Concept of History," 60.

188. Arendt, *The Human Condition*, 257–259ff.

189. Arendt, "Preface: The Gap Between Past and Future," 3–4ff.

190. Arendt, "The Crisis in Education," 189–193; Arendt, "What Is Freedom?" 152ff., 164–169; Arendt, "On Hannah Arendt," 311; Arendt, "Personal Responsibility Under Dictatorship," 45ff.; Arendt, "Some Questions Concerning Moral Philosophy," 80; Arendt, "Collective Responsibility," 151–158; Arendt, "Introduction *into* Politics," in *The Promise of Politics*, 106ff.; Arendt, *The Life of the Mind*, "Thinking," 158.

191. Arendt, "Introduction into Politics," lecture course (1963), LOC 023803; see also 023804–6.

192. Arendt, "The Crisis in Education," 189–193; Arendt, "What Is Freedom?" 152ff, 164–169; Arendt, *The Life of the Mind*, "Willing," 198.

193. Arendt, "The Crisis in Education," 189.

194. Arendt, "What Is Freedom?" 151–153ff.

195. Arendt, "History of Political Theory: Machiavelli," lecture course (1955), LOC 024022–23.

196. Ibid., 024020.

197. Ibid., 024021.

198. Ibid., 024018.

199. Arendt, "What Is Freedom?" 153.

Chapter 2

1. Arendt, "Preface: The Gap Between Past and Future," 4.

2. Arendt, *The Human Condition*, 17ff.; Arendt, *On Revolution*, 168; Arendt, *The Life of the Mind*, "Willing," 198.

3. Arendt, "Philosophy and Politics: What Is Political Philosophy?" (1969), LOC 024421. I have edited the passage slightly to smooth out the language.

4. Arendt, *On Revolution*, 114–127, 224–225, 237–238; Arendt, "Introduction into Politics" (1963), LOC 023796–806; Arendt, "Preface: The Gap Between Past and Future," 3ff.; Arendt, "What Is Freedom?" 156ff.; Arendt, *The Human Condition*, 192ff.

5. Arendt, "What Is Authority?" 120.

6. Arendt, *The Human Condition*, 199–200, 203.

7. Arendt, "The Concept of History," 43ff.; Arendt, *The Life of the Mind*, "Thinking," 131ff.; Arendt, "Philosophy and Politics: What Is Political Philosophy?" (1969), LOC 024426ff.

8. Arendt, "The Concept of History," 71–72; Arendt, *The Human Condition*, 197–199; Arendt, "Introduction *into* Politics," in *The Promise of Politics*, 123ff., 172; Arendt, "Philosophy and Politics: What Is Political Philosophy?" (1969), LOC 024434.

9. Arendt, "The Concept of History," 51, 71–72; Arendt, *The Human Condition*, 197–199; Arendt, "Philosophy and Politics: What Is Political Philosophy?" (1969), LOC 024434; Arendt, "Philosophy and Politics: The Problem of Action and Thought After the French Revolution" (1954), LOC 023364ff.

10. Arendt, *The Human Condition*, 41, 193–198.

11. Ibid., 48ff., 55ff., 197ff.; cf. Arendt, "What Is Freedom?"

12. Arendt, *On Revolution*, 20ff.

13. Ibid., 20–21; Arendt, *The Human Condition*, 32, 215; Arendt, "Introduction *into* Politics," in *The Promise of Politics*, 118.

14. Arendt, "Introduction *into* Politics," in *The Promise of Politics*, 96.

15. Arendt, *The Human Condition*, 215

16. Arendt, *On Revolution*, 96.

17. Arendt, *The Human Condition*, 28ff.

18. Ibid., 24.

19. Arendt, "Introduction *into* Politics," in *The Promise of Politics*, 119.

20. Ibid., 117.

21. Euben, "Hannah Arendt at Colonus," 41; Pitkin, "Justice," 327ff.; Wolin, "Hannah Arendt: Democracy and the Political," 3ff. See also the discussion in Arendt, "On Hannah Arendt," which shows the perplexity of several commentators, such as Richard Bernstein, Christian Bay, and Mary McCarthy.

22. Arendt, "Introduction *into* Politics," in *The Promise of Politics*, 134; see also her comment in "On Hannah Arendt," 315–318ff.

23. Arendt, "On Hannah Arendt," 316.

24. Ibid., 318.

25. Arendt, "Introduction *into* Politics," in *The Promise of Politics*, 119.

26. Ibid., 51–52.

27. Arendt, "The Concept of History," 51, 71–72; Arendt, "Introduction *into* Politics," in *The Promise of Politics*, 128–129, 166–171; Arendt, "Philosophy and Politics: What Is Political Philosophy?" (1969), LOC 024433–36.

28. Arendt, "The Concept of History," 51, 71–72; Arendt, "Philosophy and Politics: What Is Political Philosophy?" (1969), LOC 024433–36ff; Arendt, *The Promise of Politics*, 26.

29. Arendt, *The Promise of Politics*, 16–17; Arendt, "Philosophy and Politics: The Problem of Action and Thought After the French Revolution" (1954), LOC 023401.

30. Arendt, "Philosophy and Politics: What Is Political Philosophy?" (1969), LOC 024434–37.

31. Ibid., 024435.

32. Ibid., 024434.

33. Arendt, "Philosophy and Politics: The Problem of Action and Thought After the French Revolution" (1954), LOC 023359.

34. Arendt, "Philosophy and Politics: What Is Political Philosophy?" (1969), LOC 024437.

35. Arendt, *The Life of the Mind*, "Thinking," 165.

36. Arendt, "Philosophy and Politics: What Is Political Philosophy?" (1969), LOC 024441.

37. Arendt, *The Life of the Mind*, "Thinking," 177.

38. Arendt, *The Promise of Politics*, 21.

39. Arendt, "Philosophy and Politics: What Is Political Philosophy?" (1969), LOC 024439–47.

40. Ibid., 023358.

41. Ibid., 023367.

42. Arendt, "What Is Authority?" 119–120; Arendt, *The Human Condition*, 220–230; Arendt, "Philosophy and Politics: The Problem of Action and Thought After the French Revolution" (1954), LOC 023367–68.

43. Dean Hammer, "Hannah Arendt and Roman Political Thought: The Practice of Theory," *Political Theory* 30:1 (February 2002), 124–149.

44. Arendt, "Introduction *into* Politics," in *The Promise of Politics*, 163.

45. Arendt, "Introduction *into* Politics," in *The Promise of Politics*, 97; Arendt, "Karl Jaspers: Citizen of the World?" 89.

46. See Young-Bruehl, *Hannah Arendt: For Love of the World*, 158, 280–286. For her positive comments on world citizenship, see Arendt, "Karl Jaspers: Citizen of the World?" 93; Arendt, "Kant's Political Philosophy" (1964), LOC 032295; Arendt, *Lectures on Kant's Political Philosophy* (1970), 75; Arendt, "Introduction *into* Politics," in *The Promise Of Politics*, 97.

47. Arendt, "Introduction *into* Politics," in *The Promise of Politics*, 97, 163–190. Discussions of Arendt's ambivalent yet hopeful relationship with the idea of world citizenship can be found in Andrew Arato and Jean L. Cohen, "Banishing the Sovereign? Internal and External Sovereignty in Arendt," in *Politics in Dark Times: Encounters with Hannah Arendt*, ed. Seyla Benhabib (New York: Cambridge University Press, 2010), 137ff., esp. 167–168; Seyla Benhabib, "Reclaiming Universalism: Negotiating Republican Self-Determination and Cosmopolitan Norms," Tanner Lectures on Human Values (delivered at the University of California, Berkeley, March 2004); Bridget Cotter, "Hannah Arendt and the 'Right to Have Rights,'" in *Hannah Arendt and International Relations*, ed. Anthony F. Lang, Jr., and John Williams (New York: Palgrave Macmillan, 2005).

48. Arendt, "Remarks on 'The Crisis Character of Modern Society,'" *Christianity and Crisis* 26:6 (May 30, 1966), 112–114. Acknowledgments go to Margaret Canovan's *Hannah Arendt: A Reinterpretation of Her Political Thought* for pointing me to this source. There are a variety of other sources that her book also pointed me to.

49. Arendt, "What Is Authority?" 120.

50. Arendt, "Philosophy and Politics" (2004), 435–436.

51. Arendt, "The Great Tradition II: Ruling and Being Ruled," 952.

52. Arendt, "What Is Authority?" 120, 124.

53. Ibid., 124–125.

54. Ibid., 121.

55. Ibid., 122–125; Arendt, *The Promise of Politics*, 41–42, 54–55.

56. Arendt, "What Is Authority?" 123–124; Arendt, *The Promise of Politics*, 48–49.

57. Arendt, *The Origins of Totalitarianism*, 3rd ed., 126.

58. Ibid., 124–128.

59. Arendt, "What Is Authority?" 120–121.

60. Arendt, *The Origins of Totalitarianism*, 3rd ed., 208.

61. Arendt, "Introduction *into* Politics," in *The Promise of Politics*, 173. Most of Arendt's observations on Rome are based on Mommsen's dated but highly influential work.

62. Arendt, "Introduction *into* Politics," in *The Promise of Politics*, 176.

63. Ibid., 170, 178–179.

64. Ibid., 164–165.

65. Ibid., 171, 179.

66. Ibid., 189.

67. Ibid., 186.

68. Arendt, "On Humanity in Dark Times: Thoughts About Lessing," 25; Arendt, "The Crisis in Culture," 221.

69. Arendt, "On Humanity in Dark Times," 25; Arendt, "The Crisis in Culture," 220–222.

70. Arendt, "The Concept of History," 48–51.

71. Arendt, "Introduction *into* Politics," in *The Promise of Politics*, 167; more broadly, see 167–170.

72. Arendt, "Preface: The Gap Between Past and Future," 13.

73. Arendt, "Introduction *into* Politics," in *The Promise of Politics*, 187–188.

74. Arendt, "What Is Authority?" 125.

75. Ibid., 125–127; Gelasius quoted at 126.

76. Ibid., 126.

77. Ibid., 106.

78. Ibid., 127, 286.

79. Ibid., 127–128.

80. Ibid., 128.

81. Arendt, *On Revolution*, 108, 153–154, 193.

82. Arendt, "What Is Authority?" 140.

83. Arendt, *On Revolution*, 33–35; cf. 153–154.

84. Ibid., 24.

85. Ibid., 106ff., 247ff.

86. Ibid., 132–135.

87. Ibid., 137–140.

Chapter 3

1. Richard J. Bernstein, "Arendt on Thinking," in *The Cambridge Companion to Hannah Arendt*, ed. Dana Villa (Cambridge: Cambridge University Press, 2000), 277; George Kateb, *Hannah Arendt: Politics, Conscience, Evil* (Totowa, NY: Rowman & Allanheld, 1984), 188–189. It is also implied in many other discussions of the role of thinking in Arendt's thought, since most begin their discussions with the Eichmann trial. See, for instance, Robert Fine, "Judgment and the Reification of the Faculties: A Reconstructive Reading of Arendt's *The Life of the Mind*," *Philosophy and Social Criticism* 34:1–2 (2008); and Villa, "Thinking and Judging."

2. Arendt, *The Life of the Mind*, "Thinking," 5–6.

3. Arendt, "Preface: The Gap Between Past and Future," 12–13; Arendt, *The Life of the Mind*, "Thinking," 197–199ff.

4. Arendt, "Preface," 13–14; Arendt, *The Life of the Mind*, "Thinking," 85–88.

5. Arendt, "Philosophy and Politics" (2004), 437–441; Arendt, *The Life of the Mind*, "Thinking," 98–101, 179–181ff.

6. Arendt, *The Life of the Mind*, "Thinking,: 6; Arendt, *The Human Condition*, 14–17, 20–21; Arendt, "Introduction into Politics," lecture course (1963), LOC 023846.

7. Arendt, *The Human Condition*, 17.

8. Arendt, *The Life of the Mind*, "Thinking," 6ff.; Arendt, *The Human Condition*, 14–17, 20–21.

9. Arendt, *The Life of the Mind*, "Thinking," 10–11, 212.

10. Ibid., 45.

11. Ibid., 53, 72.

12. Ibid., 80–84, 88, 125, 197ff.

13. Ibid, 204ff.; Arendt, "Preface: The Gap Between Past and Future," 10.

14. Arendt, *The Life of the Mind*, "Thinking," 184ff.

15. Ibid., 56–60, 62–65, 185ff.

16. Ibid., 88.

17. Ibid., 108–121, 141–151.

18. Arendt, "Philosophy and Politics" (2004), 448–451.

19. Arendt, "The Concept of History," 46–47; Arendt, *The Human Condition*, 302–304.

20. Arendt, *The Human Condition*, 20.

21. Arendt, "Philosophy and Politics: What Is Political Philosophy?" (1969), LOC 024425–26.

22. Ibid., 024455; Arendt, *The Life of the Mind*, "Thinking," 78–79, 114–115.

23. Arendt, "Philosophy and Politics: What Is Political Philosophy?" (1969), LOC 024423.

24. Arendt, "Introduction *into* Politics," in *The Promise of Politics*, 131; Arendt, "What Is Freedom?" 145, 149, 159; Arendt, *The Life of the Mind*, "Willing," 198–200.

25. Arendt, "The Concept of History," 46–47.

26. Arendt, "Philosophy and Politics: The Problem of Action and Thought After the French Revolution" (1954), LOC 023360, 66–67.

27. Arendt, *The Life of the Mind*, "Thinking," 178.

28. Ibid., 174–175.

29. Arendt, "Preface: The Gap Between Past and Future," 13–14.

30. Arendt, *The Life of the Mind*, "Thinking," 178.

31. Ibid., 185.

32. Arendt, "On Hannah Arendt," 303.

33. Ibid., 303; Arendt, *The Life of the Mind*, "Thinking," 88–91, 132ff., 148–149.

34. Arendt, "Philosophy and Politics: What Is Political Philosophy?" (1969), LOC 024461.

35. Ibid., 023358.

36. Plato, *Republic*, 514a–517b.

37. The most well-known account of her interpretation of the cave allegory comes in "What Is Authority?"; but she had for the most part developed the line of argument well before the publication of *The Human Condition*, in materials that were more recently published in the manuscript "Philosophy and Politics" (2004), which was written primarily in the early 1950s. She also corresponded with both Heidegger and Jaspers about the argument around the mid-1950s. See Arendt and Heidegger, *Letters*, 120; and Arendt and Jaspers, *Correspondence*, 284, 288–289.

38. Arendt, "Guggenheim Proposal." Thanks go to Patchen Markell for furnishing me with this document.

39. Arendt and Heidegger, *Letters*, 120–121.

40. The evidence for this comes out most powerfully in her discussion of philosophical "wonder," or *thaumazein*. It is replete in Arendt, "Philosophy and Politics: What Is Political Philosophy?" (1969); see also Arendt, "Philosophy and Politics" (2004), 447ff.; Arendt, *The Human Condition*, 12–21, 302–305; Arendt, "The Concept of History," 46–47.

41. Arendt, "On Hannah Arendt," 305–306.

42. See Arendt, "Guggenheim Proposal"; "Tradition and the Modern Age," 17ff, 39–40; "What Is Authority?" 109–110, 127–128; Arendt, "Philosophy and Politics: The Problem of Action and Thought After the French Revolution" (1954), LOC 023418.

43. Arendt, *The Human Condition*, 185ff. The reference is to Plato's *Laws* 803 and 644. Also see Arendt, *The Promise of Politics*, 56ff., 81ff.; and Arendt, "Karl Marx and the Tradition of Western Political Thought," 312–313.

44. Arendt, *Lectures on Kant's Political Philosophy*, 22. Arendt quotes this line from Pascal in several places that stretch from well before the publication of *The Human Condition* to her final work on *The Life of the Mind* manuscript. See Arendt, "Concern with Politics in Recent European Thought," 429; Arendt, "Philosophy and Politics: What Is Political Philosophy?" (1969), LOC 024420; Arendt, *The Life of the Mind*, "Thinking," 152–153.

45. Arendt, "Philosophy and Politics" (2004), 445–450; Arendt, "Tradition and the Modern Age," 35–36; Arendt, "Philosophy and Politics: What Is Political Philosophy?" (1969), LOC 024425–26.

46. Plato, *Republic*, 516e–517a.

47. Arendt, "Philosophy and Politics" (2004), 446–447.

48. Arendt, "What Is Authority?" 106, 119–120; Arendt, *The Human Condition*, 229–230; Arendt, "The Great Tradition II: Ruling and Being Ruled," 954; Arendt, *The Promise of Politics*, 52.

49. Arendt, "What Is Authority?" 109, 114; Arendt, *The Human Condition*, 221–230.

50. Arendt, "What Is Authority?" 104–108, 132.

51. Ibid., 119–120.

52. Ibid., 105.

53. Ibid., 107–110.

54. Ibid., 110, 284 n. 13.

55. Arendt, *The Human Condition*, 139–143, 142–143 n. 7.

56. Ibid., 225–227; Arendt, "What Is Authority?" 112–113.

57. Arendt, *The Human Condition*, 227.

58. Ibid., 301.

59. Arendt, "What Is Authority?" 112–113.

60. Arendt, *The Human Condition*, 223–226, 302–303; Arendt, "Philosophy and Politics" (2004), 429–431, 451–454; Arendt, "What Is Authority?" 112–115.

61. Arendt, "Philosophy and Politics" (2004), 446–447; Arendt, "What Is Authority?" 107–113; Arendt, *The Human Condition*, 220–227.

62. Arendt, "The Great Tradition I: Law and Power," 713.

63. Arendt, "Karl Marx and the Tradition of Western Political Thought," 304.

64. Arendt, "What Is Authority?" 141; Arendt, *The Human Condition*, 228–230; Arendt, *On Revolution*, 55.

65. Arendt, "History of Political Philosophy: Machiavelli," lecture course (1955), LOC 024022–27; Arendt, "What Is Freedom?" 150–153; Arendt, "Philosophy and Politics: The Problem of Action and Thought After the French Revolution" (1954), LOC 023368–70; Arendt, "What Is Authority?" 116–117.

66. Arendt, *On Revolution*, 27.

67. Arendt, "History of Political Philosophy: Machiavelli" (1955), LOC 024026; see also Arendt, "What Is Authority?" 139–141.

68. Ibid., 115–116.

69. Arendt, "Philosophy and Politics: The Problem of Action and Thought After the French Revolution" (1954), LOC 023370.

70. Ibid., 023370–71.

71. Arendt, "What Is Authority?" 116ff.

72. Ibid., 116.

73. Ibid., 116–119; Arendt, "The Great Tradition I: Law and Power," 713.

74. Arendt, "What Is Authority?" 115, 118–120.

75. Arendt, *The Promise of Politics*, 47.

76. Arendt, "What Is Authority?" 114–115; Arendt, *The Promise of Politics*, 56; Arendt, *The Human Condition*, 14–17; Arendt, "Karl Marx and the Tradition of Western Political Thought," 314–315.

77. The most succinct statement is in Arendt, "Karl Marx and the Tradition of Western Political Thought," 304–305; see also Arendt, "What Is Authority?" 110, 127–128; Arendt, "The Great Tradition I: Law and Power," 713–716; Arendt, *The Human Condition*, 222–224ff.

78. Arendt, "Philosophy and Politics" (2004), 427ff.; Arendt, *The Promise of Politics*, 6ff.; Arendt, *The Life of the Mind*, "Thinking," 173–178ff.

79. Aristotle, *The Nicomachean Ethics*, trans. J. A. K. Thomson and Hugh Tredennick (New York: Penguin Books, 2004), 1.9–10.

80. Ibid., 10.7–8.

81. Seyla Benhabib, *Situating the Self: Gender, Community and Postmodernism in Contemporary Ethics* (Cambridge, UK: Polity Press, 1992), 124ff.; Lisa Disch, *Hannah Arendt and the Limits of Philosophy* (Ithaca, NY: Cornell University Press, 1994), 164, 210ff.

Chapter 4

1. This is Arendt's unique account of the origins of modernity. There are, of course, several other accounts one might consult, including Hans Blumenberg, *The Legitimacy of the Modern Age*, trans. Robert M. Wallace (Cambridge, MA: MIT Press, 1983); Michael Allen Gillespie, *The Theological Origins of Modernity* (Chicago: University of Chicago Press, 2008); Martin Heidegger, *The Question Concerning Technology and Other Essays*, trans. William Lovitt (New York: Harper & Row, 1977); Friedrich Nietzsche, *On the Genealogy of Morals*, trans. Walter Kaufmann (New York: Random House, 1969); Charles Taylor, *Sources of the Self: The Making of the Modern Identity* (Cambridge, MA: Harvard University Press, 1989); Max Weber, *The Protestant Ethic and the Spirit of Capitalism with Other Writings on the Rise of the West*, trans. Stephen Kalberg (New York: Oxford University Press, 2009).

2. Arendt, *The Human Condition*, 288.

3. Werner Heisenberg, *The Physicist's Conception of Nature*, trans. Arnold J. Pomerans (London: Hutchinson, 1958); Thomas S. Kuhn, *The Structure of Scientific Revolutions* (Chicago: University of Chicago Press, 2012).

4. Thomas Nagel, *The View from Nowhere* (Oxford: Oxford University Press, 1986); Hilary Putnam, *Reason, Truth, and History* (Cambridge: Cambridge University Press, 1981).

5. Kant, *Critique of Pure Reason*, A310/B366ff. I am aware that pragmatist approaches tend to emphasize the practice of error correction in an attempt to head off the criticism implied in these views. However, in my view, these approaches are simply sidestepping the critique. It seems to me that there is an unavoidable "Archimedean" point of reference implied in the notion of error correction. Where, after all, is the standard against which an "error" is judged derived from?

6. Arendt, *The Human Condition*, 11.

7. Ibid., 263.

8. Ibid., 2–5, 262–264.

9. Ibid., 4.

10. Arendt, *The Origins of Totalitarianism*, 3rd ed., 300–301.

11. Ibid., 137–138.

12. Arendt, *The Human Condition*, 262, 288.

13. Ibid., 258, 260.

14. Arendt, "The Concept of History," 54–55.

15. Arendt, *The Human Condition*, 288.

16. Arendt, "The Concept of History," 55.

17. Arendt, *The Human Condition*, 262.

18. Ibid., 288; Arendt, *On Revolution*, 130–131.

19. Arendt, *The Human Condition*, 42, 248.

20. Ibid., 259.

21. Arendt, "The Concept of History," 42–43.

22. Arendt, *The Human Condition*, 1–2, 262–264, 271.

23. Ibid., 271.

24. René Descartes, *Discourse on Method*, trans. Donald A. Cress (Indianapolis, IN: Hackett, 1998), 34–35.

25. C. J. Herington, "Introduction," in *Persians* by Aeschylus, trans. Janet Lembke and C. J. Herington (Oxford: Oxford University Press, 1981), 21–23.

26. Arendt, *The Human Condition*, 14–16, 289

27. Ibid., 14; Arendt, "What Is Authority?" 126–127.

28. Aristotle, *The Nicomachean Ethics*, 1177a35–36, 1178b20–32.

29. Arendt, *The Human Condition*, 289–290, 294–295.

30. Ibid., 290.

31. Ibid., 295; Arendt repeats the phrase on pp. 17, 228, 282. See also Arendt, "Tradition and the Modern Age," 31; and Arendt, "The Concept of History," 57, 76.

32. Arendt, *The Human Condition*, 231, 295, 298.

33. Ibid., 271.

34. Ibid., 116, 126, 133; Arendt, "Tradition and the Modern Age," 31; Arendt, *On Revolution*, 12.

35. Arendt, *The Human Condition*, 322–323.

36. See Michael Allen Gillespie, *Nihilism Before Nietzsche* (Chicago: University of

Chicago Press, 1996); Martin Heidegger, *Nietzsche*, trans. David Ferrell Krell, et al. (New York: HarperCollins, 1991); Stanley Rosen, *Nihilism: A Philosophical Essay* (New Haven, CT: Yale University Press, 1969); Taylor, *Sources of the Self.*

37. Arendt, *The Human Condition*, 126. Subsequent page references to *The Human Condition* in this section appear parenthetically in the text.

38. There is a slight terminological ambiguity concerning the idea of world alienation in *The Human Condition*. In the early chapters of "The *Vita Activa* and the Modern Age," Arendt draws a distinction between the "world alienation" begun by the accumulation of wealth that resulted from the Reformation's expropriation of church land and the "earth alienation" that was the result of the discovery of the Archimedean point's impulse to escape from the human condition (264). However, to my knowledge, this short passage is the only occasion where she ever draws this distinction, indeed, the only time she ever uses the term "earth alienation," either in the rest of *The Human Condition* or throughout the remainder of her work. Other than this instance, she typically uses the more generic term "world alienation" or some other similar designation such as "worldlessness" or "loss of the world" (115–118, 322). Thus, this ambiguity should not trouble us all that much, and I propose to use the generic term "world alienation" to signify the various turns of phrase she uses in expressing the idea that the modern world has been fundamentally characterized by a growing detachment, obscurity, and ominous unpredictability in relation to its inhabitants.

39. See also Arendt, "The Concept of History," 72–73.

40. See also Arendt, "Tradition and the Modern Age," 31ff.

41. Taylor, *Sources of the Self*, 211ff.; Gillespie, *The Theological Origins of Modernity*, 255ff.; Jeremy Waldron, *God, Locke, and Equality: Christian Foundations in Locke's Political Thought* (Cambridge: Cambridge University Press, 2002); Jeremy Waldron, "Legislation and Moral Neutrality," in *Liberal Neutrality*, ed. Robert E. Goodin and Andrew Reeve (London: Routledge, 1989).

42. Arendt, *The Human Condition*, 28–29, 41, 256–257. See also Arendt, "Karl Marx and the Tradition of Western Political Thought," 300–305; Arendt, "Introduction *into* Politics," in *The Promise of Politics*, 98, 108–110; Arendt, "Tradition and the Modern Age," 31ff.

43. Arendt, *The Human Condition*, 45, 148–152, 321ff.

44. Ibid., 3–11, 147ff.

45. Arendt, "The Cold War and the West: Symposium," *Partisan Review* 29:1 (1962).

46. Arendt, *The Human Condition*, 228ff., 305–306.

47. Ibid., 227–228; "What Is Authority?" 113; Arendt, *Lectures on Kant's Political Philosophy*, 22–23; Arendt, "Concern with Politics in Recent European Philosophical Thought," 429.

48. Arendt, *The Human Condition*, 234–236, 244–245, 305.

49. Ibid., 299–300.

50. Ibid., 222ff.; Arendt, "The Great Tradition I: Law and Power," 713; Arendt, "The Great Tradition II: Ruling and Being Ruled," 953; Arendt, *The Promise of Politics*, 63–64; Arendt, "What Is Authority?" 109–111, 116–118.

51. Arendt, *The Human Condition*, 228; Arendt, "What Is Authority?" 109–111, 116ff.; Arendt, "The Great Tradition I: Law and Power," 718ff.

52. Arendt, "The Great Tradition I: Law and Power," 718–720.

53. Thomas Hobbes, *Leviathan*, ed. Richard Tuck (Cambridge: Cambridge University Press, 1996), chap. 18.

54. It is true that the original impulse to develop political sovereignty and sovereignty-based political theories came from the immediate need to end the post-Reformation wars of religion. But the question of why exactly sovereignty was put forward as the solution to the problem, as opposed to other possible solutions, is not really addressed by this point. Arendt seems to have believed that the wars of religion were a peculiarly modern problem, and that therefore sovereignty was in all likelihood the obvious modern solution. While modern science may not have directly been the cause of the wars of religion, Michael Gillespie has shown that there were a variety of premodern sources that ultimately congealed into modernity with the emergence of modern science. See Gillespie, *The Theological Origins of Modernity*.

55. Arendt, *The Human Condition*, 228ff.; Arendt, *The Promise of Politics*, 41, 50–54, 191–192; Arendt, *On Revolution*, 108–109.

56. Arendt, *On Revolution*, 11–13, 18–31.

57. See, for example, Bernstein, "Rethinking the Social and the Political," 248ff.; Canovan, *Hannah Arendt: A Reinterpretation of Her Political Thought*, 201–238; Pitkin, "Justice," 336ff.; Villa, *Arendt and Heidegger*, 35ff.

58. Arendt, *On Revolution*, 108–109.

59. Ibid., 24.

60. Ibid., 33–35.

61. Ibid., 31–66, 102ff., 127–133.

62. Ibid., 102.

63. Ibid., 13–14, 58–59, 118–131, 163–170, 188–196.

64. Theda Skocpol, *Diminished Democracy: From Membership to Management in American Civic Life* (Norman: University of Oklahoma Press, 2003); Robert D. Putnam, *Bowling Alone: The Collapse and Revival of American Community* (New York: Simon & Schuster, 2000).

65. Arendt, *On Revolution*, 8ff., 25–31, 54–55; Arendt, "What Is Authority?" 127–141.

66. Arendt, *The Human Condition*, 200ff.; Arendt, *On Revolution*, 158ff., 170–174.

67. Arendt, *On Revolution*, 25.

68. Ibid., 38–48; Arendt, *The Human Condition*, 228ff.

69. Arendt, *On Revolution*, 48.

70. Arendt, *Lectures on Kant's Political Philosophy*, 45.

71. Ibid.

72. Arendt, "Karl Marx," seminar at University of Chicago (1966), LOC 024295, 024328.

73. Arendt, *On Revolution*, 38–48, esp. 43.

74. Arendt, *The Promise of Politics*, 70–80; Arendt, *On Revolution*, 23, 44–45, 54,103–105; Arendt, *The Human Condition*, 199ff.

75. This section, which develops the relationship between Hegel's legacy, Marx's use of Hegel, and the development of ideological political thought, is augmented by several

invaluable—though highly schematic—manuscripts and lectures that span from about 1951 to 1966, some of which I have retrieved from the Library of Congress and others that have been edited and published in various places by Jerome Kohn, along with Arendt's statements concerning Marx in "Tradition and the Modern Age."

76. Arendt, *The Life of the Mind*, "Willing," 140.

77. Arendt, "Karl Marx," seminar (1966), LOC 024295; cf. Arendt, *The Life of the Mind*, "Willing," 140.

78. Arendt, *The Promise of Politics*, 70–71, 73–74.

79. Arendt, "Karl Marx and the Tradition of Western Political Philosophy," 310.

80. Ibid.; Arendt, *The Promise of Politics*, 70.

81. Walter Kaufmann, *Hegel: A Reinterpretation* (Notre Dame, IN: University of Notre Dame Press, 1988), 154; Gustav E. Mueller, "The Hegel Legend of 'Thesis-Antithesis-Synthesis,'" *Journal of the History of Ideas* 19:3 (June 1958), 411–414.

82. Arendt, *The Promise of Politics*, 70, 74–75.

83. Arendt, "Karl Marx," seminar (1966), LOC 024295.

84. Arendt, *The Promise of Politics*, 74.

85. Arendt, "Tradition and the Modern Age," 31.

86. Arendt, "Karl Marx and the Tradition of Western Political Philosophy," 300–301.

87. Arendt, "Tradition and the Modern Age," 17–20, 31–32.

88. Arendt, *The Promise of Politics*, 75–76; Arendt, "Karl Marx" seminar (1966), LOC 024295.

89. Arendt, "Karl Marx and the Tradition of Western Political Philosophy," 310.

90. Ibid., 308–312; Arendt, *The Promise of Politics*, 75–80; Arendt, "Karl Marx," seminar (1966), LOC 024294–95.

91. Arendt, "Tradition and the Modern Age," 18ff., 23–24.

92. Ibid., 28ff., 34ff.

93. Ibid., 39.

94. Ibid., 30.

95. Arendt, "Karl Marx and the Tradition of Western Political Philosophy," 290–297.

96. Arendt, "Tradition and the Modern Age," 29.

97. Arendt, *The Human Condition*, 294ff.

98. Arendt, "What Is Authority?" 100–104.

99. Arendt, *On Revolution*, 1; Arendt, *The Origins of Totalitarianism*, 3rd ed., 468ff.

100. Arendt, *The Origins of Totalitarianism*, 3rd ed., 468–469.

101. Arendt, *The Promise of Politics*, 40–42, 102ff.

102. Ibid, 102–103.

103. Arendt, *The Origins of Totalitarianism*, 3rd ed., 457–458, 475–477.

104. Arendt, "The Great Tradition I: Law and Power," 717.

105. Arendt, *The Promise of Politics*, 87–90.

106. Arendt, "The Great Tradition I: Law and Power," 719–720; Arendt, *The Origins of Totalitarianism*, 3rd ed., 461–465.

107. Arendt, *The Origins of Totalitarianism*, 3rd ed., 468–471.

108. Ibid.; Arendt, "The Great Tradition I: Law and Power," 720; Arendt, "Tradition and the Modern Age," 26.

109. Arendt, "Ideologies," seminar given at University of California, Berkeley (1955), LOC 024126; Arendt, *The Human Condition*, 39–45, 182ff.

110. Arendt, *The Origins of Totalitarianism*, 3rd ed., 470–471.

111. For a good account of Bernstein's thought and political activities, see Sheri Berman, *The Primacy of Politics: Social Democracy and the Making of Europe's Twentieth Century* (Cambridge: Cambridge University Press, 2006), 35–46.

112. Arendt, *The Human Condition*, 6.

113. Arendt, "Tradition and the Modern Age," 26–27; Arendt, "The Concept of History," 59ff.

114. Arendt, *The Human Condition*, 6.

115. Ibid., 289.

116. Arendt, "The Concept of History," 59.

117. Arendt, "Tradition and the Modern Age," 26.

118. Arendt, "Guggenheim Proposal."

119. Arendt and Heidegger, *Letters*, 120–121; see also Jerome Kohn, "Introduction," *The Promise of Politics*.

120. Arendt, "Ideology and Terror: A Novel Form of Government," *Review of Politics* 15:3 (July 1953), 303–327.

121. Arendt, *The Origins of Totalitarianism*, 3rd ed., 460–479.

122. Ibid., 458.

123. Pages 457–459 of the "Totalitarianism in Power" chapter in the third edition, which mention the "common world," begin where this chapter concludes in the first edition on page 428.

124. Arendt, *The Origins of Totalitarianism*, 1st ed., 191–197.

125. Ibid., 216–221.

126. Ibid., 123–134.

127. Arendt, *The Origins of Totalitarianism*, 3rd ed., 473–477.

128. Arendt, "Introduction *into* Politics," in *The Promise of Politics*, 109–110.

129. Arendt, "Political Experiences in the Twentieth Century," course at the New School for Social Research (1968), LOC 023612–13.

130. Ibid., 023590; Arendt, "Tradition and the Modern Age," 26–27.

131. Arendt, "Political Experiences in the Twentieth Century" (1968), LOC 023592–93.

132. Ibid., 023593. For a similar external discussion of the profound impact of the First World War on Western society, see David Fromkin, *Europe's Last Summer: Who Started the Great War of 1914?* (New York: Vintage Books, 2004), 5–9.

133. Arendt, "Political Experiences in the Twentieth Century" (1968), LOC 023594.

134. Ibid.

135. Ibid.

136. Arendt, *The Origins of Totalitarianism*, 3rd ed., 220.

137. Ibid.

138. Ibid., 220–221.

139. Ibid., 106ff, 326ff.

140. Richard Overy, *The Dictators: Hitler's Germany, Stalin's Russia* (New York: W. W. Norton, 2004), 21–22.

141. Arendt, "Ideologies," seminar (1955). There appears to be a clerical error in the way the course was listed in the Library of Congress archive. The course is labeled "Ideologies Seminar" in the archive, but this is undoubtedly a mistake, since the first page of the course (LOC 024106) is labeled by Arendt under the course heading "Totalitarianism 212B" and therefore should be labeled in the archive as "Totalitarianism Seminar." Also, be advised that the pages of Arendt's notes are out of order, and, as a result, anyone who consults this source will first have to reorder them.

142. Ibid., 024122, 25, 53.

143. Ibid., 024130–31.

144. Ibid., 024123–24.

145. Ibid., 024137.

146. Arendt, *The Human Condition*, 230ff., 238, 268ff.

147. Arendt, "The Concept of History," 58–63, 87–90; Arendt, *The Human Condition*, 231, 262ff.

148. Arendt, "The Archimedean Point," lecture given at College of Engineers, University of Michigan (1968), LOC 031401.

149. Arendt, *Between Past and Future*, 208ff., 221, 262ff., 272ff.

Chapter 5

1. Arendt, *The Human Condition*, 283; cf. Arendt, "The Crisis in Culture," 175; Arendt, *The Origins of Totalitarianism,* 3rd ed., 475–476; Arendt, *The Life of the Mind,* "Thinking," 50–53, 81.

2. Arendt, *The Origins of Totalitarianism*, 3rd ed., 3ff, 308–318, 440ff.

3. Arendt, *The Human Condition*, 283ff.

4. Arendt, "Philosophy and Politics" (2004), 446–447; Arendt, *The Human Condition*, 283–284.

5. Arendt, "The Crisis in Culture"; Arendt, "Truth and Politics"; Arendt, *Lectures on Kant's Political Philosophy.*

6. Arendt, *Lectures on Kant's Political Philosophy*, 7–10.

7. Makkreel, *Imagination and Interpretation in Kant*; Makkreel, "Reflective Judgment, Orientation, and the Priorities of Justice," 105–110; Makkreel, "The Role of Judgment and Orientation in Hermeneutics," 29–50; Ferrara, *Justice and Judgment*; Ferrara, *The Force of Example*; Lara, *Narrating Evil.*

8. Kateb, "The Judgment of Hannah Arendt," 122.

9. Benhabib, "Judgment and the Moral Foundations of Politics in Hannah Arendt's Thought," 198–201.

10. Benhabib, *The Reluctant Modernism of Hannah Arendt*, 193–194.

11. Ronald Beiner, "Rereading 'Truth and Politics,'" *Philosophy and Social Criticism* 34:1–2 (2008), 123–136; Beiner, "Rereading Hannah Arendt's Kant Lectures"; Habermas, "Hannah Arendt's Communications Concept of Power"; Steinberger, "Hannah Arendt on Judgment."

12. Habermas, "Hannah Arendt's Communications Concept of Power," 22–23.

13. Bernstein, "Judging—the Actor and the Spectator"; Beiner, "Interpretive Essay," 134–135.

14. Bernstein, "Judging," 237.

15. Beiner, "Interpretive Essay," 92.

16. Bernstein, "Judging," 237.

17. Beiner, "Interpretive Essay," 134–135; Beiner, "Rereading Hannah Arendt's Kant Lectures," 100.

18. Dostal, "Judging Human Action"; Norris, "Arendt, Kant, and the Politics of Common Sense"; Steinberger, "Hannah Arendt on Judgment".

19. Norris, "Arendt, Kant, and the Politics of Common Sense," 191.

20. Steinberger, "Hannah Arendt on Judgment," 818–819.

21. See John D. Schaeffer, "Commonplaces: *Sensus Communis*," in *A Companion to Rhetoric and Rhetorical Criticism*, ed. Walter Jost and Wendy Olmsted (Blackwell Publishing, 2003), *Blackwell Reference Online*, 3ff., accessed 27 August 2015 at http://www.blackwellreference.com/public/book.html?id=g9781405101121_9781405101121.

22. Aristotle, "De Anima," in *The Basic Works of Aristotle*, ed. Richard McKeon (New York: Random House, 2001), 3.2; see also Pavel Gregoric, *Aristotle on the Common Sense* (New York: Oxford University Press, 2007).

23. Aristotle, "Rhetoric," in *Plato Gorgias and Aristotle Rhetoric*, trans. Joe Sachs (Newburyport, MA: Focus Publishing, 2009), 1.1–2, 2.1ff.; see also David Summers, *The Judgment of Sense: Renaissance Naturalism and the Rise of Aesthetics* (Cambridge: Cambridge University Press, 1987), 81ff.

24. Summers, *The Judgment of Sense*, 81.

25. Aristotle, *Nicomachean Ethics*, book 6.

26. Schaeffer, "Commonplaces," 3–8.

27. Arendt, "Philosophy and Politics: The Problem of Action and Thought After the French Revolution" (1954), LOC 023363.

28. Ibid., 023363–64.

29. See Gillespie, "Martin Heidegger's Aristotelian National Socialism"; and Kisiel, *The Genesis of Heidegger's "Being and Time."*

30. Heidegger, *Being and Time*, 169ff.

31. Arendt, "Understanding and Politics," 307–309, 311.

32. Ibid., 311–313ff.

33. Ibid., 311, 316–318.

34. Arendt, *Denktagebuch*, 569ff.

35. Arendt and Jaspers, *Correspondence*, 318.

36. Arendt, "Some Questions Concerning Moral Philosophy," 137–145; Arendt, "The Concept of History," 51ff.; Arendt, "The Crisis in Culture," 216ff.; Arendt, "Truth and Politics," 237–238; Arendt, *Lectures on Kant's Political Philosophy*, 41ff., 58–77; Arendt, *The Life of the Mind*, "Thinking," 94ff., 215–216.

37. Hans-Georg Gadamer, *Truth and Method*, 2nd rev. ed., trans. Joel Weinsheimer and Donald G. Marshall (New York: Continuum, 1975), 17–30ff.

38. Arendt, *Denktagebuch*, 582. Author's translation.

39. Ibid., 574, 575.

40. Ibid., 572.

41. Ibid.: "Das Urteilen erhebt Anspruch auf Gültigkeit, ohne doch im mindesten zwingen zu können."

42. Arendt, "The Concept of History," 47–54; Arendt, "The Crisis in Culture," 217–219; Arendt, "Truth and Politics," 228–230, 235–238; Arendt, *The Life of the Mind*, "Thinking," 111, 215.

43. Arendt, "Kant's Political Philosophy" (1964), LOC 032259, 69, 70, 83, 92, 94, 95.

44. Ibid., 032259.

45. Ibid., 032270.

46. Arendt, "On Hannah Arendt," 312–313.

47. Arendt, "The Crisis in Culture," 218ff.

48. In formulating my interpretation of Kant's *Critique of Judgment*, I have referenced the following works: Henry E. Allison, *Kant's Theory of Taste: A Reading of the "Critique of Aesthetic Judgment"* (New York: University of Cambridge Press, 2001); Allison, *Kant's Transcendental Idealism*, rev. and enlarged ed. (New Haven, CT: Yale University Press, 2004); Paul Guyer, *Kant and the Claims of Taste* (Cambridge, MA: Harvard University Press, 1979); Guyer, "The Transcendental Deduction of the Categories," in *The Cambridge Companion to Kant*, ed. Paul Guyer (New York: Cambridge University Press, 1992); *Kant* (New York: Routledge, 2006); Beatrice Longuenesse, *Kant and the Capacity to Judge: Sensibility and Discursivity in the Transcendental Analytic of the "Critique of Pure Reason,"* trans. Charles T. Wolfe (Princeton, NJ: Princeton University Press, 1998); Werner S. Pluhar, introduction to *Critique of Judgment*, by Immanuel Kant, trans. Werner S. Pluhar (Indianapolis, IN: Hackett, 1987); Anthony Savile, *Aesthetic Reconstructions: The Seminal Writing of Lessing, Kant and Schiller* (Oxford: Basil Blackwell, 1987); John H. Zammito, *The Genesis of Kant's Critique of Judgment* (Chicago: University of Chicago Press, 1992).

49. Arendt, *The Life of the Mind*, "Thinking," 69, 94–98, 215–216.

50. Zammito, *The Genesis of Kant's Critique of Judgment*, 42–44ff.

51. Ibid., 21–33ff.; Schaeffer, "Commonplaces," 5–8; Dabney Townsend, "From Shaftesbury to Kant: The Development of the Concept of Aesthetic Experience," *Journal of the History of Ideas* 48:2 (April 1987), 287–305.

52. Zammito, *Genesis*, 8–10, 28–44.

53. Ibid., 21–33ff.

54. Schaeffer, "Commonplaces," 5–8; Townsend, "From Shaftesbury to Kant," 288ff., 291ff.

55. Townsend, "From Shaftesbury to Kant," 299ff.; David Hume, "Of the Standard of Taste," in *Essays Moral, Political, and Literary*, rev. ed., ed. Eugene F. Miller (Indianapolis: Liberty Fund, 1987); Online Library of Liberty ebook PDF, 142ff., accessed January 22, 2010, at http://oll.libertyfund.org/titles/704.

56. Townsend, "From Shaftesbury to Kant," 287.

57. Hume, "Standard of Taste," 142–152; Zammito, *Genesis*, 30–31ff.

58. Zammito, *Genesis*, 21–30.

59. Immanuel Kant, *Observations on the Feeling of the Beautiful and Sublime*, trans. John T. Goldthwait (Berkeley: University of California Press, 2003), 58–60.

60. Zammito, *Genesis*, 46; Kant, *Critique of Pure Reason*, A21.

61. Zammito, *Genesis*, 46, 89ff.

62. Immanuel Kant, *Critique of Judgment*, trans. Werner S. Pluhar (Indianapolis, IN: Hackett, 1987), Ak. 211–216, 236–238.

63. Ibid., Ak. 177–179, 194, 196–198.

64. Ibid., "First Introduction to the *Critique of Judgment*," Ak. 225'.

65. The idea that there is a sharp distinction between intelligence and feelings, emotions, or passions is increasingly becoming suspect, and Kant may be seen as one of the modern origins of this recognition. For contemporary discussions of it, see William E. Connolly, *Neuropolitics: Thinking, Culture, Speed* (Minneapolis: University of Minnesota Press, 2002); Martha C. Nussbaum, *Upheavals of Thought: The Intelligence of Emotions* (New York: Cambridge University Press, 2001); Charles Taylor, *Sources of the Self: The Making of the Modern Identity* (Cambridge, MA: Harvard University Press, 1989), part 1; Taylor, "What Is Human Agency?" in *Philosophical Papers*, vol. 1 (Cambridge: Cambridge University Press, 1985); Leslie Paul Thiele, *The Heart of Judgment: Practical Wisdom, Neuroscience, and Narrative* (New York: Cambridge University Press, 2006), 163–200.

66. Arendt, "Kant's Political Philosophy" (1964), LOC 032284; Immanuel Kant, *Critique of Practical Reason*, trans. Werner S. Pluhar (Indianapolis, IN: Hackett, 2002), 203.

67. Arendt, "Kant's Political Philosophy" (1964), LOC 0322883–87. It is a common misconception that Arendt had no appreciation for the idea of a morally good will. Her point about the morally good, rather, was not that it did not exist, but that it had no relevance in the political realm and, indeed, was potentially dangerous when used as standard of judgment there. See Arendt, *The Human Condition*, 73–78; Arendt, "Some Questions Concerning Moral Philosophy," 80–81; Arendt, "Collective Responsibility," 154; Arendt, "What Is Authority?" 137–138.

68. Kant, *Critique of Pure Reason*, A133/B172.

69. Ibid., A133/B172–A134/B173.

70. Kant, *Critique of Judgment*, Ak. 174ff., 197–198.

71. Ibid., Ak. 225'.

72. Ibid., Ak. 244ff'. Moreover, in the second introduction, Kant writes that "in a critique of judgment, the part that deals with aesthetic judgment belongs to it essentially. For this [faculty] alone contains a principle that judgment lays completely a priori at the basis of its reflection on nature" (ibid., Ak. 193). Allison also notes "Kant's clear privileging of taste from the standpoint of transcendental critique" in *Kant's Theory of Taste*, 4–6ff.

73. Kant, *Critique of Judgment*, Ak. 188ff., 221–222.

74. Ibid., Ak. 189.

75. Ibid., Ak. 217–219; Arendt, "Kant's Political Philosophy" (1964), LOC 032278ff.; Arendt, *Lectures on Kant's Political Philosophy* (1970), 69ff.

76. Kant, *Critique of Judgment*, Ak. 212.

77. Ibid., Ak. 189–193, 204ff., 209–219.

78. Ibid., Ak. 205, 209ff.

79. Ibid., Ak. 217.

80. Ibid., Ak. 217, 238ff., 288–293ff,; Arendt, *Lectures on Kant's Political Philosophy*, 67–69.

81. Kant, *Critique of Judgment*, Ak. 238–239.

82. Ibid., Ak. 293–294.

83. Ibid., Ak. 294.

84. Ibid.

85. Ibid., Ak. 295; this is Arendt's translation from *Lectures on Kant's Political Philosophy*, 71.

86. Beiner, "Interpretive Essay," 134–136.

87. Zammito, *Genesis*, 124–131; Allison, *Kant's Theory of Taste*, 164.

88. Kant, *Critique of Judgment*, Ak. 282–283, 306–320, 355–356.

89. Ibid., Ak. 296ff., 355.

90. Ibid., Ak. 190, 215, 239, 282–283; Arendt, "The Crisis in Culture," 215, 217.

91. Kant, *Critique of Judgment*, Ak. 282–284, 296ff., 312, 355.

92. Arendt, "The Crisis in Culture," 215, 217; Arendt, "Kant's Political Philosophy" (1964), LOC 032292.

93. Arendt, "Kant's Political Philosophy" (1964), LOC 032266, 69–70, 91–92; Arendt, *Lectures on Kant's Political Philosophy*, 42–45, 56, 76.

94. Kant, *Critique of Judgment*, Ak. 293ff.; Arendt, "Kant's Political Philosophy" (1964), 032266ff.; Arendt, *Lectures on Kant's Political Philosophy*, 70ff.

95. Kant, *Critique of Judgment*, Ak. 355–356; Arendt, "Kant's Political Philosophy" (1964), LOC 032291, 98; Arendt, "The Crisis in Culture," 221–222.

96. Kant, *Critique of Judgment*, Ak. 313.

97. Ibid., Ak. 309–310.

98. Ibid., Ak. 319.

99. Arendt, *The Human Condition*, 210.

100. Allison, *Kant's Theory of Taste*, 179ff.; Guyer, *Kant and the Claims of Taste*, 318–322; Savile, *Aesthetic Reconstructions*, 99–191.

101. Norris, "Arendt, Kant, and the Politics of Common Sense," 165–191.

102. Arendt, *Lectures on Kant's Political Philosophy*, 9, 14–16.

103. Ibid., 45–46.

104. Ibid., 48ff.

105. Arendt, "Tradition and the Modern Age," 24.

106. Arendt, *Lectures on Kant's Political Philosophy*, 8, 45–54.

107. Arendt, "Kant's Political Philosophy" (1964), LOC 032253–59.

108. Arendt, *Lectures on Kant's Political Philosophy*, 26–27.

109. Ibid., 41–44.

110. Ibid., 48–65.

111. Ibid., 58–65.

112. Arendt, "The Crisis in Culture," 217; Arendt, "Kant's Political Philosophy" (1964), LOC 032268.

113. Arendt, "Kant's Political Philosophy" (1964), LOC 032270, 91–92, 98.

114. Arendt, "The Crisis in Culture," 217.

115. Arendt, "Kant's Political Philosophy" (1964), LOC 032298.

116. Arendt, *Responsibility and Judgment*, 143–146; Arendt, "The Crisis in Culture," 217–222; Arendt, "Kant's Political Philosophy" (1964), LOC 032270, 91–92, 98.

117. Arendt, "Truth and Politics," 235ff.

118. Kant, *Critique of Judgment*, Ak. 355–356; Arendt, "Kant's Political Philosophy" (1964), LOC 032295.

119. Arendt, "The Crisis in Culture," 217.

120. Arendt, *Lectures on Kant's Political Philosophy*, 62. This is Arendt quoting Kant.

121. Arendt, "What Is Freedom?" 150–153.

122. Cf. Arendt, *The Life of the Mind*, "Willing," 183–184.

123. Arendt, "History of Political Theory: Machiavelli," lecture course (1955), LOC 024022–23.

124. Arendt, "What Is Authority?" 137; Arendt, "What Is Freedom?" 151.

125. Arendt, "Some Questions Concerning Moral Philosophy," 94–106ff.

126. Arendt, *The Life of the Mind*, "Thinking," 175, 177.

127. Ibid., 193.

128. Ibid., 132; see also Arendt, "The Concept of History," 45.

129. Arendt, "The Concept of History," 44–55.

130. Arendt, "Some Questions Concerning Moral Philosophy," 78–79; Arendt, "Truth and Politics," 240–241; Arendt, "Collective Responsibility," 151–153; Arendt, "Personal Responsibility Under Dictatorship," 43–48; Arendt, "Civil Disobedience," 60ff.

131. Arendt, *Eichmann in Jerusalem*, 287ff.; Arendt, *The Life of the Mind*, "Thinking," 3ff. It should be noted that Arendt's portrait of Eichmann as a kind of mindless and banal bureaucrat was probably not accurate. David Cesarani, for instance, has uncovered a variety of flaws in Arendt's research and introduced materials that show Eichmann was a much more traditionally evil character than Arendt had allowed. See Cesarani, *Becoming Eichmann: Rethinking the Life, Crimes and Trial of a "Desk Murderer"* (Cambridge, MA: Da Capo Press, 2006).

132. Arendt, "Some Questions Concerning Moral Philosophy," 96ff.

133. Arendt, "What Is Freedom?" 151ff.

134. Beiner, "Rereading Hannah Arendt's Kant Lectures," 91ff.; Beiner, "Rereading Truth and Politics," 123; Habermas, "Hannah Arendt's Communications Concept of Power," 211ff.; Steinberger, "Hannah Arendt on Judgment," 803ff.

135. Beiner, "Rereading Truth and Politics,"130.

136. Arendt, "Truth and Politics," 222.

137. Ibid., 226–227, 234–235.

138. Ibid., 225, 232, 236–239.

139. Ibid., 237; Arendt, "The Concept of History," 44–52.

140. Arendt, "Intellectuals and Responsibility," lecture (1967). The manuscript is very rough, and so I have edited the quote somewhat.

141. Arendt, "The Concept of History," 49–62; Arendt, "Truth and Politics," 245ff.

142. Arendt, "Truth and Politics," 245–259.

143. Arendt, *The Human Condition*, 5.

144. Arendt, *On Revolution*, 270–273.

Conclusion

1. See Joyce Appleby, *The Relentless Revolution: A History of Capitalism* (New York: W. W. Norton, 2010), 24ff.; Richard Heinberg, *The End of Growth: Adapting to Our New*

Economic Reality (Gabriola Island, BC: New Society Publishers, 2011); Paul Roberts, *The End of Oil: On the Edge of a Perilous New World* (New York: Houghton Mifflin, 2005), 21ff.

2. Cocks, *On Sovereignty and Other Political Delusions*, 87ff.; Krause, "Beyond Non-Domination"; Markell, *Bound by Recognition*, 5; Villa, "Beyond Good and Evil," 275, 277–278; Zerilli, *Feminism and the Abyss of Freedom*, 116–119.

3. Markell, *Bound by Recognition*, 178.

4. See Theodor W. Adorno, *Negative Dialectics* (New York: Continuum, 1973); Herbert Marcuse, *Reason and Revolution* (New York: Routledge, 2000); Judith Butler, *Subjects of Desire: Human Reflections in Twentieth-Century France* (New York: Columbia University Press, 2012).

5. Rachel Carson, *Silent Spring* (1962; repr., Boston: Houghton Mifflin, 2002); Donella Meadows, Jorgen Randers, and Dennis Meadows, *Limits to Growth: The 30-Year Update* (White River Junction, VT: Chelsea Green, 2004); E. F. Schumacher, *Small Is Beautiful: Economics as if People Mattered* (1973; repr., New York: HarperCollins, 2010).

6. J. G. A. Pocock, *The Machiavellian Moment: Florentine Political Thought and the Atlantic Republican Tradition* (Princeton, NJ: Princeton University Press, 1975).

7. Thomas Piketty, *Capital in the Twenty-First Century*, trans. Arthur Goldhammer (Cambridge, MA: Harvard University Press, 2014); Heinberg, *The End of Growth*.

8. Karl Polanyi, *The Great Transformation: The Political and Economic Origins of Our Time* (1944; repr., Boston: Beacon Press, 2001), 60ff.

9. Piketty, *Capital in the Twenty-First Century*, 72–73ff.

10. Ibid., 146ff., 274ff.

11. Ibid., 78–79.

12. Ibid., 93–94.

13. Ibid., 93–95.

14. Heinberg, *The End of Growth*, 11, 171ff.

15. Robert J. Gordon, "The Demise of U.S. Economic Growth: Restatement, Rebuttal, and Reflections," NBER Working Paper No. 19895, National Bureau of Economic Research, Cambridge, MA, February 2014.

16. Mats Larsson, *The Limits of Business Development and Economic Growth: Why Business Will Need to Invest Less in the Future* (New York: Palgrave Macmillan, 2004), 2, 5, 121.

17. Heinberg, *The End of Growth*, 10ff.

18. Ibid., 107ff.

19. Ibid., 156–173.

20. Marco Raugei, Pere Fullana-i-Palmer, and Vasilis Fthenakis, "The Energy Return on Energy Investment (EROI) of Photovoltaics: Methodology and Comparisons with Fossil Fuel Life Cycles," *Energy Policy* 45 (2012), 576–582.

21. Heinberg, *The End of Growth*, 158.

22. Ibid., 118ff.

23. Ibid., 20ff.

24. Arendt, *On Revolution*, 11–23, 130–131, 240–273; Arendt, "On Hannah Arendt," 315–319.

25. Arendt, *On Revolution*, 118–131; Arendt, "Civil Disobedience," 82–102. In *Diminished Democracy*, Theda Skocpol showed how accurate commentators like Tocqueville and Arendt were on America's civic life. Arendt tends to undersell in *On Revolution* the amount of civic engagement that took place in America throughout the nineteenth and early twentieth century. Skocpol's book remedy's that flaw by showing how widespread the principle of federalism was in American civic life.

26. Arendt, *On Revolution*, 241–247, 265–273.

27. Arendt, "Introduction *into* Politics," in *The Promise of Politics*, 97.

28. Arendt, *Lectures on Kant's Political Philosophy*, 75.

29. Wendell Berry, *The Gift of Good Land* (San Francisco: North Point Press, 1981), 137ff.; Berry, *What Are People For? Essays* (Berkeley, CA: Counterpoint, 2010), 123ff.; Murray Bookchin, *The Ecology of Freedom: The Emergence and Dissolution of Hierarchy* (Palo Alto, CA: Cheshire Books, 1982); Bookchin, *Post-Scarcity Anarchism* (Oakland, CA: AK Press, 2004); Fred Curtis, "Eco-Localism and Sustainability," *Ecological Economics* 46 (2003), 83–102; Aidan Davison, *Technology and the Contested Meanings of Sustainability* (Albany: State University of New York Press, 2001), 179ff.; Robin Hahnel, "Eco-Localism: A Constructive Critique," *Capitalism, Nature, Socialism* 18:2 (June 2007), 62–78; Hahnel, *Economic Justice and Democracy: From Competition to Cooperation* (New York: Routledge, 2005); Heinberg, *The End of Growth*, 267ff.; Herbert Marcuse, *One-Dimensional Man: Studies in the Ideology of Advanced Industrial Society* (Boston: Beacon Press, 1964); Ivan Illich, *In the Mirror of the Past: Lectures and Addresses, 1978–1990* (New York: Marion Boyars, 1992); Schumacher, *Small Is Beautiful*, 67, 155ff.; Leslie Paul Thiele, *Sustainability* (Cambridge, UK: Polity Press, 2013), 142ff.

30. For further discussions of the debate surrounding the emerging idea of "community-based economics" as an alternative to unsustainable capitalism, see Curtis, "Eco-Localism and Sustainability"; and Hahnel, "Eco-Localism: A Constructive Critique."

31. Herman E. Daly, *Toward a Steady-State Economy* (San Francisco: W. H. Freeman, 1973), 167ff.; cf. Daly, *Ecological Economics and Sustainable Development: Selected Essays of Herman Daly* (Northampton, MA: Edward Elgar, 2007).

Bibliography

Note: The Library of Congress holdings of the Hannah Arendt Papers can be accessed at the following URL: http://memory.loc.gov/ammem/arendthtml/arendthome.html.

Adorno, Theodor W. *Negative Dialectics.* New York: Continuum, 1973.

Allison, Henry E. *Kant's Theory of Taste: A Reading of the "Critique of Aesthetic Judgment."* New York: Cambridge University Press, 2001.

———. *Kant's Transcendental Idealism*, Rev. and enlarged ed. New Haven, CT: Yale University Press, 2004.

Appleby, Joyce. *The Relentless Revolution: A History of Capitalism.* New York: W. W. Norton, 2010.

Arato, Andrew, and Jean L. Cohen. "Banishing the Sovereign? Internal and External Sovereignty in Arendt." In *Politics in Dark Times: Encounters with Hannah Arendt*, ed. Seyla Benhabib. New York: Cambridge University Press, 2010.

Arendt, Hannah. "The Archimedean Point." Lecture given at College of Engineers, University of Michigan (1968). Hannah Arendt Papers, Manuscript Division, Library of Congress, Washington, DC (Series: Speeches and Writings File, 1923–1975, n.d.).

———. "Breakdown of Authority." Lecture given at New York University (1953). Hannah Arendt Papers, Manuscript Division, Library of Congress, Washington, DC (Series: Speeches and Writings File, 1923–1975, n.d.).

———. "Civil Disobedience." In *Crises of the Republic.* New York: Harcourt Brace, 1972.

———. "The Cold War and the West: Symposium." *Partisan Review* 29:1 (1962).

———. "Collective Responsibility." In *Responsibility and Judgment*, ed. Jerome Kohn. New York: Schocken Books, 2003.

———. "The Concept of History." In *Between Past and Future: Eight Exercises in Political Thought.* New York: Penguin Books, [1968] 2006.

———. "Concern with Politics in Recent European Philosophical Thought." In *Essays in Understanding: 1930–1954*, ed. Jerome Kohn. New York: Schocken Books, 1994.

———. "The Crisis in Culture: Its Social and Its Political Significance." In *Between Past and Future: Eight Exercises in Political Thought.* New York: Penguin Books, [1968] 2006.

———. "Crisis in Education." In *Between Past and Future: Eight Exercises in Political Thought.* New York: Penguin Books, [1968] 2006.

———. *Denktagebuch: 1950 bis 1973.* Ed. Ursula Ludz and Ingeborg Nordmann. Munich: Piper, 2002.

———. *Eichmann in Jerusalem: A Report on the Banality of Evil.* New York: Penguin Books, 1963.

———. "The Great Tradition I: Law and Power." *Social Research* 74:3 (Fall 2007).

———. "The Great Tradition II: Ruling and Being Ruled." *Social Research* 74:4 (Winter 2007).

———. "Guggenheim Proposal." Hannah Arendt Papers, Manuscript Division, Library of Congress, Washington, DC, Organizations, 1943–1976, John Simon Guggenheim Memorial Foundation,1952–1975 (Series: Correspondence File, 1938–1976, n.d.).

———. "History of Political Theory: Machiavelli." Lecture course at University of California, Berkeley (1955). Hannah Arendt Papers, Manuscript Division, Library of Congress, Washington, DC (Series: Subject File, 1949–1975, n.d.).

———. *The Human Condition.* Chicago: University of Chicago Press, 1958.

———. "Ideologies." Seminar at University of California, Berkeley (1955). Hannah Arendt Papers, Manuscript Division, Library of Congress, Washington, DC (Series: Subject File, 1949–1975, n.d.).

———. "Ideology and Terror: A Novel Form of Government." *Review of Politics* 15:3 (July 1953).

———. "Intellectuals and Responsibility." Lecture (1967). Hannah Arendt Papers, Manuscript Division, Library of Congress, Washington, DC (Series: Speeches and Writings File, 1923–1975, n.d.).

———. "Introduction into Politics." Lecture course at University of Chicago (1963). Hannah Arendt Papers, Manuscript Division, Library of Congress, Washington, DC (Series: Subject File, 1949–1975, n.d.).

———. "Introduction *into* Politics." In *The Promise of Politics*, ed. Jerome Kohn. New York: Schocken Books, 2005.

———. "Kant's Political Philosophy." Seminar at University of Chicago (1964). Hannah Arendt Papers, Manuscript Division, Library of Congress, Washington, DC (Series: Subject File, 1949–1975, n.d.).

———. "Karl Jaspers: Citizen of the World?" In *Men in Dark Times.* New York: Harcourt Brace, 1968.

———. "Karl Marx." Seminar at University of Chicago (1966). Hannah Arendt Papers, Manuscript Division, Library of Congress, Washington, DC (Series: Subject File, 1949–1975, n.d.).

———. "Karl Marx and the Tradition of Western Political Thought." *Social Research* 69:2 (Summer 2002).

———. *Lectures on Kant's Political Philosophy.* Ed. Ronald Beiner. Chicago: University of Chicago Press, 1982.

———. *The Life of the Mind.* 2 vols. ("Thinking" and "Willing) in 1. Ed. Mary McCarthy. New York: Harcourt, 1978.

———. "Lying and Politics." In *Crises of the Republic.* New York: Harcourt Brace, 1972.

———. "Martin Heidegger at Eighty." Trans. Albert Hofstadter. *New York Review of Books*, October 21, 1971.

———. "The Nation." In *Essays in Understanding, 1930–1954*, ed. Jerome Kohn. New York: Schocken Books, 1994.

———. "On Hannah Arendt." In *Hannah Arendt: The Recovery of the Public World*, ed. Melvyn A. Hill. New York: St. Martin's Press, 1979.

———. "On Humanity in Dark Times: Thoughts About Lessing." In *Men in Dark Times*. New York: Harcourt Brace, 1968.

———. *On Revolution*. New York: Penguin Books, [1963] 2006.

———. *On Violence*. New York: Harcourt Brace, 1970.

———. *The Origins of Totalitarianism*. New York: Harcourt, 1951.

———. *The Origins of Totalitarianism*, 3rd ed. New York: Harcourt, 1966.

———."Personal Responsibility Under Dictatorship." In *Responsibility and Judgment*, ed. Jerome Kohn. New York: Schocken Books, 2003.

———. "Philosophy and Politics." *Social Research* 71:3 (Fall 2004). Originally published in *Social Research* 57:1 (Spring 1990).

———. "Philosophy and Politics: The Problem of Action and Thought After the French Revolution." Lecture and manuscript (1954). Hannah Arendt Papers, Manuscript Division, Library of Congress, Washington, DC (Series: Speeches and Writings File, 1923–1975, n.d.).

———. "Philosophy and Politics: What Is Political Philosophy?" Lecture course at New School for Social Research, New York (1969). Hannah Arendt Papers, Manuscript Division, Library of Congress, Washington, DC (Series: Subject File, 1949–1975, n.d.).

———. "Political Experiences of the Twentieth Century." Lecture course at New School for Social Research, New York (1968). Hannah Arendt Papers, Manuscript Division, Library of Congress, Washington, DC (Series: Subject File, 1949–1975, n.d.).

———. "Preface: The Gap Between Past and Future." In *Between Past and Future: Eight Exercises in Political Thought*. New York: Penguin Books, [1968] 2006.

———. *The Promise of Politics*. Ed. Jerome Kohn. New York: Schocken Books, 2005.

———. "Remarks on 'The Crisis Character of Modern Society.'" *Christianity and Crisis* 26:6 (May 30, 1966).

———. "A Reply to Eric Voegelin." In *Essays in Understanding, 1930–1954*, ed. Jerome Kohn. New York: Schocken Books, 1994.

———. "Some Questions Concerning Moral Philosophy." In *Responsibility and Judgment*, ed. Jerome Kohn. New York: Schocken Books, 2003.

———. "The Spiritual Quest of Modern Man: The Answer of the Existentialists." Lecture at New School for Social Research, New York (1952). Hannah Arendt Papers, Manuscript Division, Library of Congress, Washington, DC (Series: Speeches and Writings File, 1923–1975, n.d.).

———. "Tradition and the Modern Age." In *Between Past and Future: Eight Exercises in Political Thought*. New York: Penguin Books, [1968] 2006.

———. "Truth and Politics." In *Between Past and Future: Eight Exercises in Political Thought*. Penguin Books: New York, [1968] 2006.

———. "Understanding and Politics." In *Essays in Understanding, 1930–1954*, ed. Jerome Kohn. New York: Schocken Books, 1994.

———. "Walter Benjamin, 1892–1940." In *Men in Dark Times*. New York: Harcourt Brace, 1968.

———. "What Is Authority?" In *Between Past and Future: Eight Exercises in Political Thought*. New York: Penguin Books, [1968] 2006.

———. "What Is Existential Philosophy?" In *Essays in Understanding, 1930–1954*, ed. Jerome Kohn. New York: Schocken Books, 1994.

———. "What Is Freedom?" In *Between Past and Future: Eight Exercises in Political Thought*. New York: Penguin Books, [1968] 2006.

Arendt, Hannah, and Martin Heidegger. *Letters, 1925–1975*. Ed. Ursula Ludz. Trans. Andrew Shields. New York: Harcourt, 2004.

Arendt, Hannah, and Karl Jaspers. *Correspondence, 1926–1969*. Ed. Lotte Kohler and Hans Saner. Trans. Robert Kimber and Rita Kimber. New York: Harcourt Brace Jovanovich, 1992.

Arendt, Hannah, and Mary McCarthy. *Between Friends: the Correspondence of Hannah Arendt and Mary McCarthy, 1949–1975*. Ed. Carol Brightman. New York: Harcourt Brace, 1995.

Aristotle. "De Anima." In *The Basic Works of Aristotle*, ed. Richard McKeon. New York: Random House, 2001.

———. *The Nicomachean Ethics*. Trans. J. A. K. Thomson and Hugh Tredennick. New York: Penguin Books, 2004.

———. *The Politics and the Constitution of Athens*. Trans. Benjamin Jowett, with revisions by Jonathan Barnes. Ed. Steven Everson. New York: Cambridge University Press, 1996.

———. "Rhetoric." In *Plato Gorgias and Aristotle Rhetoric*, trans. Joe Sachs. Newburyport, MA: Focus Publishing, 2009.

Arrow, Kenneth J. "Economic Theory and the Hypothesis of Rationality." In *The New Palgrave: Utility and Probability*, ed. John Eatwell, Murray Milgate, and Peter Newman. New York: Macmillan, 1990.

Baehr, Peter. *Hannah Arendt, Totalitarianism, and the Social Sciences*. Stanford, CA: Stanford University Press, 2010.

Beiner, Ronald. "Interpretive Essay." In *Lectures on Kant's Political Philosophy*, ed. Ronald Beiner. Chicago: University of Chicago Press, 1982.

———. *Political Judgment*. Chicago: University of Chicago Press, 1983.

———. "Rereading Hannah Arendt's Kant Lectures." In *Judgment, Imagination, and Politics: Themes from Kant and Arendt*, ed. Ronald Beiner and Jennifer Nedelsky. Lanham, MD: Rowman & Littlefield, 2001.

———. "Rereading Truth and Politics." *Philosophy and Social Criticism* 34:1–2 (2008).

Beiner, Ronald, and Jennifer Nedelsky, eds. *Judgment, Imagination, and Politics: Themes from Kant and Arendt*. Lanham, MD: Rowman & Littlefield, 2001.

Benhabib, Seyla. "Feminist Theory and Hannah Arendt's Concept of Public Space." *History of the Human Sciences* 6:97 (1993).

———. "Judgment and the Moral Foundations of Politics in Hannah Arendt's Thought." In *Judgment, Imagination, and Politics: Themes from Kant and Arendt*, ed. Ronald Beiner and Jennifer Nedelsky. Lanham, MD: Rowman & Littlefield, 2001.

———. "Reclaiming Universalism: Negotiating Republican Self-Determination and

Cosmopolitan Norms." Tanner Lectures on Human Values. Delivered at the University of California, Berkeley, March 2004.

———. *The Reluctant Modernism of Hannah Arendt*. New ed. New York: Rowman & Littlefield, 2000.

———. *Situating the Self: Gender, Community and Postmodernism in Contemporary Ethics*. Cambridge, UK: Polity Press, 1992.

———. "Toward a Deliberative Model of Democratic Legitimacy." In *Democracy and Difference*, ed. Seyla Benhabib. Princeton, NJ: Princeton University Press, 1996.

Berman, Sheri. *The Primacy of Politics: Social Democracy and the Making of Europe's Twentieth Century*. Cambridge: Cambridge University Press, 2006.

Bernstein, Richard. "Arendt on Thinking." In *The Cambridge Companion to Hannah Arendt*, ed. Dana Villa. Cambridge: Cambridge University Press, 2000.

———. *Beyond Objectivism and Relativism: Science, Hermeneutics, and Praxis*. Philadelphia: University of Pennsylvania Press, 1983.

———. "Judging—the Actor and the Spectator." In *Philosophical Profiles: Essays in a Pragmatic Mode*. Philadelphia: University of Pennsylvania Press, 1986.

———. *Praxis and Action: Contemporary Philosophies of Human Activity*. Philadelphia: University of Pennsylvania Press, 1971.

———. "Rethinking the Social and the Political." In *Philosophical Profiles: Essays in a Pragmatic Mode*. Philadelphia: University of Pennsylvania Press, 1986.

Berry, Wendell. *The Gift of Good Land*. San Francisco: North Point Press, 1981.

———. *What Are People For? Essays*. Berkeley, CA: Counterpoint, 2010.

Birmingham, Peg. "Hannah Arendt: The Spectator's Vision." In *The Judge and the Spectator: Hannah Arendt's Political Philosophy*, ed. Joke J. Hermsen and Dana R. Villa. Leuven, Belgium: Peeters, 1999.

Blumenberg, Hans. *The Legitimacy of the Modern Age*. Trans. Robert M. Wallace. Cambridge, MA: MIT Press, 1983.

Bookchin, Murray. *The Ecology of Freedom: The Emergence and Dissolution of Hierarchy*. Palo Alto, CA: Cheshire Books, 1982.

———. *Post-Scarcity Anarchism*. Oakland, CA: AK Press, 2004.

Bourdieu, Pierre. *The Social Structures of the Economy*. Cambridge, UK: Polity, 2005.

Brogan, Walter A. *Heidegger and Aristotle: The Twofoldness of Being*. Albany: State University of New York Press, 2005.

Brzezinski, Zbigniew K., and Carl J. Friedrich. *Totalitarianism, Dictatorship, and Autocracy*. New York: Frederick A. Praeger, 1963.

Butler, Judith. *Subjects of Desire: Human Reflections in Twentieth-Century France*. New York: Columbia University Press, 2012.

Canovan, Margaret. *Hannah Arendt: A Reinterpretation of Her Political Thought*. New York: Cambridge University Press, 1992.

Caputo, John. *Radical Hermeneutics: Repetition, Deconstruction, and the Hermeneutic Project*. Bloomington: Indiana University Press, 1987.

Carson, Rachel. *Silent Spring*. 1962. Repr., Boston: Houghton Mifflin, 2002.

Cesarani, David. *Becoming Eichmann: Rethinking the Life, Crimes and Trial of a "Desk Murderer."* Cambridge, MA: Da Capo Press, 2006.

Cocks, Joan. *On Sovereignty and Other Political Delusions*. New York: Bloomsbury Academic, 2014.

Connolly, William E. *Neuropolitics: Thinking, Culture, Speed*. Minneapolis: University of Minnesota Press, 2002.

Cotter, Bridget. "Hannah Arendt and the 'Right to Have Rights.'" In *Hannah Arendt and International Relations*, ed. Anthony F. Lang, Jr., and John Williams. New York: Palgrave Macmillan, 2005.

Curtis, Fred. "Eco-Localism and Sustainability." *Ecological Economics* 46 (2003).

Curtis, Kimberley. *Our Sense of the Real: Aesthetic Experience and Arendtian Politics*. Ithaca, NY: Cornell University Press, 1999.

Daly, Herman E. *Ecological Economics and Sustainable Development: Selected Essays of Herman Daly*. Northampton, MA: Edward Elgar, 2007.

——. *Toward a Steady-State Economy*. San Francisco: W. H. Freeman, 1973.

Davison, Aidan. *Technology and the Contested Meanings of Sustainability*. Albany: State University of New York Press, 2001.

Degryse, Annelies. "*Sensus communis* as a Foundation for Men as Political Beings: Arendt's Reading of Kant's Critique of Judgment." *Philosophy and Social Criticism* 37:3 (2011).

Dennett, Daniel C. *Elbow Room: The Varieties of Free Will Worth Wanting*. Cambridge, MA: MIT Press, 1984.

d'Entrèves, Maurizio Passerin. *The Political Philosophy of Hannah Arendt*. New York: Routledge, 1994.

——. "'To Think Representatively': Arendt on Judgment and the Imagination." *Philosophical Papers* 35:3 (2006).

Descartes, René. *Discourse on Method*. Trans. Donald A. Cress. Indianapolis, IN: Hackett, 1998.

Deutscher, Max. *Judgment After Arendt*. Burlington, VT: Ashgate, 2007.

Dietz, Mary G. "'The Slow Boring of Hard Boards': Methodical Thinking and the Work of Politics." *American Political Science Review* 88:4 (December 1994).

——.. *Turning Operations: Feminism, Arendt, and Politics*. New York: Routledge, 2002.

Disch, Lisa. *Hannah Arendt and the Limits of Philosophy*. Ithaca, NY: Cornell University Press, 1994.

Dostal, Robert J. "Judging Human Action: Arendt's Appropriation of Kant." In *Judgment, Imagination, and Politics: Themes from Kant and Arendt*, ed. Ronald Beiner and Jennifer Nedelsky. Lanham, MD: Rowan & Littlefield, 2001.

——. "Time and Phenomenology in Husserl and Heidegger." In *The Cambridge Companion to Heidegger*, 2nd ed., ed Charles B. Guignon. New York: Cambridge University Press, 2006.

Dreyfus, Hubert L. "Heidegger on the Connection Between Nihilism, Art, Technology, and Politics." In *The Cambridge Companion to Heidegger*, 2nd ed., ed. Charles B. Guignon. New York: Cambridge University Press, 2006.

Euben, J. Peter. "Hannah Arendt at Colonus." In *Platonic Noise*. Princeton, NJ: Princeton University Press, 2003.

Ferrara, Alessandro. *The Force of Example: Explorations in the Paradigm of Judgment*. New York: Columbia University Press, 2008.

————. *Justice and Judgment: The Rise and the Prospect of the Judgment Model in Contemporary Political Philosophy.* Thousand Oaks, CA: Sage, 1999.

Fine, Robert. "Judgment and the Reification of the Faculties: A Reconstructive Reading of Arendt's *The Life of the Mind.*" *Philosophy and Social Criticism* 34:1–2 (2008).

————. *Political Investigations: Hegel, Marx, Arendt.* New York: Routledge, 2001.

Forman, Fonna. "Sympathy in Space(s): Adam Smith on Proximity." *Political Theory* 33:2 (April 2005).

————. "Whose Context? Which Impartiality? Reflections on Griswold's Smith." *Perspectives on Political Science* 30:3 (Summer 2001).

Fromkin, David. *Europe's Last Summer: Who Started the Great War of 1914?* New York: Vintage Books, 2004.

Gadamer, Hans-Georg. "Autobiographical Reflections." In *The Gadamer Reader: A Bouquet of His Later Writings*, ed. and trans. Richard E. Palmer. Evanston, IL: Northwestern University Press, 2007.

————. "Hermeneutics as Practical Philosophy." In *The Gadamer Reader: A Bouquet of His Later Writings*, ed. and trans. Richard E. Palmer. Evanston, IL: Northwestern University Press, 2007.

————. "Hermeneutics and Social Science." *Philosophy and Social Criticism* 2 (1975).

————. "On the Possibility of a Philosophical Ethics." In *The Gadamer Reader: A Bouquet of His Later Writings*, ed. and trans. Richard E. Palmer. Evanston, IL: Northwestern University Press, 2007.

————. *Truth and Method.* 2nd rev. ed. Trans. Joel Weinsheimer and Donald G. Marshall. New York: Continuum, 1975.

Garsten, Bryan. "The Elusiveness of Arendtian Judgment." In *Politics in Dark Times: Encounters with Hannah Arendt*, ed. Seyla Benhabib. New York: Cambridge University Press, 2010.

Gellately, Robert. *Backing Hitler: Consent and Coercion in Nazi Germany.* New York: Oxford University Press, 2001.

Gillespie, Michael Allen. "Martin Heidegger's Aristotelian National Socialism." *Political Theory* 28:2 (April 2000).

————. *Nihilism Before Nietzsche.* Chicago: University of Chicago Press, 1996.

————. "Radical Philosophy to Political Theology." In *The Oxford Handbook of Theology and Modern European Thought*, ed. Nicholas Adams, George Pattison, and Graham Ward. Oxford: Oxford University Press, 2013.

————. *The Theological Origins of Modernity.* Chicago: University of Chicago Press, 2008.

Goeschel, Christian. *Suicide in Nazi Germany.* New York: Oxford University Press, 2009.

Gordon, Robert J. "The Demise of U.S. Economic Growth: Restatement, Rebuttal, and Reflections." NBER Working Paper No. 19895, National Bureau of Economic Research, Cambridge, MA, February 2014.

Gray, John Glenn. "The Abyss of Freedom—and Hannah Arendt." In *Hannah Arendt: The Recovery of the Public World*, ed. Melvyn A. Hill. New York: St. Martin's Press, 1979.

Green, Donald, and Ian Shapiro. *Pathologies of Rational Choice Theory.* New Haven, CT: Yale University Press, 1996.

Gregoric, Pavel. *Aristotle on the Common Sense.* New York: Oxford University Press, 2007.

Griswold, Charles L. *Adam Smith and the Virtues of Enlightenment.* Cambridge: Cambridge University Press, 1999.

Guignon, Charles B., ed. *The Cambridge Companion to Heidegger.* 2nd ed. New York: Cambridge University Press, 2006.

Guyer, Paul. *Kant.* New York: Routledge, 2006.

———. *Kant and the Claims of Taste.* Cambridge, MA: Harvard University Press, 1979.

———. "The Transcendental Deduction of the Categories." In *The Cambridge Companion to Kant,* ed. Paul Guyer. New York: Cambridge University Press, 1992.

Habermas, Jürgen. "Hannah Arendt's Communications Concept of Power." *Social Research* 44:1 (Spring 1977).

———. *Moral Consciousness and Communicative Action.* Trans. Christian Lenhardt and Shierry Weber Nicholsen. Cambridge, MA: MIT Press, 1996.

———. "On the German-Jewish Heritage." *Telos* 44 (Summer 1980).

———. "Three Normative Models of Democracy." In *Inclusion of the Other: Studies in Political Theory,* ed. Ciaran Cronin and Pablo De Greiff. Cambridge, MA: MIT Press, 1998.

Hahnel, Robin. "Eco-Localism: A Constructive Critique." *Capitalism, Nature, Socialism* 18:2 (June 2007).

———. *Economic Justice and Democracy: From Competition to Cooperation.* New York: Routledge, 2005

Hammer, Dean. "Hannah Arendt and Roman Political Thought: The Practice of Theory." *Political Theory* 30:1 (February 2002).

Heidegger, Martin. *Basic Writings.* Rev. and expanded ed., ed. David Farrell Krell. New York: HarperCollins, 1993.

———. *Being and Time.* Trans. John Macquarrie and Edward Robinson. New York: Harper and Row, 1962.

———. *Being and Time.* Trans. Joan Stambaugh. Rev. Dennis J. Schmidt. Albany: State University of New York Press, [1953] 2010.

———. *Discourse on Thinking.* Trans. John M. Anderson and E. Hans Freund. New York: Harper Torchbooks, 1966.

———. "Letter on Humanism." In *Basic Writings,* rev. and expanded ed., ed. David Farrell Krell. New York: HarperCollins, 1993.

———. *Nietzsche: Volumes One and Two.* Ed. and trans. David Farrell Krell. New York: HarperCollins, 1991.

———. *Nietzsche: Volumes Three and Four.* Ed. David Farrell Krell. Trans. Frank A. Capuzzi, David Farrell Krell, and Joan Stambaugh. New York: HarperCollins, 1991.

———. "On the Essence of Truth." Trans. John Sallis. In *Basic Writings,* rev. and expanded ed., ed. David Farrell Krell. New York: HarperCollins, 1993.

———. "The Origin of the Work of Art (Early Draft)." In *The Heidegger Reader,* ed. Günter Figal, trans. Jerome Veith. Bloomington: Indiana University Press, 2009.

———. *Plato's Sophist.* Trans. Richard Rojcewicz and Andrée Schuwer. Bloomington: Indiana University Press, 1992.

———. "The Question Concerning Technology." In *Basic Writings,* rev. and expanded ed., ed. David Farrell Krell. New York: HarperCollins, 1993.

————. *The Question Concerning Technology and Other Essays.* Trans. William Lovitt. New York: Harper & Row, 1977.

————. "What Is Metaphysics?" In *Basic Writings*, rev. and expanded ed., ed. David Farrell Krell. New York: HarperCollins, 1993.

Heinberg, Richard. *The End of Growth: Adapting to Our New Economic Reality.* Gabriola Island, BC: New Society Publishers, 2011.

Heisenberg, Werner. *The Physicist's Conception of Nature.* Trans. Arnold J. Pomerans. London: Hutchinson, 1958.

Herington, C. J. "Introduction." In *Persians* by Aeschylus. Trans. Janet Lembke and C. J. Herington. Oxford: Oxford University Press, 1981.

Hinchman, Lewis P., and Sandra K. Hinchman. "In Heidegger's Shadow: Hannah Arendt's Phenomenological Humanism." *Review of Politics* 46:2 (April 1984).

Hobbes, Thomas. *Leviathan.* Ed. Richard Tuck. Cambridge: Cambridge University Press, 1996.

Honig, Bonnie. *Political Theory and the Displacement of Politics.* Ithaca, NY: Cornell University Press, 1993.

————. "The Politics of Agonism: A Critical Response to 'Beyond Good and Evil: Arendt, Nietzsche, and the Aestheticization of Political Action' by Dana R. Villa." *Political Theory* 21:3 (August 1993).

Howe, Irving. "Banality and Brilliance: Irving Howe on Hannah Arendt." *Dissent*, June 5, 2013. Accessed at http://www.dissentmagazine.org/online_articles/banality-and-brilliance-irving-howe-on-hannah-arendt.

Hume, David. "Of the Standard of Taste." In *Essays Moral, Political, and Literary*, rev. ed., ed. Eugene F. Miller. Indianapolis: Liberty Fund, 1987. Online Library of Liberty, ebook PDF. Accessed January 22, 2010, at http://oll.libertyfund.org/titles/704.

Illich, Ivan. *In the Mirror of the Past: Lectures and Addresses, 1978–1990.* New York: Marion Boyars, 1992.

Kant, Immanuel. *Critique of Judgment.* Trans. Werner S. Pluhar. Indianapolis, IN: Hackett, 1987.

————. *Critique of Practical Reason.* Trans. Werner S. Pluhar. Indianapolis, IN: Hackett, 2002.

————. *Critique of Pure Reason.* Trans. Werner S. Pluhar. Indianapolis, IN: Hackett, 1986.

————. *Observations on the Feeling of the Beautiful and Sublime.* Trans. John T. Goldthwait. Berkeley: University of California Press, 2003.

Kateb, George. *Hannah Arendt: Politics, Conscience, Evil.* Totowa, NY: Rowman & Allanheld , 1984.

————. "The Judgment of Hannah Arendt." In *Judgment, Imagination, and Politics: Themes from Kant and Arendt*, ed. Ronald Beiner and Jennifer Nedelsky. Lanham, MD: Rowman & Littlefield, 2001.

Kaufmann, Walter. *Hegel: A Reinterpretation.* Notre Dame, IN: University of Notre Dame Press, 1988.

Kisiel, Theodore. *The Genesis of Heidegger's "Being and Time."* Berkeley: University of California Press, 1993.

Kohn, Jerome. Introduction to *The Promise of Politics*, by Hannah Arendt. Ed. Jerome Kohn. New York: Schocken Books, 2005.

———. Introduction to *Responsibility and Judgment*, by Hannah Arendt. Ed. Jerome Kohn. New York: Schocken Books, 2003.

Krause, Sharon. "Beyond Non-Domination: Agency, Inequality and the Meaning of Freedom." *Philosophy and Social Criticism* 39:2 (January 2013).

Kuhn, Thomas S. *The Structure of Scientific Revolutions*. Chicago: University of Chicago Press, 2012.

Lara, Maria Pia. *Narrating Evil: A Post-Metaphysical Theory of Reflective Judgment*. New York: Columbia University Press, 2007.

Larsson, Mats. *The Limits of Business Development and Economic Growth: Why Business Will Need to Invest Less in the Future*. New York: Palgrave Macmillan, 2004.

Lobkowicz, Nicolas. *Theory and Practice: History of a Concept from Aristotle to Marx*. Notre Dame, IN: University of Notre Dame Press, 1967.

Longuenesse, Beatrice. *Kant and the Capacity to Judge: Sensibility and Discursivity in the Transcendental Analytic of the "Critique of Pure Reason."* Trans. Charles T. Wolfe. Princeton, NJ: Princeton University Press, 1998.

Machiavelli, Niccolo. *The Prince and Other Writings*. Trans. Wayne A. Rebhorn. New York: Barnes & Noble Classics, 2003.

MacIntyre, Alasdair. *Whose Justice? Which Rationality?* Notre Dame, IN: University of Notre Dame Press, 1988.

Makkreel, Rudolf A. *Imagination and Interpretation in Kant: The Hermeneutical Import of the "Critique of Judgment."* Chicago: University of Chicago Press, 1990.

———. "Reflective Judgment, Orientation, and the Priorities of Justice." *Philosophy and Social Criticism* 27:3 (2001).

———. "The Role of Judgment and Orientation in Hermeneutics." *Philosophy and Social Criticism* 34:1–2 (2008).

Marcuse, Herbert. "Heidegger's Politics." In *The Essential Marcuse: Selected Writings of Philosopher and Social Critic Herbert Marcuse*, ed. Andrew Feenberg and William Leiss. Boston: Beacon Press, 2007.

———. *One-Dimensional Man: Studies in the Ideology of Advanced Industrial Society*. Boston: Beacon Press, 1964.

———. *Reason and Revolution*. New York: Routledge, 2000.

Markell, Patchen. "Anonymous Glory." *European Journal of Political Theory*, January 18, 2015. Digitally accessed before appearance in print at http://ept.sagepub.com/content/early/2015/01/16/1474885114567344.abstract.

———. "Arendt's Work: On the Architecture of *The Human Condition*." *College Literature* 38:1 (Winter 2011).

———. *Bound by Recognition*. Princeton, NJ: Princeton University Press, 2003.

———. "The Surprising Platonism of Hannah Arendt." Paper delivered at "Tragic Vision, Democratic Hope: A Conference in Honor of J. Peter Euben," Duke University. November 9, 2012.

Marshall, David L. "The Origin and Character of Hannah Arendt's Theory of Judgment." *Political Theory* 38:3 (2010).

————. "The Polis and Its Analogues in the Thought of Hannah Arendt." *Modern Intellectual History* 7:1 (2010).

Marx, Karl. "Communist Manifesto." In *The Marx-Engels Reader*, 2nd ed., ed. Robert C. Tucker. New York: W. W. Norton, 1978.

McCarthy, Mary. "Editor's Postface." In *The Life of the Mind*, by Hannah Arendt. Ed. Mary McCarthy. New York: Harcourt, 1978.

McCarthy, Michael. *The Political Humanism of Hannah Arendt.* New York: Lexington Books, 2012.

McClure, Kirstie M. "The Odor of Judgment: Exemplarity, Propriety, and Politics in the Company of Hannah Arendt." In *Hannah Arendt and the Meaning of Politics*, ed. Craig Calhoun and John McGowan. Minneapolis: University of Minnesota Press, 1997.

Meadows, Donella, Jorgen Randers, and Dennis Meadows. *Limits to Growth: The 30-Year Update.* White River Junction, VT: Chelsea Green, 2004.

Montgomery, Henry A., William R. Miller, and J. Scott Tonigan. "Does Alcoholics Anonymous Involvement Predict Treatment Outcome?" *Journal of Substance Abuse Treatment* 12:4 (July–August 1995).

Mueller, Gustav E. "The Hegel Legend of 'Thesis-Antithesis-Synthesis.'" *Journal of the History of Ideas* 19:3 (June 1958).

Nagel, Thomas. *The View from Nowhere.* Oxford: Oxford University Press, 1986.

Nietzsche, Friedrich. *On the Genealogy of Morals.* Trans. Walter Kaufmann. New York: Random House, 1969.

Norberg, Jakob. "Arendt in Crisis: Political Thought in *Between Past and Future.*" *College Literature* 38:1 (Winter 2011).

Norris, Andrew. "Arendt, Kant, and the Politics of Common Sense." *Polity* 29:2 (Winter 1996).

Nussbaum, Martha C. *Upheavals of Thought: The Intelligence of Emotions.* New York: Cambridge University Press, 2001.

Overy, Richard. *The Dictators: Hitler's Germany, Stalin's Russia.* New York: W. W. Norton, 2004.

Piketty, Thomas. *Capital in the Twenty-First Century.* Trans. Arthur Goldhammer. Cambridge, MA: Harvard University Press, 2014.

Pitkin, Hanna Fenichel. *The Attack of the Blob: Hannah Arendt's Concept of the Social.* Chicago: University of Chicago Press, 1998.

————. "Justice: On Relating Public and Private." *Political Theory* 9:3 (August 1981).

Plato. *Republic.* Trans. G. M. A. Grube; rev. C. D. C. Reeve. Indianapolis, IN: Hackett, 1992.

Pluhar, Werner S. Introduction to *Critique of Judgment*, by Immanuel Kant. Trans. Werner S. Pluhar. Indianapolis, IN: Hackett, 1987.

Pocock, J. G. A. *The Machiavellian Moment: Florentine Political Thought and the Atlantic Republican Tradition.* Princeton, NJ: Princeton University Press, 1975.

Polanyi, Karl. *The Great Transformation: The Political and Economic Origins of Our Time.* 1944. Repr., Boston: Beacon Press, 2001.

Polt, Richard. *Heidegger: An Introduction.* Ithaca, NY: Cornell University Press, 1999.

Putnam, Hilary. *Reason, Truth, and History.* Cambridge: Cambridge University Press, 1981.

Putnam, Robert D. *Bowling Alone: The Collapse and Revival of American Community*. New York: Simon & Schuster, 2000.

Rasmussen, Dennis. *The Pragmatic Enlightenment: Recovering the Liberalism of Hume, Smith, Montesquieu, and Voltaire*. Cambridge: Cambridge University Press, 2013.

Raugei, Marco, Pere Fullana-i-Palmer, and Vasilis Fthenakis. "The Energy Return on Energy Investment (EROI) of Photovoltaics: Methodology and Comparisons with Fossil Fuel Life Cycles." *Energy Policy* 45 (2012).

Ricoeur, Paul. "Aesthetic Judgment and Political Judgment According to Hannah Arendt." In *The Just*. Trans. David Pellauer. Chicago: University of Chicago Press, 2000.

Roberts, Paul. *The End of Oil: On the Edge of a Perilous New World*. New York: Houghton Mifflin, 2005.

Rojcewicz, Richard. *The Gods and Technology: A Reading of Heidegger*. Albany: State University of New York Press, 2006.

Rosen, Stanley. *Nihilism: A Philosophical Essay*. New Haven, CT: Yale University Press, 1969.

Savile, Anthony. *Aesthetic Reconstructions: The Seminal Writing of Lessing, Kant and Schiller*. Oxford: Basil Blackwell, 1987.

Schaeffer, John D. "Commonplaces: *Sensus Communis*." In *A Companion to Rhetoric and Rhetorical Criticism*, ed. Walter Jost and Wendy Olmsted. Blackwell Publishing, 2003. *Blackwell Reference Online*. Accessed on August 27, 2015 at http://www.blackwellreference.com/public/book.html?id=g9781405101121_9781405101121.

Schumacher, E. F. *Small Is Beautiful: Economics as if People Mattered*. 1973. Repr., New York: HarperCollins, 2010.

Sen, Amartya. *Freedom, Rationality, and Social Choice: The Arrow Lectures and Other Essays*. Oxford: Oxford University Press, 2000.

Shapiro, Ian. *The Flight from Reality in the Human Sciences*. Princeton, NJ: Princeton University Press, 2005.

Skocpol, Theda. *Diminished Democracy: From Membership to Management in American Civic Life*. Norman: University of Oklahoma Press, 2003.

Smith, Adam. *The Theory of Moral Sentiments*. Ed. D. D. Raphael and A. L. Macfie. Indianapolis, IN: Liberty Classics, 1982.

Steinberger, Peter J. "Hannah Arendt on Judgment." *American Journal of Political Science* 34:3 (August 1990).

Strong, Tracy B. "Martin Heidegger and the Space of the Political." In *Politics Without Vision: Thinking Without a Banister in the Twentieth Century*. Chicago: University of Chicago Press, 2012.

———. "Without a Banister: Hannah Arendt and Roads Not Taken." In *Politics Without Vision: Thinking Without a Bannister in the Twentieth Century*. Chicago: University of Chicago Press, 2012.

Summers, David. *The Judgment of Sense: Renaissance Naturalism and the Rise of Aesthetics*. Cambridge: Cambridge University Press, 1987.

Taminiaux, Jacques. *The Thracian Maid and the Professional Thinker: Arendt and Heidegger*. Trans. and ed. Michael Gendre. Albany: State University of New York Press, 1997.

Taylor, Charles. "Engaged Agency and Background." In *The Cambridge Companion to Heidegger,* 2nd ed., ed. Charles B. Guignon. New York: Cambridge University Press, 2006.

———. "Explanation and Practical Reason." In *The Quality of Life,* ed. Martha Nussbaum and Amartya Sen. Oxford: Oxford University Press, 1992.

———. Introduction to *Philosophical Papers,* vols. 1 and 2. Cambridge: Cambridge University Press, 1985.

———. "How Is Mechanism Conceivable?" In *Philosophical Papers,* vol. 1. Cambridge: Cambridge University Press, 1985.

———. "Rationality." In *Philosophical Papers,* vol. 2. Cambridge: Cambridge University Press, 1985.

———. *Sources of the Self: The Making of the Modern Identity.* Cambridge, MA: Harvard University Press, 1989.

———. "The Validity of Transcendental Arguments." In *Philosophical Arguments.* Cambridge, MA: Harvard University Press, 1995.

———. "What Is Human Agency?" In *Philosophical Papers,* vol. 1. Cambridge: Cambridge University Press, 1985.

Tetlock, Philip E. *Expert Political Judgment: How Good Is It? How Can We Know?* Princeton, NJ: Princeton University Press, 2005.

Thiele, Leslie Paul. *The Heart of Judgment: Practical Wisdom, Neuroscience, and Narrative.* New York: Cambridge University Press, 2006.

———. "Judging Hannah Arendt: A Reply to Zerilli." *Political Theory* 33:5 (October 2005).

———. *Sustainability.* Cambridge, UK: Polity Press, 2013.

Townsend, Dabney. "From Shaftesbury to Kant: The Development of the Concept of Aesthetic Experience." *Journal of the History of Ideas* 48:2 (April 1987).

Villa, Dana R. "The Anxiety of Influence: On Arendt's Relationship to Heidegger." In *Politics, Philosophy, Terror: Essays on the Thought of Hannah Arendt.* Princeton, NJ: Princeton University Press, 1999.

———. *Arendt and Heidegger: The Fate of the Political.* Princeton, NJ: Princeton University Press, 1996.

———. "Arendt, Heidegger, and the Tradition." *Social Research* 74:4 (Winter 2007).

———. "Beyond Good and Evil: Arendt, Nietzsche, and the Aestheticization of Political Action." *Political Theory* 20:2 (May 1992).

———. "Hannah Arendt, 1906–1975." *Review of Politics* 71:1 (2009).

———. "Introduction: The Development of Arendt's Political Thought." In *The Cambridge Companion to Hannah Arendt,* ed. Dana Villa. New York: Cambridge University Press, 2000.

———. "Thinking and Judging." In *The Judge and the Spectator: Hannah Arendt's Political Philosophy,* ed. Joke J. Hermsen and Dana R. Villa. Leuven, Belgium: Peeters, 1999.

Waldron, Jeremy. *God, Locke, and Equality: Christian Foundations in Locke's Political Thought.* Cambridge: Cambridge University Press, 2002.

———. "Legislation and Moral Neutrality." In *Liberal Neutrality,* ed. Robert E. Goodin and Andrew Reeve. London: Routledge, 1989.

Weber, Max. *The Protestant Ethic and the Spirit of Capitalism with Other Writings on the Rise of the West.* Trans. Stephen Kalberg. New York: Oxford University Press, 2009.

Wellmer, Albrecht. "Hannah Arendt on Judgment: The Unwritten Doctrine of Reason." In *Judgment, Imagination, and Politics: Themes from Kant and Arendt,* ed. Ronald Beiner and Jennifer Nedelsky. Lanham, MD: Rowman & Littlefield, 2001.

White, Stephen K. *Sustaining Affirmation: The Strengths of Weak Ontology in Political Theory.* Princeton, NJ: Princeton University Press, 2000.

Wolin, Richard, ed. *The Heidegger Controversy: A Critical Reader.* Cambridge, MA: MIT Press, 1993.

Wolin, Sheldon S. "Hannah Arendt and the Ordinance of Time." *Social Research* 44:1 (Spring 1977).

———. "Hannah Arendt: Democracy and the Political." *Salmagundi* 60 (Spring–Summer 1983).

———. *Politics and Vision: Continuity and Innovation in Western Political Thought.* Expanded ed. Princeton, NJ: Princeton University Press, 2004.

Wrathall, Mark A. "Truth and the Essence of Truth in Heidegger's Thought." In *The Cambridge Companion to Heidegger,* 2nd ed., ed. Charles B. Guignon. New York: Cambridge University Press, 2006.

Yazicioglu, Sanem. "Arendt's Hermeneutic Interpretation of Kantian Reflective Judgment." *Philosophy Today* 54:4 (December 2010).

Young-Bruehl, Elisabeth. *Hannah Arendt: For Love of the World.* 2nd ed. New Haven, CT: Yale University Press, 2004.

———. "Reflections on Hannah Arendt's *The Life of the Mind.*" In *Hannah Arendt: Critical Essays,* ed. Lewis P. Hinchman and Sandra K. Hinchman. Albany: State University of New York Press, 1994.

———. *Why Arendt Matters.* New Haven, CT: Yale University Press, 2006.

Zammito, John H. *The Genesis of Kant's Critique of Judgment.* Chicago: University of Chicago Press, 1992.

Zerilli, Linda. *Feminism and the Abyss of Freedom.* Chicago: University of Chicago Press, 2005.

———. "Response to Thiele." *Political Theory* 33:5 (October 2005).

———. "'We Feel Our Freedom': Imagination and Judgment in the Thought of Hannah Arendt." *Political Theory* 33:2 (April 2005).

Index

French revolution, 132–33; as disclosing political phenomena to Kant and Hegel, 135–37, 172
French Resistance, 57, 60, 63, 145

Gadamer, Hans-Georg, 157–61, 210 n. 40
Galilei, Galileo, 113, 122
Gap between past and future. *See* thinking ego
Genealogy, 10, 20–24, 64, 104; "pearl diving," 10, 23, 37
Genius, 160, 163, 168–71, 174–76. *See also* taste
Gillespie, Michael Allen, 33, 214 n. 73, 228 n. 54, 253
Global politics, 18, 189, 202. *See also* cosmopolitanism
Gordon, Robert, 197–98
Greek politics, 11, 16, 38–39, 55, 64–72; and activity of founding, 64–66
Guyer, Paul, 171

Habermas, Jürgen, 2, 153–55, 180, 182
Hegel, G. W. F., 93–94, 136–40, 193, 212 n. 34, 228 n. 75
Heidegger, Martin, 15, 21–37, 39, 41, 44–46, 51, 88–90, 95, 127, 157–61, 163, 211 n. 16, 211 n. 27, 213 n. 50, 213 n. 60, 214 n. 73, 214 n. 75
Heinberg, Richard, 196, 198–200
Herder, Johann Gottfried, 163
Hermeneutic philosophy, 24–34, 158; theories of judgment, 158–61
Historicity. *See* narrative ontology of humans
Historiography, 19–24, 36, 77, 108
History, 3, 19, 21, 24, 27, 72, 77, 86, 177; and human agency, 15, 20–21, 23–24, 31, 35–37, 51, 57–61, 86, 104, 108, 112; and immortality, 39, 49, 56, 59, 61; modern misconceptions of, 20, 35, 61, 131–32, 137, 139, 141–49, 152, 173; philosophies of history, 15, 36, 61, 136–39, 142, 144, 173; and politics, 15, 20–21, 23, 26, 37, 56–61, 136, 155, 173, 177. *See also* historiography; ideology; narrative ontology of humans; philosophy of history; politics
Hitler, Adolf, 48, 147
Homo faber, 57, 119–20, 130
Howe, Irving, 3
The Human Condition (book), 2–3, 23, 25, 27–28, 37, 41, 48, 52, 55, 57–58, 64, 68–69, 73, 75, 83, 86–87, 89, 95, 99–100, 104, 108–9, 112, 116–17, 123–24, 126, 128–29, 143–44, 148–49, 151, 160, 176, 186, 214 n. 75, 223 n. 37, 224 n. 44, 227 n. 38; as

depicting only a portion of the human condition (*vita activa*), 5–11; imprecise writing of, 51; influence on how Arendt is interpreted, 15, 133. *See also The Origins of Totalitarianism*
Human condition (concept), 8, 40–42, 49, 77, 104, 109, 122, 132, 149, 158, 174; possibility of altering, 108, 110–16, 119, 121, 148–49
Human artifice, 41–43, 54, 66, 111–12, 123, 128, 181–82, 184, 204
Hume, David, 163–64

Identity, 20, 31, 35–36, 39, 45, 47, 56, 126, 191–92, 195
Ideology, viii, 36, 127, 141–48, 184
Imagination, 23, 87, 90, 150, 153, 165–67, 171, 204
Immortality. See *athanatizein*
Impartiality, 69, 80, 106, 159, 175; vs. objectivity, 79, 181–84. *See also* common sense; enlarged mentality; impartiality; intersubjective validity; *sensus communis*
Industrial revolution, 119, 124, 188, 195–98
Institutions, 18, 21, 54, 67, 75, 108, 116, 153, 189, 194–95, 201. *See also* markets
Instrumentalism, 19–20, 56–57, 66, 68, 79, 104–5, 115, 120, 123, 130, 132
Intellectuals, 2–4, 24, 146, 154, 163, 179–84
Interpretation, 21–24, 106, 158–61, 163
Intersubjective validity, 11, 14, 17, 153, 161–72, 179, 189; articulated in Kantian aesthetics, 153, 161–72 ; as general validity, 160–61, 170–71, 174; as hypothetical validity, 169–70, 174; vs. universal validity, 11, 152–53, 155, 160, 165, 170–71, 189. *See also* common sense; enlarged mentality; impartiality; *sensus communis*

Jaspers, Karl, 5–6, 25, 73, 89, 159
Jesus, 81
Justice: as a-telic, 57; and freedom, 191–92; global, 189; social justice, 54, 56, 189, 191–93; in modern era, 127–28

Kafka, Franz, 90, 116
Kant, Immanuel, viii, 7, 9, 11–12, 17–18, 46, 73, 110, 131, 136–37, 143, 152–79, 202, 212 n. 34
Kaplan, David E., 92
Kateb, George, 12, 153, 155
Kierkegaard, Søren, 140
King, Martin Luther, viii, 50, 83
Kohn, Jerome, 6

Acknowledgments

This project would not have been possible without the support, in a variety of forms, of a number of individuals and institutions. Thanks should first go to the University of Pennsylvania Press. My editor, Damon Linker, along with managing editor Erica Ginsburg and copy editor Jennifer Shenk, has done sterling work that has greatly improved the book. This book is also the result of the generous support of The Center for the Study of Liberal Democracy at the University of Wisconsin–Madison. Thanks must go to its directors: Richard Avramenko, Donald Downs, John Sharpless, and Howard Schweber. I have also received support for this project from Duke University and the Kenan Institute for Ethics. Several individuals contributed important ideas and criticism to this project. These include Ruth Grant, Thomas Spragens, Tracy Strong, and especially Michael Gillespie, who was instrumental in refining the project's overall argument. I would also like to thank the reviewers of this book, whose comments were extremely helpful, and particularly Ronald Beiner, who revealed his identity in order to facilitate his gracious and comprehensive notes on the book's initial draft. Obviously, Beiner is one of the major interlocutors of the book's argument, and the fact that I addressed him so often solely indicates the exceptional quality of his scholarship and his in many ways foundational importance for this particular debate. Last, I would like to thank my family for trusting and believing in me while I pursued this project, and especially my children, Lavi and Ila, who have kept my work grounded in the real world. Though they may not understand my work very well, they are what give it meaning.